LOUISIANA LEGACY

EDWIN W. EDWARDS
Governor of Louisiana
Commander-in-Chief of the Louisiana National Guard

Louisiana Legacy

A History of the State National Guard

by
EVANS J. CASSO

Foreword by Maj. Gen. O. J. Daigle, Jr.

Paintings by
ROBERT M. RUCKER

Sketches by
CAPTAIN J. SIDNEY BECNEL
Chaplain, Louisiana Army National Guard

A FIREBIRD PRESS BOOK

PELICAN PUBLISHING COMPANY
Gretna 1998

Copyright © 1976
By Evans J. Casso
All rights reserved

Library of Congress Cataloging in Publication Data

Casso, Evans J.   1914-
   Louisiana legacy.

   Bibliography: p. 265-69.
   Includes index.
   1. Louisiana. National Guard—History. I. Title.
UA220.C37   355.3'7'09763   76-10175
ISBN 1-56554-546-X

Manufactured in the United States of America
Published by Pelican Publishing Company, Inc.
1000 Burmaster Street, Gretna, Louisiana 70053

TO ALL THE GENERATIONS
   WHO PAID THE BLOODY PRICE—
FOUGHT FOR OUR STATE AND NATION
   AND GAVE THEIR LIVES IN SACRIFICE,
THIS BOOK IS RESPECTFULLY DEDICATED

*The publication of this book was made
possible through support of the
National Guard Association of Louisiana and
the Louisiana Guard Enlisted Association.*

Contents

Foreword ix
Preface xi
Acknowledgments xiii
Chapter 1   Evolvement and Establishment 3
Chapter 2   Colonization, Trial, and Traumas 17
Chapter 3   Birth of the Louisiana Militia 29
Chapter 4   Politics, Intrigue, and the Pawn 41
Chapter 5   The American Merger 47
Chapter 6   Prelude to Peace 63
Chapter 7   Rehearsal and the Battle of Brothers 73
Chapter 8   Conquerors, Carpetbaggers, and Home Rule 89
Chapter 9   Rebuilding and a New Rehearsal 101
Chapter 10   Blood on the Horizon 109
Chapter 11   Reorganization and Natural Disasters 133
Chapter 12   World War II, Lineages, and Heroism 139
Chapter 13   An Asian Adventure 183
Chapter 14   Reflections and the Future 195
Chapter 15   The Adjutants General 207
Chapter 16   Jackson Barracks 251
Chapter 17   Redemption and Resurrection 263
Bibliography 265
Index 271

MAJOR GENERAL O. J. DAIGLE, JR.

(Portrait by Charles Richards)

Foreword

With the arrival of the Bicentennial of this great country, a host of unsung heroes and heretofore unknown patriots will emerge to receive due recognition for their unselfish contributions to the restoration of peace in time of war, order in time of natural disaster, and tranquility in time of civil uprising. Not the least among these is our citizen soldier whose story will unfold through the pages of this book.

To date, relatively little has been written about these dedicated men, but a deligient search through narrative reports, chronicles, individual memoirs, journals, state papers, archives, and interviews has revealed their rightful place in the history of state and nation. This richly deserved legacy evolves from a nucleus of early settlers who had the foresight to band together as militiamen for the purpose of survival against hostile forces of men and of nature. Their purpose has passed through the annals of history as an everlasting inspiration to guide the destiny of our country. I respectfully salute these loyal citizens and am proud of my small part in preserving this legacy for future generations of Louisianians and Americans.

O. J. Daigle, Jr.
Major General
The Adjutant General
State of Louisiana

Preface

In writing a book of this magnitude and about an institution almost as old as the name *Louisiana*, many requisites were necessary. The confidence that Major General O. J. Daigle, Jr., expressed by commissioning me to do this study was in itself an impetus. He put at my disposal the resources of his office and staff; for that and for the trust he placed in me, I shall be forever grateful. But at no time did he in any way impose his ideas on the book's contents. He asked me to do a complete, impartial history of the Louisiana National Guard; and with the help of the Guard and individuals knowledgeable in various fields of Louisiana and its military history, I have endeavored to do this.

In a letter, General Daigle said, among other things, "I am pleased to know you will be directing the production of this endeavor which will become a legacy of Louisiana." He had inadvertently given me the title, *Louisiana Legacy*.

When I got into the research for this book, curiosity was soon replaced by wonder. Here was a facet of Louisiana's rich and unique history that had never been treated with any degree of depth or perspective.

I do not consider this history of the Louisiana National Guard complete; no military history ever is; for as time goes on new sources and materials are frequently uncovered. Opinions change as events of the past are viewed in different perspectives. Over two hundred thousand books have been written about Napoleon I and his times; numbers of new books have appeared annually since his death a century and a half ago. About forty thousand books have been written about the American Civil War, and new ones are in production for the future.

There was no method for collection or depositing historical papers pertaining to the Louisiana National Guard until the administration of General Raymond H. Fleming whose tenure began in 1928. Since then there has been a permanent repository which is now under the care and direction of Mary Burk Oalmann, military historian, of the Louisiana Military Department. Since Jackson Barracks has passed alternately from Federal to the state military administrations, through the years, records of those years prior to General Fleming have been lost or destroyed. In Louisiana, political upheavals and chaotic events have taken place in a subtropical climate, and neither the events nor climate was conducive to the preservation of military records. In some cases, public records were simply taken by individuals who considered them their personal property, particularly if the papers pertained to them. All these circumstances contributed to the loss of much valuable material.

I began the project by reconstructing events while I gathered all available material in the military files at Jackson Barracks and all that could be garnered from private individuals, public libraries, and other institutions. Presented here is a factual history of the Louisiana National Guard based upon available material.

Illustrations were copied from paintings that Robert M. Rucker created for this book and for commemoration of the important eras of Louisiana National Guard history for the Bicentennial.

The sketches featured as chapter headings are the work of Captain J. Sidney Becnel, a Louisiana Army National Guard chaplain. They highlight crucial events from each chapter as the narrative unfolds and pay tribute to important figures. The portrait of Major General Daigle is by Charles Richards.

I am grateful to Mr. Rucker, to Mr. Richards, and to Chaplain Becnel for the added dimension created by their splendid creativity. The originals of the illustrations will become part of the art collection of General and Mrs. Daigle.

Acknowledgments

During the preparation of this book, several persons were of inestimable help to me. First and foremost was Major Ernest N. Souhlas, who through the entire project acted as liasion officer between me and the adjutant general's office. His constant aid and enthusiasm have been indispensable, and I shall always be grateful to him.

Brigadier General Karl N. Smith, chief of staff of the Louisiana National Guard counseled me on protocol, terminology, and lineage of the various military units. I appreciate his considerable assistance and that of his secretary, Lynn Mary Wigginton.

Mary Burk Oalmann, military historian and custodian of the annals of the Louisiana National Guard, put the Guard files at my disposal. Her courtesy and cooperation are deeply appreciated. Lieutenant Colonel Edwin P. Roux and Captain Michael L. Brown were particularly helpful in promoting the book among Guardsmen.

Sergeant-major Stanley Sirgo attended to details in the artwork and made the photographs of the cannons Redemption and Resurrection. Mary-Alice Roy transcribed all my material for study and editing. Her job was enormous, and she has my thanks for her patience and excellent work.

Several personal friends contributed of their talents toward this volume: William E. Rooney read my manuscript, and I appreciate his critical analysis. Beverly Senat LeBlanc, as a special aide, saved time for me and helped me to meet the publisher's deadline. Annamae Stieffel Silbernagel handled vital correspondence with cheerful and efficient dispatch.

I extend my thanks to my thorough and expert proof readers, Paula Gremillion de Priest, Virginia Brinson Glade, and Markey Casso Swails. I also wish to thank Charles L. Dufour and Mr. and Mrs. Francis R. Barnard (Sue Calogne) for lending me books from their exceptional libraries. Simone de la Souchere Delery, my long-time friend, helped me with some of the French translations for which I thank her.

Librarians and their staffs at public and private institutions assisted me: Ann Gwyn, head of the Special Collections Division of the Howard-Tilton Memorial Library at Tulane University, was most kind and helpful. Equally helpful was M. Stone Miller, Jr., head of the Department of Archives and Manuscripts, at Louisiana State University. Marvin E. Wright, director of the New Orleans Public Library accorded me every courtesy, and I would like to cite in particular Mr. Collin B. Hamer at the Louisiana Division of the library.

Gratefully, I offer a bouquet of thanks to my wife and helpmate, Madeleine, for her forebearance through the duration of my work.

Finally, I assume all responsibility for the contents of this book. If there a there are errors or omissions, the fault is mine.

LOUISIANA LEGACY

The central figure depicts General Andrew Jackson, a military forefather, great in his ability to summon and rally the citizenry to the cause of common defense. At bottom right are symbols of security in the life of the American pioneer: his flintlock, his peaceful homestead, and his "powder and pocket of lead." At bottom left stands in readiness the forerunner of the present-day citizen-soldier Guardsman, ever prepared to defend his loved ones and property from aggressors.

CHAPTER 1

Evolvement and Establishment

The rights of the American people to bear arms, as incorporated by amendment to the United States Constitution, has become a basic American tenet. The second of the original ten amendments reads, "A well-regulated militia, being necessary to the security of a free State, the right of the people to keep and bear arms, shall not be infringed."

The appellation *National Guard* was given first to the Seventh New York Regiment on August 16, 1824, when it served as an honor guard for the visit of the Marquis de Lafayette to the United States, and did not come into general use until the beginning of the twentieth century. The organized militia system is a grass roots institution, distinctively American and with no similarity to any other armed force in the world. It derives its strength from the people who fill its ranks and from the citizens who support it. It was once the only line of defense against marauding hostile Indians who threatened or attacked the early colonists. In its beginning the militia was, as the Guard is today, a band of citizen soldiers. Although the National Guard now has more personnel, more sophisticated weaponry, and a higher degree of mobility by land and, now, by air, its purpose is the same—to maintain the peace and tranquility of the respective states and to protect the interests and integrity of the nation's borders.

The nature of the National Guard's composition makes it a viable military arm that can be mobilized quickly and adroitly. It has met every challenge during a history that reaches back into three centuries, to a time when early colonists banded and armed themselves to protect their families in those bleak and almost forsaken settlements that dotted the coasts of New England and Virginia. Initially clothed in the homespun garments fashioned from spinning wheels, thimble, thread, and homemade dye, the guard recalls the rifle over the fireplace, the loaded gun in the corner of the room; it is our protection, the immediate means at hand to repulse an enemy or to maintain the integrity of our laws, and sometimes to keep peace among ourselves. It is the natural offspring of our democracy, and it is the army at home beyond the reach of a dictator's power.

Militia is an all encompassing word defining any force that carries arms. The term became *organized militia* during colonial times and later under the auspices of the individual states began a more objective direction as the immediate protector of a given territory. It was natural that the men who forged early principles with politics and who had some misgivings about creating and maintaining a standing army that could be a tempting tool of powerful politicians, eventually succumbed to sound reason.

George Washington experienced much difficulty in persuading a cautious Constitutional Convention about the need of a federal force. His convictions, declared in the "Sentiments on a Peace Establishment," which he wrote at Newburgh in 1783, reflect his philosophy gained through personal experience. He suggested that a reserve force be made up from the general militia and manned by young men to "form a Corps in every State, capable of resisting any sudden impression which might be attempted by a foreign enemy while the remainder of the National forces would have time to assemble and make preparations for the field." Washington knew the necessity of that margin of safety—a fully armed reserve capable of mobilizing in a matter of hours. He actually pressed for an organized system with federal supervision and regulated periods of training. He was not successful in gaining recognition for his proposal, but the 1792 Congress did grudgingly concede the necessity and the duty of such a force to serve in time of need. It was not until 1903 that a federal law was passed appreciably supporting the National Guard. Major General Charles Dick, then a representative from the state of Ohio, wrote the Dick acts of 1907 and 1908 and was largely responsible for the emergence of the National Guard as a distinct national force supported by federal resource and technology. These acts, however, provided insufficient support.

The National Defense Act promulgated in 1916 provided that the Guard, when called into service, would become an integral part of the armed forces of the United States. An act of June 4, 1920, joined the National Guard with the Regular Army as the United States Army. At last, most of Washington's hopes were realized and to an extent the great general and president never expected. It took almost a century and a half for the National Guard to take the form that he had designed. But like the greatest establishments of the United States, it had embryonic beginnings that were nurtured by national pride and sustained by the free and voluntary enthusiasm of generations.

The Guard has withstood the test of history, outlasting lesser ideas and the occasional attack by politicians.

By commissioning Washington and his generals and inducting them into emergency active duty, the Continental Congress in effect created the National Guard. Significantly, the initial commissions made by the Continental Congress were first appointed or created by the governors of the respective states or their congressional delegations. The colonies' revolt against England was initiated by the organized militia. Even the Minute Men of Lexington County, Massachusetts, who participated in the events that brought armed revolt against the British, were basically a National Guard unit. They, in time, became part of Washington's army, as did all the organized militia. When asked to explain the status of his army to the first Continental Congress in 1780, Washington replied: "If in all cases ours was one army or thirteen armies allied for common defense, there would be no difficulty in solving our question; we are occasionally both, and I should not be much out if I were to say we are sometimes neither but the compound of both." So fearful were the original thirteen states of a standing army that it was not until September 29, 1789, that the first Congress made a move to create a Regular Army. During the interim from 1775, when the revolution actually began, until 1789, well after the defeat of the British, the young nation had no Regular Army. The organized militia of the respective colonies formed the army that defeated England. And it was this precursor of the National Guard that stood by to defend the country until the Constitutional Convention or Congress made up its mind to create a Regular Army. After the Regular Army became a reality, the National Guard formed a reserve adjunct that, through the years, has supported the Regular Army which, alone, has never been strong enough to serve the nation in time of war.

It took generations for the National Guard to evolve into today's highly competent and efficient forces, though the Guard met every exigency and long before the colonists ever thought of independence from England. The first federal subsidy came about in 1808 when Congress provided $200,000 annually to the State Militias. The appropriation signified the beginning of an appreciation among members of Congress for the mechanics of a home-oriented militia. The colonists' early fears of a standing army grew out of their sufferings at the hands of English troops and the German Hessian mercenaries. The colonists did not want to create a potential monster that might destroy their tender republic. Fearing a national army as they did, they surely would not foster individual strong armies within each of the states. The new nation had not yet reached unity of opinion; each of the former colonies considered itself individually sovereign. At the beginning of the nineteenth century the unanimity and mutual trust as understood today had not yet come about.

Fortunately, during this period of indecision the state militias (National Guards) were still intact. The early Congress' unwillingness to deal realistically with security almost cost the country its independence in the War of 1812. Out of a population of 7,239,000, the United States was able to account for a potential of 719,499 officers and men, around a nucleus of the National Guard. Not by any standards were these men choice troops. Most furnished their own arms; their uniforms were invariably homemade; and their entire accouterments in most instances were a long-arm flintlock, powder horn, and a pocket of lead pellets. But they had an indispensable *esprit de corps*, gained, no doubt, from having beaten the crack British troops in the Revolution. They also desperately desired to preserve their newly won freedom. Their adversaries would develop a new respect for the figurative American with a musket in one hand and a plow in the other.

Of over 700,000 potentials, only about 67,000 men were actually drawn into a force that could be called an army. The beginning of the War of 1812 found the Americans making a good showing at Fort McHenry and Baltimore but routed at Lundy Lane. Their enthusiasm almost exceeded their capability. The capture and burning of the national capitol was a frightening symbol of the country's peril.

General Pakenham's British troops, with their bagpipes, colorful

Evolvement and Establishment

banners, and splendid regalia of red and white, topped with jaunty kepis, presented quite a contrast to the nondescript Americans who awaited their initial charge. Andrew Jackson, who had risen from a general officer in his native Tennessee organized militia to active duty in command of the state's volunteer regiments, came into New Orleans with 2,982 officers and men, mainly from Tennessee and Kentucky. He was quickly reinforced with 515 Louisianians—some infantrymen and some artillerymen, and another local battalion. The others who made up his army were quickly recruited from local military manpower units, strengthening Jackson's army to 5,690. This figure represents the majority of local citizen-soldiers, or the National Guard of their day.

Frontier life had superbly prepared the average American for warfare; his gun was an ever-present necessity. Physical stamina, developed by exposure to the elements, and manual farm labor strengthened his body. Actually, most Americans were better shots than their English counterparts, since hunting was their way of life. They had learned Indian fighting—shooting from concealed position—a new tactic. All these ingredients added up to a strong army of individuals representing various ethnic elements not theretofore assembled. Consider America's cosmopolitan aggregation, the Anglo-Saxon ancestry of the Kentuckians and Tennesseans plus the French, German, Spanish, and Negro from Louisiana spiced with Laffite and his buccaneers, many speaking their native language or dialects. The bulk of that force was equivalent to the present National Guard.

The Mexican War was the first war in which American troops were in an action entirely beyond United States borders. It was fought by volunteers from the state militias and by the Regular Army. The Federal Militia Act did not give the president the power to draft any state militia units for a service beyond three months, but Congress could change this and did on occasions. Men of patriotic zeal more often than not joined for long service or the duration of the war, or at least as long as their respective units were needed. The total aggregate for the Mexican War was 104,284 officers and men, including marines. Of this total, 30,000 served in Regular Army units, and abut only half of these joined the army in Mexico. At least half of the officers and men in the army were citizen soldiers from what was then the equivalent of the National Guard of the respective states. Seven regiments, four battalions, and a battery of artillery left Louisiana to engage in the Mexican War. Every regiment was recruited and often armed and equipped by the state which was entitled to reimbursement from the U.S. Treasury if the unit became part of the military force for potential action.

At the time of the firing on Fort Sumter, the first armed action of the Civil War, the Regular Army numbered slightly more than 16,435 men. Each state, however, had its own militia. The immediate gathering of all these forces, North and South, provided the opposing armies of the first battles of the war, notably First Manassas. The North fielded 37,000 men and the South 35,000, indicating the means of quick recruiting, assembling, and deploying armies through the American system of state National Guards.

The successes of the South during the early part of the war were due to the excellent morale and quality of training in the home militias. Pride and tradition and regular training programs had prepared the southerners for an action that came up rather unexpectedly. It seemed unlikely that relatively large armies would oppose each other within eighty-eight days after the firing of Fort Sumter. The South had only 29 percent of the officers of the Regular Army, but having the remaining 71 percent of these highly trained officers proved to be of little avail to the North, and they suffered inglorious defeats during the first phase of the war. The poor condition of their state militias was a contributing factor, and the battles of First and Second Manassas were examples of unpreparedness. Had the South possessed the resources and manpower of the North, or had they pressed on and captured Washington, this country surely would have had different a history since 1861.

One of the oddities of the Civil War was that Robert E. Lee was a Regular Army officer. His counterpart, Ulysses S. Grant, though a West Pointer, had retired from the army and was residing in a sleepy Illinois town serving only in occasional drills of the state militia. William T. Sherman, also a graduate of West Point, had given up the military and was president of Louisiana State Seminary of Learning and Military Academy—now Louisiana State University—when hostilities broke out.

George Washington was a National Guardsman of his day since he was immediately commissioned from his service in the colony of Virginia to the service of all the colonies to fight England. Andrew Jackson, as stated, was no more than a general officer of his state militia, and he rose to greatness in Indian wars and achieved brilliant victory at New Orleans over the British. Then came Grant and

Evolvement and Establishment

Sherman, who were not practicing professional soldiers when the Civil War began, but who led the North to victory after four years of hellish fighting. Admittedly, the North developed superior manpower and resources as the war wore on, but if lesser men had been in charge of the deteriorated homeguard, the outcome would no doubt have been different.

The United States has suffered through many critical tests. First, was the war for independence; then the next generation had to fight the same, but much wiser and better equipped enemy to really establish national sovereignty. The Mexican War settled a territorial dispute and secured the southwest border. The successive defeats of England had assured northern borders, and the Louisiana Purchase provided a western frontier. What was not secure by land was protected by the Atlantic and Pacific oceans. In all the uncertain periods of this nation the home militia arose to defend against any threat. Every early trial that tested the body politic worked to ultimate advantage. Diverse ideas, principles, and peoples made up a nation that would withstand the trials of two centuries. The National Guard has progressed with the dynamic country.

Following the Civil War, states' rights gave way to a strong federal union. Each conflict and every added state have strengthened the Union and, more important, have brought the realization that compromise is the foundation of democracy. Some American institutions, like the National Guard, developed gradually through generations. The great compromises effected by people of varying ethnic and cultural antecedents brought about a oneness, and that homogenous composition is reflected in the musters of National Guard units throughout the land.

With the end of the Civil War, a trend began for a strong federal government. By the time the Spanish-American War, the National Guard had become an integral part of the armed forces. Guardsmen from seventeen states were sent to Manila with the Seventh Corps. The Guardsmen comprised a majority in the corps, a most significant recognition of this unique institution. Of special importance during this period was a provision whereby a Guard formation could be accepted into U.S. volunteers as a unit, but with loss of identity. The motive was to procure officers and men from the Guard and fuse them into the Regular Army, the Guard being a "farm" from which the Regular Army could call up or recruit men considered above average and place them and their units accordingly. A little-known fact about the Spanish-American War is that National Guard units stayed on for a year beyond their enlistments to keep the peace in the Philippines.

Elihu Root, secretary of war under Presidents William McKinley and Theodore Roosevelt, made it possible for National Guardsmen to become officers in the Regular Army. Any man under twenty-eight with certification of graduation from a state university that had a military program could become a second lieutenant in the Regular Army. Root also founded the War College, and though he retained the seniority rule, he did make national recognition possible for men of the state militias. Up to this period of the nation's history the Regular Army had never won a war without the active participation of the home guard. Root stressed the fact that if the Regular Army was to maintain the status of small but adequate peacetime units that relied on the National Guard for wartime expansion, there should be some uniformity in its training and weaponry. But pressure from Regular Army proponents induced him to provide that engineers, cavalry, and artillery should be composed only of Regulars. And there were still some men in the War Department who considered the National Guard merely a farm from which the Regulars could derive trained officers and men. The best summation of the whole mentality of the War Department during this time—the turn of the century—is that they were obsessed with professional jealousy.

The Dick Act of 1903 required that within five years of its promulgation, the regulations and weapons of the National Guard must be the same as those of the Regular Army. Of all the legislation affecting the Guard between 1792 and 1903 the Dick Act was the most important. From the time of its enactment the National Guard enjoyed equal military status with the Regular Army. Due recognition had been given, even if given grudgingly.

The Dick Act also brought renewed interest into the local National Guards, and each units hastened to meet all the requirements. Many units were found to be far behind normal expectations; some were good; and some were exceptional. But each was concerned with meeting specifications to be determined by officers of the Regular Army. There was, naturally, a period of transition before the Guard reached the demanded specifications. An entirely restructured program was launched along lines of the Regulars' own assessments of what the American army should be. An act of May 27, 1908, furthered the importance of the National Guard by determining that

Evolvement and Establishment 11

they would be called to service before volunteers in case of an emergency. This act made the National Guard an official adjunct to the Regular Army and, therefore, vital to the security of the country. Also, as a result of the Dick Act, the condition of National Guardsmen, their materiel, and their weapons would be the onus of the Regular Army, and any criticism of the Guard would also be criticism of the Regulars.

Because of the revoltion in Mexico in 1912 and its effect upon border security, U.S. Attorney General George W. Wickersham declared the National Guard's duty in Mexico unconstitutional. Others, who pleaded that constitutionality was established as early as 1846–1848, when the organized militias of the respective states had served in Mexico, were ignored.

Attorney General Wickersham's opinion almost wrecked the National Guard. Many proponents of the Guard thought the Dick Act had resolved the issue. True, the judge advocate of the Regular Army had cited the Dick Act as unconstitutional. But it was only an opinion of an appointed official and not debated and passed upon as the Dick Act was in the Congress of the United States. Here was another instance where professional jealousy precluded reason. Representative Charles Dick, who had championed the National Guard in 1903 and who had gone on to become U.S. Senator, had by 1912 retired from public life and was practicing law in Ohio.

For four years the status of the National Guard was in doubt and had few champions in the national administration. Had it not been for its grass roots supports, the Guard might well have passed into oblivion. But the National Defense Act of June 3, 1916, fully restored it to its rightful place within the fabric of the country. The instability of Mexico and its potential threat to the U.S. border added to the warlike designs of Kaiser Wilhelm made a strong national reserve imperative. So it was that the National Guard again officially became a potent component of the United States Army.

The Selective Draft Law of May 18, 1917, reconfirmed the status of the National Guard. The numbers within divisions would also be differentiated by numbers in regard to the three classes of soldiers; Regular, National Guard, and draftees.

Major Douglas MacArthur made a proposal to create a National Guard Division from men and units not being assembled into the initial Guard divisions. His proposition was accepted and the name *Rainbow* was given MacArthur's Forty-second Division which went on to fame in World War II. The Division was called Rainbow because its men and officers represented twenty-six states of the Union and the broad ethnic complexities of America, "it covered the land like a rainbow."

Although the great bulk of National Guard manpower was subservient to the Regular Army, its contributions at home and to the expeditionary forces are great. The adjutants-general of the respective states handled problems associated with the draft, and as a consequence there was a steady flow of ample manpower. The National Guardsman in his role as "doughboy," the name given American infantrymen in World War I, performed as well as any other soldier. Killed or wounded in action were some 103,731 Guardsmen, over twice the number of casualties of the Regular Army.

In 1920 the National Defense Act passed, allotting eight hundred troops per Congressional representative to the National Guard.

The act was modified in 1923, and allocations were cut by more than one-half. Congress, in its appropriations, limited the strength of the Guard to 190,000, somewhat less than the allotments. This was typical treatment: An act by Congress for so many troops but with insufficient appropriation; or like the Act of 1908 that ran afoul of an interpretation by Attorney General Wickersham; or as in the case in World War I, when the National Guard units were in so many instances lost in reassignments and deployments of military logistics of the Regular Army. It was a long, tough march along the avenues of national history before the National Guard gained the status it enjoys today.

In 1940 the National Guard was authorized to recruit 300,000 men, and this was realized within a short time. These figures were considered to be one-fourth of necessary wartime strength. Despite all preceding legislation, the states were not completely happy; they preferred that the Guard be a permanent component of the army, not just during a national emergency. An Act of June 15, 1933, did embrace those aspirations; it created the Federal Reserve Force, which was actually the National Guard, and it was to be considered a separate arm of the United States military potential. Unfortunately, the people who made the laws affecting the Guard did not always fully understand them. After Omar N. Bradley became chief of staff, he included a course of instruction at the United States Military Academy dealing with relations between the National Guard and the Regular Army. This move helped immeasurably and there has been

Evolvement and Establishment

less confusion since.

There are two ways in which the Guard may be used in federal service—by *call* of the president or by *order* of Congress. The president has the authority to call all or part of the Guard into active military service whenever (1) the country is invaded or is in danger of invasion; (2) there is a rebellion or danger of rebellion against the authority of the government; (3) if the president is unable, with the Regular forces, to execute the laws of the United States. He may also call the Guard units to suppress insurrection, rebellion, or interference with state and federal law. They retain their status as federally recognized units and members of the National Guard, but officers continue to be appointed by the states, and neither officers nor enlisted men may be held to serve beyond the terms of their existing commissions and enlistments.

Congress orders units to active duty, and when such is accomplished, units and members are relieved from duties in the Guards of the their respective states, regardless of the term of their current commission or enlistment. They may be retained on active duty for the duration of the war or emergency and six months thereafter or such other period as may be authorized by law.

The president, through congressional approval, has precedence over all state prerogatives. This was clearly demonstrated during the integration crisis at the University of Mississippi during the 1960s. President Kennedy called the National Guard of Mississippi to implement the integration law and maintain the peace when the governor was dilatory in acting.

In the integration crisis at Little Rock, President Eisenhower, on September 24, 1957, sent federal troops to enforce a federal court order for schools to operate on an integrated basis. The president had the prerogative to call the Arkansas National Guard, but chose to send federal troops instead.

On September 16, 1940, the National Guard of the United States was ordered into active service. The United States Army immediately grew in strength by about 300,000, including 21,000 officers. During the war about 40 percent of the enlisted National Guardsmen became second lieutenants. Statistics like these demonstrate the value of a quick and ready source of manpower in cases of emergency. Replacements from Selective Service, or Draft, provided enough replacements for the National Guard to rapidly acquire a wartime strength.

War games of immense proportions were staged in Louisiana to train the forces for overseas duty. By January, 1941, the active army had reached a total of 730,000 men of whom 200,000 were Guardsmen. By September an additional 800,000 selectees swelled the ranks. Engaged in the war games in Louisiana were 460,000 officers and men or about one-fourth of the total strength of the army. The contours of the land in Louisiana and the warm climate were ideal for infantry and tank maneuvers, and General Raymond H. Fleming, Louisiana adjutant general, was instrumental in acquiring two million acres in central Louisiana for these purposes.

The Thirty-fourth Infantry Division, composed of National Guard units from Minnesota, North Dakota, South Dakota, and Iowa, was the first contingent of troops to land overseas during World War II. Far removed from those colonial days of "trained bands," the first line of defense at home became the first line of offense against an enemy on foreign soil. The National Guard had come a long way to gain the recognition it deserved: It served on all fronts in World War II, producing no fewer than twenty-one permanent major generals. More Guard general officers carried their induction ranks through the course of the war than did those from the Regular Army. By the end of the war the National Guard had put eighteen infantry divisions, or 300,000 men, into the field. More important, at the time of mobilization the Guard doubled the strength of our Army. Of the eighteen divisions mobilized from the Guard, nine went to Europe and Africa and nine to the Pacific. This did not include twenty squadrons of the Air National Guard fliers and ground crews.

The Korean emergency created a new problem for the National Guard, one-third of which, or approximately 138,000 men, were ordered into active service. The Guard had urged that it be mobilized completely and that instead of relieving individuals it be used to replace battle-worn units with fresh units of similar equipment and potential. This did not meet with universal approval. Further, there was much confusion in the system of numbering the various units of the Regular Army and the remaining National Guard units; some had the same numbers even when they performed similar duties.

The Selective Service Extension Act of 1950, extended to July 1, 1953, and increasing enlisted service from twenty to twenty-four months, also had an effect on the National Guard. The Guardsmen could be called as units though most of the army Reservists could be

Evolvement and Establishment 15

called as individuals. There seemed to be a constant aura of uncertainty about the Guardsmen's place in the echelons of commands. Most members of the Air National Guard who were initially ordered into federal service were sent to Korea and were followd by some infantry divisions. In the meantime, others were sent to Germany and Iceland as part of the North Atlantic Treaty Organization's deployments.

The fighting in Vietnam, though not officially designated as an emergency, brought U.S. troops again onto Asian soil through the Tomkin Resolution. A gradually accelerated role drained the manpower and materiel resources of the country far in excess of its original intent.

The foregoing pages of Chapter 1 are intended to give the reader a perspective on the national character of the Guard, its beginning, when this land was all frontier with few settlers, and its gradual evolution into what it is today. Succeeding chapters will be concerned with the history of the Louisiana Territory, from which thirteen states, or portions thereof, were formed. The area that first successfully colonized and retained its earliest name—Louisiana—will be of primary interest and more particularly the development of its National Guard.

As founder of the city of New Orleans, in April of 1718, Jean Baptiste Sieur de Bienville is the central figure of this chapter. Other highlights include (left to right): Pierre le Moyne, Sieur d'Iberville, brother of Bienville, colonizer of the lower Mississippi; a typical Acadian house characteristic of that peaceful farming people removed from Nova Scotia to Louisiana; a copy of the *Moneteur*, the first newspaper established in New Orleans in 1794; and a front view of St. Louis Cathedral, the most easily identified landmark of the Crescent City.

CHAPTER 2

Colonization, Trial, and Traumas

The colonization of Louisiana was one of the most difficult experiments in American history. The territory was vast, but its value lay in its colonization. Diseases proliferated in the warm, moist, subtropical climate of the southern extremity where initial efforts were made toward settlement. France wanted to rid itself of the territory by giving it to Spain, and Spain was dubious about accepting the gratuitous grant. Its eventual purchase by the new United States solved the problem of France and resolved Louisiana's destiny.

Although followers of Hernando De Soto descended the Mississippi River to its mouth in 1542, the history of Louisiana logically begins in 1682 when La Salle took possession of all the territory drained by the river. Of course, no one, at this time, had any idea how large the territory was, for its western extremity could not be clearly defined. Some of its eastern boundary was even in doubt. La Salle did, however, claim the territory, and he named it for his king, Louis XIV.

All attempts by La Salle to colonize the area on the river were failures. The failures were miserable enough to deter further attempts until 1699 when Pierre Le Moyne, Sieur d'Iberville, founded a settlement near the present Biloxi, Mississippi, and proceeded westward to build a fort on the Mississippi. The colony was not a thriving one, and the monopoly of trade granted Antoine Crozat in 1712 actually retarded rather than helped its growth.

In 1717 Crozat willingly transferred his interest to John Law's Company of the West. Law, it seems, changed the name of his company as often as he changed his mind. The Company of the West soon became La Compagnie des Indies, which became the basis of the ill-fated "Mississippi scheme." The Mississippi scheme was a plan, sanctioned by the French regent, to exploit the territory. This company now under the name of La Compagnie de la Louisiane ou d'Occident, issued shares that at first depreciated in value and then rose rapidly when Law, a director of the Royal Bank of France, promised to take over the stock at par value at a future date. This, of course, created the illusion that an investor could not lose. Law became obsessed with his own importance and deluded with imagined prospects of wealth. In 1719 he expanded the original company to include the development of the Indies, China, and Africa. His ideas went far afield of their original intent—the colonization of the Louisiana Territory. His grandiose plans must have impressed everyone of power in France, for Law was given absolute control of French colonial trade. The enlarged company began to issue stock and was permitted to control its own finances, thus escaping the scrutiny of wiser heads and making impartial audits impossible. This would prove Law's undoing. The company became known by yet another name—the Mississippi Company—and was given the power to invest its revenues. It assumed the state debt, and an outward appearance of prosperity caused public confidence to grow to such proportions that there were wild speculations with its shares. Law proceeded too fast; consequently he undercapitalized and overexpanded, causing the entire operation to become an enormous, unwieldy gargantua that quickly dissipated his funds. Public confidence began to wane, and speculators, in an attempt to salvage some of their investments, tried to sell their shares. So great was the number of shareholders who wanted to sell that panic resulted, and desperate men, in their endeavor to save some of their fortunes, lost all. The scheme was a colossal failure, and the great dream of colonization and developing Louisiana had suffered another setback.

The new colony had gotten off to a bad beginning, and for a while it seemed that colonization of the vast Louisiana Territory would never occur. However, there were some redeeming factors of Law's great enterprise. In his efforts he had sent many colonists to the territory, and hundreds of slaves were imported to cultivate rice, tobacco, indigo, and other crops. After the financial collapse of his Mississippi scheme all that remained were these human beings.

Germans had been sent over by Law from the Palatinate area of the Teutonic Empire. No accurate count of these people is possible, but it has been estimated with some reliability that six thousand Germans left their homeland to settle Louisiana. Deaths, diseases, starvation, and capture by the buccaneers who plied the seas, decimated their number. About two thousand eventually settled the territory, where they endured bad drinking water, tropical diseases, and bad food. Only the healthiest survived, and it soon became evident that the Germans had the temperament and stamina to conquer the wilderness. They were industrious, energetic, and thoroughly self-reliant. Since French colonization had failed, the successful settlement of the Germans marked an epic transition from the old world to the new, of people and progress. More French settlers would come later in greater numbers but by a circuitous route.

Much credit must be given to the younger brother of Iberville, Jean Baptiste Sieur de Bienville, who founded the city of New Orleans in April of 1718. Bienville had served with Iberville in an expedition into Hudson's Bay in 1697, and the following year accompanied him on a venture to found a colony at the mouth of the Mississippi. He had also been prominent in preliminary explorations, going up the Mississippi to the mouth of the Red River. Bienville's greatest asset, other than dogged perseverance, was his ability to communicate with Indians in their native tongues. He was able to negotiate personally with tribal chiefs and not suffer from inaccurate translations as so often happened to others in authorative positions.

When Iberville left Biloxi, he placed Bienville second in command to de Sauvele de la Villantray. When Sauvele died in 1701, Bienville became the leader of the settlement and expeditionary forces. He then selected a site on Mobile Bay to which he transferred the colony in 1702. Unfortunately, Iberville died in 1706, and his death portended dire consequences for the colonists. But Bienville's heroic efforts in the face of famine, Indian hostilities, the covetous threats of the Spanish, plus the jealousy of French Canada, saved the colony. Coincidental with all these problems, France neglected the colonists to a point where they had to fend for themselves. But when Louisiana was transferred to the Compagnie de la Louisiane ou d'Occident, Bienville was again made governor. The colony grew rapidly, and by

1724 the population had grown to approximately five thousand, including thirteen hundred Negroes. In addition to the growing human population there were domesticated animals to serve on the farms, for transportation, and work chores. There were eleven hundred cows, three hundred bulls, two hundred horses and mares, one hundred sheep, about the same number of goats, some swine, and poultry. In New Orleans there were sixteen hundred people, including the troops; the remaining colonists were at Biloxi, Mobile, and intervening points. New Orleans actually was a citadel in the wilderness since, finally, an establishment was created on the banks of the Mississippi. From this point on, Louisiana grew with spasmodic bursts caused by periodic influx of people seeking a home.

Neither the French nor the Spanish knew the exact limits of Louisiana during this period of history. The French in Canada seemed to administer all the area north of the Illinois River while the southern portion was administered by Bienville. Spain, however, laid claim on Louisiana on the contention that Ponce de Leon in 1512, Vasquez de Coronado in 1510, Panfile de Narvaez in 1528, and Hernando de Soto in 1538 had indeed occupied it in the name of his majesty, the king of Spain. This was true, but France contended that since Spain had not colonized these sectors, it could not rightly claim the territory. Also, France avowed to have constructed forts and settlements in Florida which Spain now claimed as its own. In fact, Spain had for centuries encompassed much of the southeastern part of the continent in defining the territory known as Florida. The inevitable course of history with its wars, treaties, and compromises would determine the destiny of Louisiana and indeliby inscribe its borders.

By the secret Treaty of Fontainebleau, November 3, 1762, France transferred all her territory west of the Mississippi and the Island of New Orleans. The geographical limits of the Island of New Orleans were considered to be the Mississippi River, Bayou Manchac, the Amite River, Lakes Maurepas and Pontchartrain, and the Gulf of Mexico, including its indentations of bays and lakes. France, wishing to be rid of this constant drain on its treasury, considered its colonization efforts a dismal failure. Crozat's and Law's bankruptcies actually shook the financial foundation of continental France, and the further depletion of French resources by continual subsidies to the colonies made the disposal of the territory imperative. France had already lost Canada; and most of the eastern side of the Mississippi, with the exception of New Orleans, had been lost to the English.

Colonization, Trial, and Traumas 21

But a few years before the Treaty of Fontainebleau, some of the French colonists who had been expelled from Canada settled in the Attakapas region of southwest Louisiana and along the Mississippi River above New Orleans. They were peaceful farming people from Acadia, formerly a French province of Canada. These colonists, who began to arrive in Nova Scotia in 1632, later found themselves English subjects because of the province's transfer to England by the Treaty of Utrecht in 1713. By 1775 these Acadians numbered about ten thousand, and in that year the fanaticism accompanying the last French and Indian wars expressed itself in the decision by the English to expel them from their lands and homes. The English doubted their loyalty since they were French and considered them a potential threat to the crown. Nearly seven thousand were deported and distributed up and down the coast from Maine to Georgia. Some endured further hardships in their efforts to reach French settlements in Quebec and Louisiana. Thus were planted the seeds for the future population of Louisiana and an abiding dislike for the English which would manifest itself by superb performances against them during the American Revolution at Baton Rouge in 1778 and in 1815 at New Orleans during the War of 1812.

The Louisiana colony had different problems from those of the thirteen colonies along the continental eastern seaboard. Louisiana was still in the throes of birth when the original colonies had established trade, laws, and governing bodies. Unlike their Anglo-Saxon counterparts whose king, George III, coveted his minions and their possessions in our new world, France was searching for means to be rid of Louisiana with its vast wilderness, disease, and hostile Indians.

Spain's Charles III, cousin of France's Louis XV, realized he needed a buffer to protect the Spanish West on the North American continent against England's expansionist ambitions. The Treaty of Fontainebleau was a secret compact, but France did prepare a notice of cession which, at Spain's request was not sent to the governor of Louisiana. Three years elapsed before the Spanish emissary arrived at New Orleans. In the summer of 1764 news of the imminent transfer of the territory to Spain reached New Orleans, but the official and prominent citizens met in January of 1765 to discuss the transfer hoping to prevail upon France to abrogate the treaty. Nicolas Chauvin de Lafreniere, the attorney general, made an impassioned speech, and all present agreed that a delegation be sent to France to plead for the return of Louisiana to the mother country. Bienville and John Milhet, a prominent New Orleans merchant, sailed to France and called on the Duke de Chioseul with their request, but they returned with the melancholy news of their failure.

Antonio de Ulloa, a distinguished scientist and mathematician, who had had a colorful career while serving Spain in Peru and Chile arrived in New Orleans on March 5, 1776, with only ninety soldiers. Ulloa expected the three hundred French troops in New Orleans to join him, but there was a great difference between the pay of the Spanish and that of the French soldiers. A French soldier received only seven livres a month ($7) while the Spanish received thirty-five. Since Ulloa was instructed not to change prevailing conditions, he immediately lowered the pay of his Spaniards, which, of course, contributed nothing to their morale. Ulloa's attempt to take possession of an empire with only ninety soldiers must be one of history's most optimistic endeavors.

Ulloa's landing provoked angry protests, and decrees restricting Louisiana commerce to Spain added fuel to fiery temper. LaFreniere, leading a band of four hundred Acadian and German civilians came to New Orleans bent on physically forcing Ulloa and his troops from Louisiana, the first attempt by any indigenous force to eject a foreign power from the North American continent. The date was October 28, 1768, eight years before colonists on the eastern seaboard began their war against England. The courageous action by the hardy band of tough Acadians and Germans marked the beginning of a new era for Louisiana because they were in effect a home guard or precursor of today's National Guard. Their action expressed the will of the people. No military institution more aptly demonstrates the personality of its people than the National Guard.

Ulloa departed on the *El Volante* for Cuba. Alexander O'Reilly succeeded Ulloa as Spain's governor of the Louisiana Territory. He and his party took formal possession of New Orleans on August 18, 1769. O'Reilly had the support of two thousand mercenary soldiers and volunteers. He arrested the ringleaders of the revolt of October, 1768, and tried and executed them. He then issued a general amnesty to all the remaining citizens and laid down laws to govern Louisiana. A census the following year (1770) indicated a population of 13,513 for Louisiana. O'Reilly also issued laws regarding landgrants; the Spanish were intent upon colonizing Louisiana.

Luis de Unzaga y Amezaga, the next governor of Louisiana, served until he was replaced by Bernardo de Galvez in 1777. One notable event during Unzaga's term was the repulse of an English expedition against upper Louisiana by Pierre Laclede, an agent of Gilbert Antoine de St. Maxent, and his St. Louis militia.

Bernardo de Galvez, more than any other man, influenced Louisiana's ultimate success at colonization, trade, and coping with the Indians who constantly threatened its people and its commerce. Only thirty years of age when appointed governor, Galvez tackled his responsibilities with the fervor and skill of an experienced administrator and, in time, gained the respect and admiration of the French and German elements in the territory, a task that seemed, before his arrival, insurmountable. Bold and enterprising, Galvez, despite Spain's announced neutrality during the American Revolution, supplied arms, money, and provisions to the Americans along the frontiers. On September 7, 1789, a Galvez expedition captured the British Fort Bute at Manchac and soundly defeated them at the Battle of Baton Rouge on September 21 and 22 of the same year. On February 5, 1780 he forced the surrender of the British at Mobile, and in the same year a combined British and Indian attack on St. Louis was repulsed. Pensacola was captured from the British in 1781, thereby relieving all of West Florida from English domination. Also in 1781 a Spanish force was successful against a British post of St. Joseph in upper Louisiana. Galvez was also responsible for restoring Spanish rule to Natchez, an important post along the Mississippi. Another important milestone in Galvez' administration was the reestablishment of trade with France.

One of the most notable achievements of Governor Galvez was the impetus his administration gave to colonizing Louisiana. Spanish families from the Canary Islands were imported as settlers. Gilbert Antoine de St. Maxent assisted in establishing colonies at Galveztown, Bayou Manchac, and Valenzuela on Bayou Lafourche. Pedro de Marigny de Mandeville led a band to Terre aux Boeufs, and Francisco Bouligny organized five hundred immigrants from Malaga to found the settlement of New Iberia. Colonization was not limited to people of Spanish extraction, for over eleven hundred Acadian immigrants were settled near Galveztown.

Estevan Miro succeeded Galvez as governor of Louisiana after a brief term as governor ad-interim. On July 14, 1785, Miro was officially named governor. Among his most worthy accomplishments was the establishment of the West Florida districts of Manchac, Baton Rouge, and the Felicianas where he settled a number of

Acadian families. By 1785 the population of Louisiana had grown to 31,433; New Orleans had 5,000 inhabitants. The Acadians, who had returned to France after their expulsion from Canada, were brought to Louisiana by the Spanish government; they numbered about 1600.

Francois Louis Hector, baron de Carondelet, a Belgian by birth but in service to Spain, succeeded Miro, beginning his administration on January 1, 1792. The first newspaper of the colony, the *Moneteur de la Louisiane*, was established in New Orleans in 1794 by Carondelet who became its editor. Street lamps, drainage, and a night police force were other additions that Carondelet brought to the city in the wilderness. Fearing the strength of the British and the potential threat of the Americans upriver he had surrounding fortifications built. Carondelet prepared for all eventualities in considering the animosity between his government and that of the Americans.

Despite the solicitous consideration given the United States by Spain during the Revolutionary War, there was a great deal of friction between them. The Spanish refusal to open the Mississippi to free navigation was the cause of much discontent in the American settlements west of the Alleghenies, and several moves for detaching Louisiana from Spain or for seizing New Orleans were planned in this connection. Spain removed restrictions on commerce coming down the Mississippi in 1794, but three years later, Americans were again denied the right to use New Orleans as a port of deposit. Agitation for seizing the city was renewed. In view of all these rumblings and as a means of quelling the threats of dissidents, Spain and the United States signed the Treaty of San Lorenzo on October 20, 1795, which restored the port of New Orleans to the Americans' use, along with other privilege.

During Carondelet's administration much progress was made in the sugar industry. When Etienne de Bore, by mass producing sugarcane, proved that sugar could be commercially profitable by planting huge acreages, sugar became Louisiana's economic mainstay and remained so for generations.

On August 5, 1797, Brigadier General Manuel Luis Gayoso de Lemos, governor of Natchez, succeeded Carondelet. Two years later he was dead of yellow fever in the epidemic of 1799. He was the last of the more distinguished Spanish governors. Francisco Bouligny, Nicolas Maria Vidal, the Marquis de Casa Calvo, and Brigadier General Juan Manuel de Salcedo served brief, undistinguished terms during the two years from Gayoso's term until Louisiana was returned to

Colonization, Trial, and Traumas

France. The secret Treaty of San Ildefonso retroceded Louisiana back to France from Spain in exchange for Tuscany and recognition of the king of Etruria. The date of this treaty was October 1, 1800.

President Thomas Jefferson, upon learning of this transfer of Louisiana, immediately put into action a plan for acquiring the port of New Orleans since, "it is New Orleans through which the produce of three-eighths of our territory must pass to market." Robert Livingston, the American representative, pressed the French minister, Talleyrand, for news concerning Louisiana but could get no enlightening reply.

A crisis developed when Juan Ventura Morales, on October 16, 1802, acting as intendant for the territory, arbitrarily canceled the rights of deposit on the port of New Orleans, thus denying the Americans a vital means of marketing their commerce. Though the agreement contained in the Treaty of San Lorenzo had provided rights to the port only until 1798, there was, nevertheless, a gentleman's agreement between Spain and the Americans, and they had continued to bring their commerce there.

President Jefferson declared to Congress on December 15, 1802, that should France again occupy Louisiana, it would change their attitude in foreign relations. He then sent James Monroe as his personal emissary to treat with France for the purchase of Louisiana. Monroe joined Livingston in France while leaders at home raged against Spain and France. It was even suggested that the president seize New Orleans by calling out fifty thousand militiamen from the Mississippi Territory and neighboring states.

Napoleon considered the colony lost even though New Orleans was the main bargaining point of the Americans' interest. Of course, there was the delicate matter of transfer from Spain to France to be resolved. But negotiations went on. Talleyrand discreetly inquired of Livingston if the United States was interested in the whole of Louisiana. Livingston replied that they were only interested in New Orleans and Florida. Since Louisiana without New Orleans would be of little value, Talleyrand suggested that they consider purchasing the entire Louisiana Territory. After much banter back and forth probing for each other's motives, they finally agreed that Louisiana could be purchased for $15 million which included $11,250,000 in francs and reparations of $3,750,000, the claims American citizens made against France. The date of this purchase was April 30, 1803, though they did not get around to signing it until May 2.

Much has been made of the bargain the United States received. It is true the Louisiana Purchase was a bargain, but the astute Napoleon had gotten rid of a huge colony he would have had difficulty in defending against the superior English navy. He also strengthened the United States, an enemy of his British adversary. He received what was then an enormous amount of cash to bolster his treasury, Napoleon also perpetuated the good will that existed between France and the United States, a friendship that would persevere through generations. England and Spain, who tried to hold onto their New World colonies, received more headaches: administering the dissident minorities, draining their national treasuries and eventually losing their investments, all for which they received nothing but ill will.

The Louisiana Purchase increased the national domain by 140 percent; from its territory were carved all or part of thirteen states; Louisiana (admitted 1812), Missouri (1821), Arkansas (1836), Iowa (1846), Minnesota (1858), Kansas (1861), Nebraska (1867), North Dakota (1889), South Dakota (1889), Montana (1889), Wyoming (1890), and Oklahoma (1908). The greatest asset, of course, was that the United States was in complete control of the Mississippi River.

The Louisiana Purchase brought, besides territorial expansion, a measure of international prestige. Since this new territory was now under the protection of a nation in residence, an added impetus for colonization was created. Louisiana was finally and inexorably attached to the destiny of a young nation pulsating with inhabitants avid to explore and settle its frontiers. It was the dawn of a new era, but more important, Louisiana also brought with its addition, ethnic elements of a cosmopolitan nature. French, German, Spanish, Negroes, and a smattering of Anglo-Saxons, all tempered and hardened by the battle with the wilderness, would be the composite whole that typified the Louisianians of 1803.

Few governors offered as much hope for land ownership as did Governor Alexander O'Reilly, an Irish-born Spanish governor. In this chapter other significant notes include: a listing of the Louisiana Militia of 1770; the heartbreak to families scourged by disease, an unusually warm, moist climate, and constant threats from Indians; the "pathfinder" who exhibited great ability to cope with dense forests, broad rivers, and undefined terrain of every sort; and finally the settlers who took Governor O'Reilly up on his offer to make Louisiana their home.

CHAPTER 3

Birth of the Louisiana Militia

Civilians volunteered or were pressed into service to help the troops of France of Spain in the Louisiana Territory. As the colonists became established, units of militia were formed from the population to repulse invaders and to maintain peace during critical times. This creation of small armed forces representative of the people whom they were to protect was an innovation uniquely American.

During the era of mercenary armies the motivation for the average soldier was money or booty. Because the mercenaries protected the ruling class, they not only enjoyed an estimable status, but they became indispensable. As a consequence, their equipment, sustenance, and health were of primary importance to those dependent upon them. The uncertainties of the Louisiana wilderness—hostile Indians, diseases—rendered the mercenary soldier somewhat unreliable. There developed more and more reliance upon the home militias in the Louisiana Territory as was the case in the original thirteen colonies to the east.

The western pioneer, in his glorified role, had one major lethal enemy—the American Indian—whom the United States Cavalry helped him to conquer and dispossess. The pioneers of south Louisiana, however, had in addition to hostile Indians a more subtle and elusive enemy in the virulent diseases that proliferated in the warm climate and attacked with cruel constancy. Yellow fever, diphtheria, scarlet fever, croup, smallpox, influenza, and lockjaw were among the vicious decimaters of the population. The immigrants were trying to colonize a land held in dispute between France and Spain and threatened by England. Louisiana was probably the most difficult place to colonize in all the Americas. The odds were incalculable, and it came about after five decades of experimentation, trial and error, and through the unconquerable will of a cosmopolitan people—Frenchmen, Germans, Spaniards, and Negroes, principally.

One never knew the odds one might face upon parting the foliage of the wilderness. On March 22, 1700, Bienville, with only twenty-two Canadians, a Charanon Indian, and a Ouachita guide, attempting to ascertain the eastern position of the Spanish, arrived at the Mississippi settlement to find Don Andres de Arriola, governor of Pensacola at Ship Island with three ships and four hundred men. His purpose was to dispossess the French from the territory claimed by Spain. Fortunately, a French naval squadron appeared upon the horizon causing Arriola to give up his plan. In keeping with the entire early history of Louisiana, improbable chance and coincidence saved a colony and the founder of New Orleans. Settlers and part-time soldiers are the stars of the saga portrayed upon the scenes of dense forests, underbrush, broad rivers, and subtropical climate all to the accompaniment of droning mosquitoes. Travel was difficult; horses were not yet in use there, and the topography demanded the use of canoes or flatbottom boats with shallow draughts. Iberville, on one of his trips, was able to make 125 miles in thirty-four hours going downstream on the Mississippi; but the return trip was an arduous battle of men against exceptionally swift, high water. The bayous and rivers intersticed the land affording natural water navigation, and though the shallowness or depths of connecting streams varied to a great degree, crafts which drew little water could traverse Louisiana with few portages between points. The usual walking pace on land was five miles an hour with a short rest, each hour. The reason for slow pace was to preserve energy; stamina was more important than speed, for extreme exertion could make the party vulnerable to attack. It was imperative to be ready to fight upon a moment's notice, and if for any reason one had spent himself with a taxing physical chore, it rendered him less effective to a waiting enemy. All these odds were calculated at the outset by men who lived by chance and by the gun. A man could load, ram, aim, and fire his musket at the rate of four shots per minute. How many arrows could be discharged in the same time! An arrow was more accurate than the musket whose smooth bore merely discharged a pellet in the general direction of the target. Three hundred years were required to perfect the repeating rifle that dispossessed the American Indian; before the repeating rifle, the odds were virtually even.

After 1766, when Spanish troops first arrived in Louisiana, the regime brought about two important innovations: First, it fortified the far-flung outposts of a wilderness by establishing military posts at the mouth of the Mississippi River as far north as St. Louis and St. Genevieve, west to Natchitoches on the Red River, and as far east as the Apalachicola River including the nearby fort of San Marcos de Apalchee which formed the boundary between East and West Florida. The Spaniards also created more forts at intervening points and occupied former French forts, actions that secured the frontiers of the new settlement. Second, militia units were organized which provided a home guard that was representative of the colonists and capable of maintaining peace and repulsing threats from Indians, Englishmen, and the frontiersmen of the United States. Militias effected a citizen participation in home defense. These two memorable actions gave the needed impetus for permanence in the Louisiana Territory. Once the Louisiana settlers were given a voice in their government—though initial expression was through participation in the militia—Louisiana began to progress. The home militia, with a secure frontier, protected an arena where people could prosper.

For generations, life in wild Louisiana was of necessity based upon military security and action; without armed might and vigilance there was no survival. Though much emphasis has been given the regular army in detailing our national history, the role of the home militias in the drama of Americana has often been overlooked. When wars or internal cries arose, the home militias formed a nucleus of volunteers to supplant the regulars or quickly assembled and restored order to areas under martial law. The spirit that motivated them was born in the swamps and highlands of the southern extremity of the huge Louisiana Territory, and due credit should be given Spain and the benevolence and direction of those early governors.

As early as 1764 Spain began experimenting with changes in the militias and in the regular army among Mexican colonists. Instead of relying solely upon fixed stations of fortifications, there were instituted permanent regiments at strategic positions. These regiments were mobile and the forts were not. Therefore the regiments could be dispatched to threatened points. The office of inspector general was created to supervise the infantry; others inspected the artillery, cavalry, and engineers. The inspector general raised, instructed, trained, and disciplined the troops through men responsible to him alone. The entire responsibility of creating an armed force and maintaining its morale was the onus of a man answerable directly to the governor. This, of course, established a rigid chain of command, as well as peacetime surveillance of the military upon which the survival of the Spanish colonists depended. The militia was thereby insured against disintegration through inactivity. Further, the office of inspector general eliminated whatever friction arose between the regulars and the militiamen.

Spain began to depend more and more upon the colonists to fill its army. Trained at weekly instruction and drill, they were to be the force to meet the first onslaught of any invading force. Captain General Alexander O'Reilly, representing the king of Spain, with absolute power, organized the first Louisiana militia on February 12, 1770—1,040 men representing thirteen companies who were drilled regularly and were provisioned by the government of Spain. In New Orleans, there were four of these companies; one company was assigned to each of the following: St. Louis, St. Genevieve, and the parishes of St. Charles, St. John the Baptist, Lafourche de Chetimaches, including Ascension Parish, Cabahonocy, including St. James, Natchitoches, Pointe Coupee, and Opelousas. Each company comprised a captain, a lieutenant, sublieutenant, three sergeants, four first-class corporals, four second-class corporals, and sixty men. Legends persist that a battery was formed among the French at the junction of Bayou Lafourche and the Mississippi which eventually became known as the Donaldsonville Cannoneers. Routine Sunday military drills and target practice provided a common denominator under which all the ethnic elements could perform collectively for the good of the colonies. This was the beginning of harmonious relationships among people whose ancestors had fought so many bloody battles on the European continent and whose contemporary kinsmen were still bitter enemies in quest of territorial expansion in the New World. A feeling of mutual reliance was the immediate result, and the brilliant O'Reilly should be credited with this move which portended so much good for Louisiana. The wide range in the age requirement for eligibility in the militia—fifteen to fifty—gave Spain a means of indoctrinating the young and middle aged—sometimes father and son—and an intimate contact with the adult population, current and future.

Birth of the Louisiana Militia

The English under General Thomas Gage, British commander in chief in North America, viewed the Spanish fortifications and the training of the colonists for the militia with apprehension concerning future relationships with Spain. When Unzaga succeeded O'Reilly, the defenses of Louisiana were in a good state. But Unzaga was still unconvinced that Louisiana would withstand an attack by England either on the frontier or from the Gulf. He therefore called for and received 100 more regulars plus 800 guns and bayonets. An attack had been planned by General Gage, but Unzaga through his own intelligence learned of it. Intense reinforcements of defenses resulted, with special attention given to the militias. Veteran regulars were employed to train the militia. The total force of men in the cosmopolitan militias at this time numbered 1,630 including free Negroes and mulattos. Unzaga created a battalion of New Orleans militia on June 1, 1775, and fitted it out in resplendent uniforms of blue jacket with a white front, red collars and lapels, all highlighted with shiny gold buttons. It was an era of beautiful uniforms that flattered the aging and accented the beauty of youth. By the 1760s martial music had been popularized by the Prussian Frederick the Great, whose genius the world was recognizing. Elegant uniforms, the stirring strains of blaring brass music set to the beat of drums, providing a vivid contrast to the wilderness, inspired the young colony. The outlands were alerted: St. Charles, St. James, St. John, Bayou Lafourche, Natchitoches, Pointe Coupee, Opelousas, and all the intervening points stood ready to fight against the British. The only attack that materialized was that made against Spanish Illinois, and it was quickly repulsed. But the militia had mobilized for the first time in the Louisiana Territory and not as an individual contingent with a remote objective but as a unified force intent upon defending Louisiana from a trespasser, a potential oppressor. For the first time in the Americas there was a unification of nationalities and races forged together in the heat of expectant danger. They did not get to fight the British; the dispute was resolved diplomatically. But they did get to wear their handsome uniforms and to revel collectively in the excitement. They paraded, celebrated, and danced, and the pride they derived from belonging to the land was contagious, spreading from one to the other. Finally, Louisiana was worth fighting for.

When Bernardo de Galvez became governor in 1777, he quickly determined by a census that of the Louisiana population of 17,926 there were 1,956 white men capable of meeting his army requirements. Like his predecessors, he pushed for excellence in the militias. By this time the first-generation Louisianians of wealth had developed a society that excluded wage-earners, tradesmen, and the indigent. In a delicate but firm maneuver Galvez inveigled this elitist group into organizing a company of cavalry equipped with sabers, carbines, and pistols. The men supplied their own mounts and uniforms consisting of dark jackets, white vests and breeches, and the usual gold buttons. They represented the most affluent males of Louisiana and were the first of the elite to form a militia in the state. Galvez also added to the strength of the militia by organizing more artillery units. A study of the military roster at this period of Louisiana history reveals French and German names familiar today in the state. With certain spelling variations, some of the rosters of 1770 to 1789 include such names as: Duplessis, Villars, Duforest, Cavelier, Guenard, Dejean, Jolibert, Ferrand, Laurent, Tondeau, Bertrand, Paul, Limier, Bertaud, Fourtin, Picou, Honore, Moise, Gaspard, Janvier, Millet, Perrin, Chamont, Roche, Tournoir, Maxent, Lafitte, Bienvenu, Veber, Fortier, Plauchet, Belluc, Fauche, Vivarest, Laugon, Judice, Simon, Lemaire, Dubuisson, Jourdan, Gaubert, Normand, Lacoste, Benoist, Roussy, Millon, Carriere, Costa, Grenet, Olivier, Ficher, Blaise, Duvernay, Lemair, Grau, Paillet, Prevost, Goudeau, Guidroz, Marachal, Zeringue, Biert, Lacroix, Dupre, Minard, Lauve, Lavergne, Lachappelle, Gignon, Brunet, Marchand, Poiree, Ferrand, Gernier, Langlois, Wiltz, Barbier, Sicard, Gaillard, Boutte, Veillon, Duroche, Boucher, Blanc, Daublain, Gilbee, Robert, Mouton, Lemoine, Dubois, Stillet, Adam, Ledue, Schmith, Landau, Durand, Giraux, Lorio, Daigle, Roman, Trepagnier, Rousseau, Lemelle, Jonas, Vibert, Chenier, DiMarco, Bertrand, Bourgeois, Quillain, Massicot, St. Amant, Albert, Lepine, Rixnaer Menard, Vagenback, Kindler, Graber, Gottier, Delanded, Verret, Labranche, Toups, Baudoin, Champagne, Edelmayrer, Krim, Houvre, Belson, Sechschneyder, Dorvain, Borne, Pieux, Zisclaer, Pochet, Materne, Badoux, Duval, Himel, Hautin, Triche, Rixner.

Vichof, Lesch, Keller, Conrad, Rouque, Jacob, Naexigre, Monts, Bouillon, Periguex, Michel, Vicner, Kerner, Kamer, Dupont, Harois, Treger, Stader, Andre, LeBouef, Lambre, Bossier, Folse, Dubier, Denoyer, Lagrange, Loup, Frederic, Becnel, Delatre, Dupuy, Rodrigue, Seghneiter, Weber, Blanchard, Haidel, Trudel, Dufrene, Romel, Ducarreaux, Maillet, Reine, Lacin, Lesage, Martin, Lanber, Barron, Colmar, Dauphin, St. Amand, Focheux, Dexte, Vasquespacq, Graber,

Birth of the Louisiana Militia

Insler, Arcenaux, Focheux, Ydlemaire, Deslone, Labranche, Boutellie, Pertuy, St. Elloy, Bauvais, Chovin, Dorvin, Brou, Troxlere, Falgout, Parre, Canue, Darensbour, Simonette, Badau, Pinatelle, Romme, Rouselle, Himelle, Andry, Verloin, Mellieure, Degruize, Dotrive, Rillieux, Delhommer, Robain, Emme, Pizare, and Mather.

Many of the names prominent in the militia of the 1770s and 1780s are still outstanding today. For instance, two Daigles appear in the rosters of the state militias during its earliest history, and two hundred years later Major General O. J. Daigle, Jr., serves as adjutant general, the highest military office in the state.

Galvez recruited soldiers and their families from the Canary Islands, and by July, 1779, over 1,500 of these immigrants had arrived in Louisiana. Of these, 329 were married men and 153 single; the rest were women and children. The emphasis now was on more colonization and the strengthening of Louisiana's defenses. By recruiting soldiers and their families from Spain's possessions, Galvez was able to do both. The average pay for a soldier was twenty cents per day. The prospect of war between England and Spain seemed imminent, and the American colonies were now in rebellion against the British. In its designs on New World territory, Spain began wooing the eastern colonies by sending supplies to Americans along the frontiers.

Galvez sent agents to all outposts to gather intelligence relative to British strength and positions. They ascertained that England's main strongholds were Manchac, Natchez, Baton Rouge, and Pensacola, and a small force at Mobile. The militia was immediately put on the alert and mobilized. The British had fortified Manchac with a small citadel called Fort Bute, named after an English diplomat. On August 27, 1779, Galvez moved out of New Orleans at the head of his troops, intent upon capturing Fort Bute. Included in his army were 60 militiamen from New Orleans, the regular army, 80 free Negroes, plus the militiamen who joined him along the way from such points as Pointe Coupee, Opelousas, Attakapas (now the Teche country), settlements along Bayou Lafourche, and the Mississippi River, making a total of 1,427. At last the preparedness that the Spanish governors had envisioned manifested itself in a cohesive multinational unit capable of offensive action—the first army of any consequence recruited and trained in the Territory of Louisiana. Most of it turned out to be militia.

Eleven days after the first segments of Galvez' army left the city of New Orleans they arrived at the site of Fort Bute. The British, in anticipation of Galvez' arrival, decided Fort Bute's position was not defensible and removed most of its forces to a stronger position at Baton Rouge. Only twenty-seven British men defended the fort, and in a matter of hours their captain surrendered. Coincidental with this operation, the Galveztown militia captured Post Green near the Iberville River (Bayou Manchac) and then took two British ships moored on Bayou Galveztown near Lake Maurepas. The quick successes emboldened the men in Galvez' army and increased their eagerness to take the redoubt at Baton Rouge. Upon reconnaissance of Baton Rouge, Galvez devised a plan of siege and immediately began digging trenches and placing his cannons in strategic positions while his army, to confuse the defendants, began divergent maneuvers. A force of over six hundred men, excluding local civilians and Indian sympathizers pressed into service, defended Baton Rouge.

Beginning with an exchange of cannon fire, the battle accelerated into concentrated musket fire that raged for twenty-four hours. By then the British realized the hopelessness of their situation and capitulated. The terms were unconditional and embodied conditions for the surrender of all posts England held on the Mississippi, foremost of which was the strong fortification upriver at Natchez.

Galvez took Mobile in the campaign of the following year (1780) and Pensacola in 1781, which together with the action at Fort Bute and Baton Rouge were the major events in which the Louisiana militia participated in the American Revolution. Louisiana now had a stake in the larger North American continent.

The militiamen were idolized in their respective villages and countrysides for their participation in the defense of their homeland. Privileges were accorded them such as preferential treatment in obtaining licenses to operate saloons, inns, restaurants, and other businesses. After years of rugged unglamourous pioneering, they enjoyed the thrills attendant to returning home as heroes.

> Hail our heroes far and near!
> In our country's service, proud
> Know them by the clothes they wear
> Their uniforms, their soldier shrouds!

Estevan Miro succeeded Governor Galvez, and under his direction military preparedness underwent the same stringent supervision. Miro actually increased the regular army, strengthening the territory's eastern defenses. Even though they fought as allies with the

Americans against the British, there was still a bit of resentment towards Spain's control of the mouth of the Mississippi. There was also a measure of mutual distrust. By the power of his office, Miro was commander in chief of the military in Louisiana, and he considered the integrity of the borders of his domain of paramount importance. By 1784 his regular army consisted of over 1,400 men and officers. Added to this were twenty-two companies of ready militias strung along the Mississippi River and Bayou Lafourche, including six companies of infantry and one of artillery in New Orleans.

Distrust between Spain and the American colonies posed many threats. Georgia, exhibiting its sovereignty in an action independent of any of the other colonies, threatened to march on New Orleans because of a territorial dispute. Perhaps intelligence of Louisiana's strong militia deterred them. The closing of the port of New Orleans also brought precipitate action. In 1787 John Sullivan, of the defunct state of Franklin, was dissuaded from a plan to capture New Orleans by the United States War Department. Similar threats were made in 1790 and 1791.

Baron Francois Luis Hector de Carondelet, who succeeded Miro as governor of Louisiana, had a long distinguished record as an administrator. He attacked the problem of defense in Louisiana with vigor and perseverance. Aided by Joseph Xavier Delfau, baron de Pontalba, Carondelet laid out some grandiose schemes, foremost of which was to put the militias on the same footing as the Regular Army. The nucleus of the militia would be to establish companies from Baton Rouge, Pointe Coupee, the Felicianas (north of Baton Rouge), Galveztown, Attakapas, and Opelousas. These units would be capable of assembling at Manchac within five days and could serve within short notice at strategic points in case of attack, delaying the enemy while New Orleans amassed its troops for counterattack. Carondelet also wanted the militia to equal the Regular Army in regard to chains of command, training, and equipment. Louisiana had a natural defense in the seasonal rise and fall of its waterways, particularly the Mississippi River. The swamps were another deterrent to attacks on New Orleans, therefore waterway protection was an essential. The average Louisianian had, by this time, become acclimated to his homeland; he traversed its rivers and swamps with equal ease. His mode of life like that of other frontiersmen required the ready rifle for game or enemy, and as a result he was, in most cases, a superb marksman.

Naturally, Carondelet's revolutionary idea of putting the militia on the same footing as the Regular Army met with opposition. People in high places were appalled at the thought of being trained and armed like ordinary civilians. Carondelet met the same resistance that Washington had regarding the retention of trained militia among the sovereign colonies. Carondelet did win out, however, and though he is seldom acknowledged for his achievement, the most advanced method of fostering and sustaining a militia in direct proportion to the strength of its population was initiated. It is to Spain's credit that her autocratic regime was more liberal in respect to the creation of a people's army than those American champions of democracy.

Under the Spanish governors, Louisiana continued great advances in securing its frontiers. The population was relatively sparse but concentrated; therefore males of eligible ages for service in the militias were actually soldiers in residence. By 1803 the strength of the militias in Louisiana was considerable, and Louisiana's secure frontier attracted American colonists. Through the dense woods Anglo-Saxons came westward to settle along tributaries of the Mississippi River—the Illinois, Ouachita, Red rivers, and others—that led to the sea by use of the port of New Orleans. The tedious, incendiary problems of the past except control of the port were resolving themselves, and the port question would be resolved by the Louisiana Purchase. Slowly, surely, wilderness had become a thriving, growing territory dotted with villages and populated countrysides that would spawn towns and cities. And as the population grew the militia grew proportionately.

It has been estimated that by the end of the Spanish domination Louisiana had over 10,000 militiamen. The Island of New Orleans and its vicinity, which included the east and west side of the Mississippi River up to Bayou Lafourche, contained 5,000 militiamen. Manchac, including Pointe Coupee, and as far as the Red River 800; Ancapas, that region along the coast from the mouth of the Mississippi to the Sabine River, 350; Opelousas (the territory, not the present city) 750; Red River, which included settlements along Bayou Boeuf, Rapides, Natchitoches and Avoyelles 1,000; Ouachita 300; Concord 40; Arkansas 150; New Madrid 350; Illinois and Missouri 1,000; scattered to the east in areas now the state of Mississippi 600; plus militiamen in the area of the Calcasieu River and west of the Sabine as far west as Nacogdoches.[1] The Spanish

---

[1] Jack D. L. Holmes, *Honor and Fidelity* (Birmingham, 1965), 53.

governors prepared Louisiana for its appointment with destiny: transfer of the territory to the United States. Jefferson and his adherents had bargained for a wilderness with an established port, New Orleans. They received far more than they bargained for; thriving settlements along the Mississippi Valley, growing commerce, a stable economy, an ever increasing population, and a ready-made army, the Louisiana militiamen.

No one was better prepared, or more welcomed, to become the first American governor of Louisiana than the central figure of this chapter, William C.C. Claiborne. Beneath him is Marquis de Lafayette of France, an honorary citizen of the newly acquired territory. The American flag rose first in the Place d'Armes accompanied by a gun salute. Responsible for the transference of the territory from France was Jefferson's emissary, James Monroe, depicted in the lower lefthand corner.

CHAPTER 4

Politics, Intrigue, and the Pawn

After the secret Treaty of San Ildefonso of October 1, 1800, whereby Spain retroceded Louisiana to France, rumors of the retrocession plus the closing of the port of New Orleans disturbed the tranquility of the area. Some blamed the French; but those of French sympathies felt a measure of relief that they were again going to be French citizens. Historians have had a difficult time in piecing together all the details and motivations for this enigmatic diplomacy. The Louisianians' preoccupation with the ambivalences of France and Spain's mysterious negotiations left them open to surprise when the United States purchased Louisiana.

The Spaniards were relieved that they were not going to belong to France; citizens of French ancestry were outraged and some threatened to forsake Louisiana and settle elsewhere. The Anglo-Saxon settlers, however, were delighted with the transaction. Pierre Clement De Laussant, Napoleon's emissary, who had been sent to Louisiana to officially begin the transfer of Louisiana back to France now also had the official duty of transferring the territory to the United States. By appointment of President Jefferson, William Charles Cole Claiborne was designated to receive the territory, but only after it was officially transferred to France from Spain. In a ceremony on November 30, 1803, the red and yellow flag of Spain was lowered, and in its stead rose the brilliant tricolor of France. The site was the Place D'Armes, the square in front of the cathedral of St. Louis in New Orleans.

Twenty days later on December 20, 1803, the Territory of Louisiana was officially transferred to the United States of America. It was a new beginning for Louisiana's people. The Louisiana Purchase brought into the United States vast quantities of land, forests, and great rivers. It also brought a cosmopolitan, somewhat exotic society composed principally of French, Spaniards, Germans, Negroes, and Anglo-Saxons (English, Welsh, Scottish, and Irish). These diversified ethnic elements, the first amalgamation of so many races in the New World, portended even greater events to come, the mass migrations of Europe's varying nationalities to America.

The military ceremony transferring Louisiana to the United States was festive. Prominent among the soldiers of France and Spain were three hundred militiamen, who pledged allegiance to the new flag. Besides participating in the impressive ceremony, the soldiers were assigned the duties of keeping peace and order. It was a Monday morning. Eight thousand New Orleanians joined with the usual transients—tradespeople who came to market, and crewmen and passengers from the ships docked along the wharves. The territory's population was about fifty thousand, and all but six thousand lived in what would become the state of Louisiana.

The militiamen, upon the request of Daniel Clark, Jr., American consul in New Orleans, were to serve until the arrival of United States troops. It is significant that the militiamen, or National Guardsmen, were the first official local and American armed force present when Louisiana became part of the United States. The militia commander was Colonel Joseph Bellechasse, a prominent plantation owner and soldier. J. W. Monette, noted historian, claims that the militiamen's first muster was a brief march on the streets of the Vieux Carre.

Governor Claiborne, only twenty-eight years old, but already worldly wise, educated, articulate, and discerning, made an impassioned speech that fell on a lot of deaf ears since most of the population did not understand English. The Babel of languages—French, Spanish, German, Negro dialects, and English resounded in the only area added to this country where a majority of the population did not understand or use the language of the nation to which they belonged.

Historians, in their haste to pay homage to the first American governor, William C. C. Claiborne and his splendid service at Chalmette during the Battle of New Orleans, have tended to overlook the ingeniously designed psychology wrought by Galvez, Miro, and Carondelet. These Spanish leaders took advantage of the martial enthusiasm emanating from the successful military exploits of Frederick the Great and Napoleon. Louisianians were also influenced by settlers from the French Caribbean Isles, principally Martinique and Santo Domingo, who came to Louisiana during the slave uprisings of 1801, and brought with them a martial spirit indigneous to Napoleonic France. In Spanish Louisiana, uniforms of magnificent beauty and design clothed the soldiers and set them apart from the rest of society. Frederick's martial music, developed to an exalted degree by Napoleon's masters, was also a source of inspiration. All these components—brilliant uniforms with equally colorful flags and banners, martial music, and heroes to emulate—proved a respite from the drudgery of everyday chores in conquering a wilderness and sustaining the human body. It was exciting to be a soldier.

Governor Claiborne indicated to President Jefferson that he wished Louisiana to become a state immediately, but in the same dispatch he expressed fear that the time was inopportune. There was apprehension between Claiborne and his Latin constituents, but the southern portion of Louisiana was declared by Congress on March 26, 1804, to be the Territory of New Orleans. Creation of the state of Louisiana would follow.

Jefferson considered many men for governor of Orleans. Among them was the Marquis de Lafayette, of France, an honorary citizen of the United States, and capable of relating to the Creole population and its language; James Monroe was also offered the post. Both men refused. Thereupon, Jefferson appointed Claiborne permanent governor of Orleans, and he was sworn in on October 2, 1804. But this by no means settled the issue because its people had hoped that Louisiana would be given statehood. American law was in conflict with theirs, and land titles were unclear. Spanish officials were still occupied with the delicate machinery of transition while rumors persisted that Louisiana would revert to France or even Spain; general unrest prevailed.

The Territory of Orleans gained representative government by an act of Congress in March, 1805, and in June, 1806, had its first territorial legislative session. Added to the problems of Claiborne and other officials was trouble on the western borner. Spain claimed that the Mexican territory extended to a point just west of Natchitoches, though the United States asserted the line of demarcation to be the

Sabine River. But Spain immediately occupied Los Adaes, little more than a spot on the map in Natchitoches Parish. The militia was immediately alerted and sent to reinforce the garrison at Natchitoches. In the meantime, General Wilkinson, with troops from St. Louis, hastened to the era. The Spainsh commander, General Herrera, sensing the gravity of the situation, retreated his army across the Sabine while the Americans followed in their wake, stopping at the east bank of the river. Thus matters stood with opposing armies facing either side of the Sabine River. Wilkinson and General Herrera avoided war by letting the matter rest until Washington and Spain could resolve the dispute.

Governor Claiborne, on April 10, 1805, created a regulatory agency for maintaining the first American militia in Louisiana according to specific regulations. It was officially referred to as the Militia Of The Territory of Orleans. Claiborne realized, as did the Spanish governors, that Louisiana was extremely vulnerable along its borders. The only protection lay in maintaining and expanding the local militias, which would be on constant alert to meet every contingency. Each militia would be capable of a delaying action in its area until reinforcements arrived. This was the overall strategy, and emphasis was placed on the maintenance of a strong militia throughout the territory.

There were many American settlers in the west of Florida whose borders abutted the southern end of eastern Louisiana. These people, seeing their western neighbors free from the yoke of foreign rule, asserted themselves by open rebellion against their Spanish masters as early as 1805. In 1810 they staged another full-scale rebellion. Baton Rouge, a short distance away from the border of Florida was attacked; the fort there fell, and its commander, Lieutenant Louis de Grand Pre, among others, was killed. Governor Claiborne, under orders from President Monroe, mobilized his forces and moved into West Florida, occupied it, quelled the rebellion, claimed it, and annexed it to the Territory of Orleans, where it has remained ever since. This section of the state is still known as the Florida Parishes and it comprises St. Helena, Washington, St. Tammany and Tangipahoa.

By 1810 the census indicated that the population of the Territory of Orleans was in excess of seventy thousand, comfortably enough over the required sixty thousand for eligibility for statehood. Julien Poydras, the territory's delegate, on January 2, 1811, broached the matter of statehood to Congress. At first the proposal was received with much opposition; the Federalists of New England fought the bill, and Massachusetts, through the voice of Josiah Quincy, threatened secession if the Territory of Orleans was granted statehood. However, on January 14, 1811, the Territory was empowered to establish itself as a state. Orleans became Louisiana, and on April 30, 1812, entered the Union as the eighteenth state. In an election for governor of the new state of Louisiana, William C. C. Claiborne won over General Jacques Villere, becoming its first American territorial governor and the first to head the state of Louisiana.

Perhaps Louisiana should have entered the Union earlier, as a state. Its relatively sparse population was one obstacle. The initial disillusionment Louisianians experienced with the hierarchy governing the territory and the reciprocity of the Americans discouraged harmony. Distrust because of ethnic contrasts and languages lent nothing to the reconciliation of differences. Colonel Bellechasse, who commanded the noble band of militia on Monday morning of December 20, 1803, when the American flag first went up the mast in Louisiana, became so disgusted with ensuing events that he left and settled in Cuba. Others with similar feelings departed. The extreme humid weather, yellow fever, and the isolation from other settled areas delayed statehood. As far as Washington and the eastern states of the Union were concerned, Louisiana's main, and perhaps only, asset then was the city of New Orleans.

But if the people of Louisiana had conquered the wilderness, diseases, especially yellow fever and malaria, would continue to take their toll. There was, however, optimism during the period of early statehood. After being bandied from pillar to post by the Spanish and French, Louisiana had finally found its destiny as part of the United States. It had attributes: the Mississippi River, fast becoming that Main Street of America, a thriving and growing port at the city of New Orleans, an energetic cosmopolitan society, and an excellent militia.

With the threat to his beloved city outweighing the threat to his own life, Pirate Jean Laffite raised a warning of the approaching British, released his brother, Pierre, from jail and became the central figure of this chapter. The historic location was the battlefield at Chalmette. Drawn at bottom center is the legendary cannon of the Donaldsonville Cannoneers. In the bottom right corner is depicted Jacques Philippe Villere, the first Creole chosen to control the destinies of his native state, having served as governor and major general of the state militia in the Battle of New Orleans.

CHAPTER 5

The American Merger

The acquisition of Louisiana almost precipitated the dissolution of the United States. Actually the New England states had threatened secession over the Louisiana Purchase. The constant menace of England's high-handed methods on the seas, which threatened American commerce, unified the people for defense. The War of 1812 was the anvil upon which American unity was forged. This war came when a unifying force was sorely needed, and the results of the bloody conflict underlined the importance of Louisiana and its people to the common defense of an expanding nation.

A brief review of the furor which the purchase of Louisiana created will help the reader to fully understand the importance of the War of 1812.

The constitutionality of secession was debated in the North more than fifty years before the Civil War. Thomas Jefferson in his first inaugural address on March 4, 1801, said: "If there be any among us who would wish to dissolve the Union . . . let them stand as monuments of the safety with which error of opinion may be tolerated when reason is left to combat it." Early in the nineteenth century, William Plumer of New Hampshire stated: "State Justice and State Power were the only remaining shelter of the wise, the good and the rich, from the wild destroying rage of Southern Jacobins." Remarks such as Jefferson's and Plumer's imprinted in the minds of the dissidents the idea of secession as a protective measure against domination by forces whose interests were contrary to that of the New England states. Samuel Hunt, a Congressman from New Hampshire, clarified the New England position with these remarks: "It was necessary for the commercial States north of Maryland to separate from the tobacco planters and establish an authoritarian regime more favorable to a mercantile aristocracy," But Senator Plumer pressing this point further said that the situation was becoming one "which every year will add power and influence to the South and to the West at the expense of the East." And he asked this question: "Should New England support and submit to a government directed by slaveholders?"

The Louisiana Purchase fanned the flames of disunity and almost caused some of the New England states to secede from the Union. Louisiana's appointment with destiny ran the gantlet of emotion, caused by political suspicions, monetary interests and regional preoccupation. Timothy Pickering of Massachusetts, the leader of a secessionist movement declared, "We had the right to acquire new territory . . . and the right to rule it as a dependent province. But the right to incorporate it into the Union? Never!" And Uriah Tracy of Connecticut, in quick agreement, orated, "No doubt we can attain territory . . . even all of Louisiana, and a thousand times more if we please, without violating the Constitution . . . but to admit the inhabitants into the Union, to make citizens of them, and States, by treaty, we cannot constitutionally do." Tracy added that ratification of the Louisiana Purchase, "would be absorbing the Northern States and rendering them as insignificant to the Union as they ought to be, if by their own consent, the measures should be adopted."

New Hampshire's Plumer revealed the New Englanders' plan for secession by saying, "Admit this western world into the Union and you destroy at once the weight and importance of the Eastern States, and compel them to establish a separate, independent empire." Fortunately, John Quincy Adams, though not concurring with Jefferson and the validity of the Louisiana transaction, did give it his wholehearted endorsement thereby neutralizing, to a degree, the bitter opposition. The motion for the ratification of the Louisiana Purchase carried by a vote of twenty-four to seven.

There were valid causes for alarm on the part of the New Englanders. The third paragraph of Section 2 of the first article of the new Constitution of the United States gave the southern states representation in Congress based in part on their slave populations.

Under such a provision, a southern planter who owned fifty slaves had as much voice in federal affairs as thirty northern free men. (Representation was apportioned among the several states according to their respective numbers, which was determined by adding to the whole of free persons—excluding Indians not taxed—three-fifths of all other persons. All other persons, of course, meant slaves.

Also, Louisiana brought with it a system of French and Spanish law which many felt was incompatible with the common law of England on which all the other states' laws were based. Barely a month after the ratification of the Louisiana Purchase, Jedediah Morse of Massachusetts stated in a letter to Plumer, "I have long been of the opinion that a division of the States would become indispensable to the preservation of our dearest interests. . . . If the States east of the Potomac and Allegheny Mountains could be peaceably erected into a separate government, under the present constitution without the Amendments which have been made since its adoption, I should hope that the reign of New England liberty would be prolonged." Judge Richard Peters of Pennsylvania added his opinions with this, "I will rather anticipate a new confederacy exempt from the corrupt and corrupting influences and oppression of the aristocratic Democrats of the South."

By January, 1804, the demand for secession became an obvious conspiracy as Senators Plumer, Tracy, Pickering, and Hillhouse and Congressmen Griswold and Hunt, plus other representatives of the New England states, met in Washington to plan the dissolution of the Union. They were to meet later at Boston to consider future action.

Senator Pickering, the leader of the secession plot, indicated in a letter to his nephew that Massachusetts should take the lead; Connecticut would join, too; New Hampshire was certain; Rhode Island would follow; there was no great difficulty with Vermont; New York would also concur; New Jersey would assuredly become an associate, and Pennsylvania might be persuaded to join their confederacy. They envisioned a northern Union to which England would not object. In a letter to George Cabot, Pickering said: "The people of the East cannot reconcile their habits, views and interests with those of the South and West. . . . I do not believe in the practicability of a long-continued union. A Northern confederacy would unite congenial characters, and present a fairer prospect of public happiness; while the Southern States, having a similarity of habits, might be left to manage their own affairs in their own way." In a bitter letter to a

Mr. Wolcott, Griswold stated, "We may also liberate ourselves entirely from the Louisiana stock, and leave that to be paid by those for whose benefit it was created."

There were, of course, many New England leaders who saw no cause for alarm by the purchase of Louisiana. George Cabot said as much in a letter to Pickering, "All the evils you describe and many more are to be apprehended, but . . . a separation is now impractical because we do not feel the necessity or utility of it." But momentum was added to the secession movement when Aaron Burr, vice-president of the United States, resigned his high office to join the secessionists to run for governor of New York in the hopes that his elevation to this office would ultimately make him head of a northern confederacy. His bitter foe, Alexander Hamilton, warned the secessionists that Burr would use the movement to foster his own aims. After Burr's defeat for the governorship of New York, Hamilton was challenged to the fatal duel because Burr claimed Hamilton's disparaging remarks had caused his defeat. Hamilton's death, on June 11, 1804, convinced most of the secessionists that separation from the Union would be folly, and they went to some lengths to rectify the harm caused by the movement. The idea lay dormant until January 14, 1811, when Congressman Josiah Quincy of Massachusetts stated on the House floor that if the Territory of Orleans became a state, it would mean the dissolution of the Union and free the states from their moral obligation.

In dramatic fashion the statehood bill did pass; Louisiana was admitted to the Union; the New England states did not secede, and their resentments and hopes died out together. But no state in the Union had the scrutiny that Louisiana had; nor were any ever subjected to such fiery denouncements.

As early as 1808 Governor Claiborne gave attention to the state militias and managed an appropriation of $200,000 which he applied to equipment. This was the first money set aside for the militias after Louisiana became a state. On September 7, 1812, the state assembly, in a resolution, instructed the governor to ask for four thousand stands of arms, four hundred sabers, and other necessary military supplies. By authority of an act of February 12, 1813, Claiborne reorganized the militia, and hundreds of printed copies of new regulations and instructions were sent to all commanders throughout the state. These created uniformity, harmony, and purpose among a membership of great cultural diversity. The act contained fifty-one

The American Merger

sections denoting every aspect of military regulations relevant to Louisiana. Male citizens from sixteen to fifty were eligible for enrollment, and by the hundreds they joined Louisiana's military. They were eager to parade, to learn military tactics, and to defend Louisiana.

When war with England was declared on June 18, 1812, Louisiana initially provided a volunteer company under the command of Captain George Thompson. This company was formed by July 27 and was composed principally of Anglo-Saxons; the exact number of men in the contingent is unknown. Louisianians had become apathetic toward frequent rumors of invasion, but a threatened attack by the Creek Indians aroused fear. On December 23, 1813, General Andrew Jackson, whose forces included a brigade of Louisiana and Mississippi Volunteers, destroyed Holy Ground, the capitol of the Creek nation, and the scene of a massacre at Fort Mims, now in Alabama. The initial fear was that the Choctaws and runaway slaves would join the Creeks in a march on New Orleans. But Jackson's victory over them was so complete that they ceased to be a threat to Louisiana. The brigade of Louisianians and Mississippians returned to Baton Rouge and on March 22, 1814, were discharged. At this late date the threat of England invading Louisiana did not receive the urgent attention it needed, but Governor Claiborne did continue to improve home defenses and strengthen the militias.

Patrols were established to reconnaissance vulnerable points along the Louisiana frontier, particularly on its eastern border. Some of the runaway slaves did join the Choctaws, but Lake Pontchartrain and Maurepas afforded a ring of defense. There were some forts in defense of the city of New Orleans: Fort Petite Coquilles (later to become Fort Pike in 1827) on the Rigolets; Fort St. Charles at the foot of Esplanade Avenue; Fort St. John at the mouth of the bayou on Lake Pontchartrain; Fort St. Leon about twelve miles south of New Orleans at what is known as English Turn; Fort Bienvenu, later called Battery Bienvenu on Bayou Bienvenu; and Fort St. Phillip about fifty-eight miles south of the city on the Mississippi River. There was also a small redoubt at Balize near the mouth of the river. None of these forts, however, were of major importance. They were places at which a small band could perhaps create a delaying action until troops were sent to reinforce the position. An adjutant general's survey indicated at once that all these fortifications were in need of repair; none had adequate supports for cannons; nor were they of a size to garrison a large body of men. At best each could be a lookout and shelter for patrols. But General Jackson did order the repairs, particularly at Fort St. Phillip since from there any ship coming up the Mississippi could be sunk.

The inclusion of West Florida in Louisiana prompted Governor Claiborne, on February 24, 1813, to completely reorganize the militia. Two divisions were set up as follow:

FIRST DIVISION: Major General Jacques Phillipe Villere

REGIMENT	MEN	LOCALITY
1st	235	City of New Orleans and Faubourgs.
2nd	358	City of New Orleans and Faubourgs.
3rd	285	Plaquemines Parish.
4th	361	City of New Orleans and Faubourgs.
5th	568	German Coast (St. Charles & St. John parishes)
6th	488	Ascension, St. James, and Acadia parishes
7th	264	Assumption and Lafourche parishes
8th	464	Iberville Parish
9th	?	Iberville Parish Pointe Coupee and West Baton Rouge parishes

SECOND DIVISION: Major General Philemon Thomas

REGIMENT	MEN	LOCALITY
10th	+	Feliciana Parish
11th	?	East Baton Rouge Parish
12th	*	St. Helena Parish
13th	*	Florida parishes east of Tangipahoa River
14th	231	St. Mary Parish
15th	280	St. Martin Parish
16th	573	Opelousas
17th	236	Rapides
18th	319	Natchitoches
19th	56	Ouachita (some in the Continental army)
20th	+	

+*The Tenth and Twentieth regiments were consolidated, totaling 546 men.*
†*The Twelfth and Thirteenth regiments were also consolidated totaling 255 men.*

In addition to the above, a total of 667 men were drafted into the militia. Claiborne's reorganization of the militias was along the order established by the Spanish governors. The overall strategy was to be able to quickly assemble a sufficient number of militiamen anywhere within the state to affect a delaying action until troops from other points could reinforce the attacked position. Since New Orleans would be the prize of any invasion of Louisiana, a greater number of troops were stationed in the city, and toward that aim free men of color were organized into companies.

In the ceremonies attendant to the transfer of Louisiana from France to the United States, two small companies of free Negroes participated in a parade. The Spanish regime had begun the practice of arming a separate militia unit composed exclusively of free men of color but with white officers. Remnants of these units petitioned Governor Claiborne to be part of Louisiana's militia. Claiborne agreed but specifically stated that membership would be confined to those who served under the Spanish regime. Major Michael Fortier, a white man, was made commander of battalion and Lewis Kerr was named junior major.

Naturally, there was some uneasiness in New Orleans about Negroes bearing arms in such numbers. The slave revolt in San Domingo was still a fresh memory, and New Orleans' black population outnumbered the whites. In 1809 about six thousand persons had come to Louisiana from San Domingo; some of them were free Negroes.

There had been a slave uprising on the German Coast; some of the slaves set fire to plantation buildings and marched to New Orleans in large numbers hoping the slaves there would join their revolt. Ironically, a great number of free Negroes owned black slaves themselves; perhaps this had a quieting effect upon the charged atmosphere. Negroes under arms, whatever their social status, did not meet with the approval of most white Louisianians.

Acting on a legislative mandate of 1812, Governor Claiborne was authorized to reestablish a battalion of free blacks limited to four companies, each of sixty men. Other stipulations were that they be landowners or sons of landowners and taxpayers; the commanding officer had to be a white man. At the Battle of New Orleans, this unit was referred to as Fortier's Battalion. Senator Sebastian Heriard from Pointe Coupee Parish served this battalion as adjutant in the battle. When the British threat became a reality, General Jackson asked the free black citizens to help defend Louisiana. He promised the same inducements that were given the white soldiers—sixty acres of land and a sum of $124. This proclamation was made public on October 24, 1814. There was some mention of increasing the number of free blacks under arms to six hundred. But Governor Claiborne stated to Jackson that this would be feasible only if they were to serve on out-of-state duty; he feared such a concentration in New Orleans. Joseph Savory, a mulatto, appeared on the roster as a second major by "Order of the Governor." Despite repeated claims of large desertions from this battalion of free blacks, the records show only two substantiated instances.

There were other units of free blacks under arms in Louisiana. A record shows a company of fifty under Captain Alexandre Lemell. This company was mustered out of service on March 3, 1815, from St. Martin Parish; it had been part of the Fifteenth Regiment of the Louisiana militia. Another crack unit of free men of color was D'Aquin's Battalion.

The muster roll of the Fourth Regiment revealed that a first sergeant had been appointed to serve a company of free men of color. No other information is apparent.

A legislative act, dated January 30, 1815—after the Battle of New Orleans—authorized the organization of a company of free blacks, limited to eighty men. Its requirements were the same as those of the New Orleanians; each member must be the owner or son of the owner of real estate and a taxpayer. There is no outstanding evidence that this company was ever organized, but the act does indicate a measure of liberality in terms of white and Negro relations.[1]

Although the Spanish governors had established cavalry units. Claiborne set about on methods of his own. As early as 1808 five cavalry units, comprising 160 men from Orleans, Opelousas, Pointe Coupee, and Natchitoches, were formed. The elite corps, invariably sons of large landowners, provided their own fine horses and all equipment except their resplendent uniforms.

There were five water approaches to New Orleans or its environs —the Mississippi River, Lake Borgne, Lake Maurepas, Lake Pontchartrain, Barataria Bay. Another important tributary was Bayou Lafourche, then a branch of the Mississippi. A small fortification, named Fort Hopkins, was established on Bayou Lafourche in October, 1814, and garrisoned by Lieutenant Henry S. Thibodaux and his command of Lafourche Volunteers. His detachment of about forty men was in service from October 30, 1814, to April 6, 1815, and was mustered out at New Orleans. There was a practice of

[1] Powell A. Casey, *Louisiana in the War of 1812*, 36.

bringing rural militias to the city to parade amid fanfare and ceremony to mark the end of their service.

Legend persists that an artillery unit was established in the area now known as Donaldsonville, composed principally of people of French extraction. Folklore says this band of redoubtables volunteered their services to Jackson at the Battle of New Orleans and blended into those forces, thereby losing their identity. Known later as the Donaldsonville Cannoneers, they are supposed to have captured a cannon from the English troops. During the Peninsular Campaign (in Spain) the British had captured a cannon from the French troops during a battle. This cannon had been cast during the height of the French Revolution, and inscribed on its barrel were the words, *Liberte, Egalite, et Fraternite* (Liberty, Equality, and Fraternity), the battle cry of those who liberated themselves from king, queen, and monarchial government. The Cannoneers are supposed to have captured this prized piece of artillery during the Battle of New Orleans. It was a redemption for the soldiers of French extraction to recapture a cannon that the English took from their French cousins far across the sea in an earlier battle. There have been many persons in the Bayou Lafourche area who could describe the cannon in detail.

The Donaldsonville Cannoneers also served in the American Civil War, and somewhere along the way the cannon became lost. It was either captured by the Union troops, or the Cannoneers buried it or hid it to prevent its capture during the last days of the war. Historians continue their search for it to substantiate the legend.

The Washington Artillery Company was organized at New Orleans, according to records, on September 7, 1838. If as legend claims, it took part in the Battle of New Orleans, this longest continuing volunteer force in Louisiana's history can officially list its participation on the Plains of Chalmette with their other battle gallantries.

Cavalry units from St. Charles, Feliciana, Attakapas, and Opelousas were from time to time alerted but put on a standby basis. Incidents on the German Coast led to an open revolt by that militia. Incensed by New England politicians and believing the British threat to be exaggerated, they turned their anger upon the Louisiana authorities. These dissidents were joined by some insubordinate New Orleans units, but Claiborne managed to communicate assurance to them that they would not be sent out of the state to perform under an "American officer." Taking a cue from the New Englanders, some Louisianians were expressing their own version of states' rights.

The British envisioned support from French and Spanish people in their invasion of Louisiana, and the threat of secession by the New England states raised their hopes. Once the threat became a reality, British intelligence was shocked to see diverse populations rally to a common cause—the defense of Louisiana!

President Madison, on August 6, 1814, directed the governor of Louisiana to do officially what Claiborne had already done mobilize the militia. Louisiana's quota was 1,000 infantry out of the national requisition of 93,500 men. The 1,000 were to be divided into two units of four companies, each with a captain, a first lieutenant, 2 junior lieutenants, 4 sergeants, 4 corporals, a drummer, a fifer, and 90 privates. The rest were to be assigned to the artillery. The drummer and fifer would set the tempo of the march, create the military aura, and echo the commands. Claiborne, however, mobilized all at his disposal, and a martial spirit enveloped Louisiana. Every Sunday or holiday, the militiamen could be seen practicing the manual of arms, marching, and generally becoming accustomed to the rigors of soldiery. On August 15, 1814, General Jackson, in a communique to Governor Claiborne, asked that the full quotas of Louisiana militias be activated immediately, because he considered an attack imminent. Because of his foresight, Claiborne was prepared to comply.

General Villere personally visited each militia unit in the state. His purpose was twofold; to insure that each was ready to fight and to see that they would help enlist more men. Military activity increased, and the citizen response was favorable; former dissidents became enthusiastic for the common cause. As in fighting Mississippi River floods, yellow fever, and other ills indigenous to the region, Louisianians responded with typical unity to defend against the British.

The pirate Jean Laffite, on whose head Claiborne had placed a price and who usually secreted himself with his band in the swamps west of the river near New Orleans, warned the local authorities of a British attack on the city. Lafitte had been offered the rank of captain in the British navy, plus an estimate $30,000 in gold. England also promised Laffite a large amount of land when peace was established. Their most compelling offer was the release of his brother, Pierre, whom they held in captivity. Spurning their promises, however, Laffite relayed the documented offer to Jean Blanque, a Louisiana legislator, with a note, part of which said, "I make you the depository of the secret on which perhaps depends the tranquility of our country." Coincidental with Laffite's revelation of the British plans, a force under Commander Daniel T. Patterson of the United States Navy and Colonel George T. Rose of the Forty-fourth Infantry were preparing to attack the pirate's refuge in Barataria Bay.

On December 2, 1814, General Andrew Jackson arrived in New Orleans. Jackson had risen from a general officer in the Tennessee militia as a famous Indian fighter to become one of the best generals of the Regular Army in American history. Upon arriving in New Orleans he immediately went on a tour of inspection and began shoring up the defense of the city. Every entrance was barricaded, including canals and bayous; he created an obstacle course for the British. He then began reinforcing his army with state militia units. Volunteer Mississippians, Choctaw Indians, and free Negroes were also pressed into service. The new additions to Jackson's army were in sharp contrast to the Tennesseans and Kentuckians who composed the main body of his troops.

The state militiamen arrived by horseback, pirogues, skiffs, bateaus, and those in the vicinity of New Orleans simply marched to unite with the forces of Jackson. It was a most disparate assemblage. The men spoke four languages—English, French, German, and Spanish, and some of those Kentuckians and Tennesseans spoke their own brogue spiced with archaic Chaucerian terms.

On December 14, 1814, a task force of five gunboats and two tenders set out in Lake Borgne to intercept the arrival of a strong British flotilla. Barges of British troops completely overwhelmed the Americans and their boats, easily landing and dispatching their troops.

News of the naval disaster reached Jackson, and he ordered his troops ready for action. He immediately asked Claiborne to convene the state legislature in order to suspend the writ of habeas corpus. When the legislators were dilatory in responding to his request he, in his typical fashion, declared martial law, which gave him absolute power. The urgency of the situation restrained anyone from taking legal action against Jackson's despotic maneuver; but Jackson, more than anyone else, realized the precariousness of the situation. There was no accurate intelligence to predict the strength of the British force; nor could anyone foretell at which point they would strike.

The vanguard of the British under General Sir Edward Pakenham landed, then moved parallel to Bayou Bienvenu to a point barely six miles below the city, near the plantation of General Villere, commander of the First Division of the Louisiana militia. Jackson learned of this on December 23 at 2 P.M. That day Major Latour, who caught sight of the Britishers while on reconnaissance, reported to Jackson that their estimated number was sixteen or eighteen hundred men.

Every available man from the city's defense perimeter was gathered to march south on the British. Along the way someone brought a handbill to General Jackson that announced: "Louisianians! Remain quiet in your houses; your slaves shall be preserved to you, and your property respected. We make war only against Americans." The propagandists depended on Louisianians feeling that they were not American. Prisoners captured by the British on their march toward New Orleans were released as an example of goodwill.

Under cover of darkness and contrary to usual military tactics, Jackson attacked the British on signal from the gunboat *Carolina* at precisely 7:30 P.M. The unorthodox method of attack startled Pakenham and checked his advance. But Jackson, knowing the English would regroup and prepare, fell back behind the Rodriguez Canal and erected ramparts of mud. This line extended three quarters of a mile running from the river to the swamps. On December 27 a small British force was repulsed on Jackson's eastern flank, and on January 1 the first artillery duel occurred. The gunboats, *Louisiana* and *Carolina*, fired shells into the mass of Britishers while Jackson's hillbilly sharpshooters dispatched their pickets in the manner of a turkey shoot.

Pakenham set up artillery at strategic points on the levee and successfully blasted and demobilized U.S. gunboats. He then prepared his major offensive by placing Colonel William Thornton at the head of a large force to occupy the west bank of the river, aiming to attack Jackson's defense there and outflank the main U.S. force which Pakenham correctly judged to be just behind the Rodriguez Canal. But Colonel Thornton was delayed and only six hundred men set out, less than half of the intended force, a fact unknown to Pakenham until after his overall plan had begun.

At sunrise on January 8, 1815, the British attacked. As they emerged from the early morning haze they were met with a lethal concentration of firepower, accentuated with cannons, sharpshooters, and the masses of stationary infantry shielded behind the ramparts. Rockets lit the sky revealing the silhouettes of red-clad Englishmen, targets as clear as roosters sitting on a fence in daylight.

The brave British were clearly visible and the Americans were not. Had it been a contest between Indians and the British, the battle would have been called a massacre.

On into the hail of lead and iron the Redcoats marched, falling like grain before the scythe. They faltered once and sought refuge in the underbrush, but urged on by their officers they again proceeded. Finally the hail of firepower was too much; they broke and sought safety at the rear. General Pakenham, wounded once in the knee and his horse shot from under him, tried gallantly to rally his forces, but a bullet shattered his spine, and he died in the arms of his subordinates as he was being carried from the field. British General Sam Gibbs was killed and General John Keane was wounded.

Meanwhile, Thornton, on the west bank, despite his limited force, did manage to rout the Americans and seize some cannons, but he had no way of combining his efforts with Pakenham's since his attack came very late in the engagement. General John Lambert, who was fourth in command, took charge and sent word to Thornton to retreat and join him to avoid more casualties. Thornton's retreat ended the battle. British ships down the river went on pounding Fort St. Phillip but after eleven days gave up, and the entire English force set out for a rendezvous at Ship Island.

The statistics showed the British loss at almost 400 dead, over 1,500 wounded, and 522 missing while Jackson's casualties came to only 333 killed, wounded or missing. Ironically, the Treaty of Ghent (Belgium) had been signed by the United States and England on December 24, 1814, ending the war, but the news had not reached either Jackson or Pakenham. Had England won a victory, the temptation to maintain control of the Mississippi Valley may have been too great. She may have laid some territorial claim on New Orleans and its environs and caused further dispute. The Battle of New Orleans secured the state of Louisiana and the territory, and even more important, it brought its people into the American nation. It also shut up, for a while, the wild orations of self-righteous New England politicians, who had disparaged Louisiana.

Jackson's victorious army, exclusive of the men stationed along the city's perimeter of defense and out of battle, was composed mainly by militiamen. With Jackson in the battle were: 66 Marines; 22 Regular Army artillerymen; 465 Seventh Regular Regiment infantrymen; 331 Forty-fourth Regular Regiment infantrymen; 2,982 officers and men from Tennessee and Kentucky militia regiments; 515 Louisiana artillerymen and a battery of St. Domingo men of color and Planche's Battalion; 1,309 Louisianians recruited from manpower pools and unorganized militia. These total 5,690 men.[2]

[2]The 7th Infantry Unit was commanded by Major H. D. Peire who was commissioned from a volunteer regiment of Louisiana from the organized militia. Major Peire held the same rank (Major) in the state militia. Jim Dan Hill, *The Minute Men in Peace and War* (Harrisburg, Pa.: The Stackpole Company).

First as a general, later as a president, Zachary Taylor led the Louisiana soldier to exhibit concern for more than his southern state. He is depicted at the bottom, center, flanked by other members of his presidential cabinet. In the upper left corner is Etienne de Bore, a noted planter who demonstrated, in 1796, the profitable results of planting sugarcane in quantity. Sharing the attention with him was the steamboat, newly arrived in Louisiana, making transportation along the Mississippi economical and attractive.

CHAPTER 6

Prelude to Peace

The interval between the War of 1812 and the Civil War has been called a period of peace by Alcee Fortier and "The Lush Years" by Charles L. Dufour. During the three decades of peace between the wars, Louisiana established an economy based almost entirely upon sugar. The sugar industry coupled with the trade brought about by the port of New Orleans, the gateway to the Mississippi Valley as well as to Central and South America, brought enormous wealth and stability to the Louisiana economy.

Sugar farming and the coming of the steamboat to New Orleans in 1812 heralded a new dawn; and in time north Louisiana began its boom with cotton. Huge plantations, which were really an expansion of the English manorial system, lined the rivers. River transportation was easy in Louisiana through the Mississippi, Red, Ouachita, Black, Atchafalaya, and such large streams such as Bayou Teche, Bayou Lafourche, Bayou Boeuf, and countless others. Virtually every farm or plantation was within wagon distance of some stream that could convey agricultural products to New Orleans and a ready market.

By 1822 Louisiana's population was in excess of 150,000 and by 1840 it had reached 350,000. Economically and culturally, Louisiana was on its way to becoming one of the wealthiest areas in the Western Hemisphere.

France, meanwhile, had been bled by the armies of occupation after Waterloo. Napoleon's soldiers, then called *demi-soldes* because they were on half pensions, could not feed and clothe themselves and their families. Funds were collected to send some of them to America, and a good portion of them settled Louisiana. The *Minerve*, a French newspaper, acquainted its reader with the country along the Mississippi River, which it called *Meschacebe,* the name given by the early French explorers. And the southerners were called *Meridionaux.*

No one knows exactly how many of Napoleon's soldiers settled in Louisiana, but there were many. South Louisiana's French culture was a natural attraction to people fearful of reenthronement of the Bourbons. The state had adopted a civil code in 1808 based on the Code de Napoleon which had been formulated in 1804, thereby obliterating what remained of the Spanish influence. The French language, too, had become dominant. In many south Louisiana communities and in New Orleans there were French-language newspapers. When Napoleon died on May 5, 1821, their banner headlines carried the news, and Frenchmen shouted, "Napoleon is dead!" Memorial services were held in New Orleans drawing people from hamlet, town, and countryside. Napoleonic soldiers paused to pay homage to the man they idolized and who had conquered half the world. His death further unified Louisianians of French ancestry.

Napoleon's death also spurred a martial spirit among all French Louisianians, and they flocked to join the local militias. In their soldiers' raiments they marched, paraded, and trained, reliving in their hearts the glories of a yesterday. A contemporary observed that the Napoleonic soldier in any company of the militia clearly stood out. There was something about the erectness of his shoulders, the set of the jaw, even the lifting of his feet that singled him out.[1]

Pierre Banjamin Buisson, born in Paris, served in the Sixth Artillery Regiment of Napoleon's Army. After Waterloo he settled in New Orleans where he became prominent in civic affairs. He reorganized the Orleans Battalion that had distinguished itself in the Battle of New Orleans, and every able Napoleonic soldier in the area rallied around him. They drilled in Jackson Square (then Place d'Armes), or in Beauregard Square (then Congo Square), that area between the Municipal Auditorium and Rampart Street. Former Colonel Vignie commanded the cavalry, Captain Buisson the artillery, and Louis Gally and Cuvilier, subordinates in the battalion were all Napoleon's soldiers.

[1]Simone de la Souchere Delery, *Napoleon's Soldiers in America* (Gretna, La.: Pelican Publishing Co., 1972).

Prelude to Peace 65

With the Ascension and Assumption regiments along Bayou Lafourche were such former luminaries of Napoleon's armies as Dr. Joseph St. Martin, who was an assistant surgeon; Victor Charbonnet was another and who became superintendent of schools in that locale; and Francois Prevost, who served as a surgeon with General Victor Emmanuel Leclerc in the West Indies Campaign. A hospital in Donaldsonville perpetuates the memory of Prevost.

Leclerc, who married Napoleon's sister, Pauline Bonaparte, commanded an expedition in 1801 to reconquer the island of Santo Domingo after the slave uprising. It was a fiasco partly because of an epidemic of yellow fever which decimated the ranks—including Leclerc. Some of the survivors sought refuge in Louisiana where they soon merged into French society. Some of these former soldiers also served in the local militia, like Prevost.

The militia remained prepared, of course. The War of 1812 had taught the value of preparedness, and the state legislature by an act of March, 1820, provided that the governor be authorized to organize a brigade anytime a thousand men enrolled in the local militia. This brigade would be commanded by a brigadier general and would be known as the Louisiana Legion—a new name for the militia.

In February, 1821, the legislature again authorized the governor to buy cannons for the New Orleans militia companies of the artillery. The law prescribed monthly drills. The Orleans companies were the first to be organized into a brigade under the new law and were given the title of First Brigade. The act also provided that there be four inspections annually—January 8 (to mark the victory at the Battle of New Orleans) and the first Saturdays in April, July, and October.

In 1829 the legislature established that only commissioned officers could elect brigadier generals. It had become a normal procedure for the men of the companies to elect their officers, but in the case of the brigadier generals, only commissioned officers were allowed to vote on their election. Fines for nonattendance at drills were enacted. By the year 1829, there were 14,800 men in the state militias with many more seeking to enlist.

On March 8, 1835, the state legislature enacted laws to modernize the militia. Eligibility for enlistment was confined to males between the ages of eighteen and forty-five, with emphasis on youth: Those between eighteen and thirty were called first class and those from thirty-one to forty-five were second class. A company required fifty privates, a captain, a first lieutenant, a junior lieutenant, five sergeants, and six corporals. An indeterminate number of men of the second class could be part of that company, which must have made some units unwieldly. This move was innovative, and the militias remained basically the same until the Civil War. But Louisiana had effectively established a militia system which could put first-class soldiers in the field in a matter of hours.

When a Congressional resolution for the annexation of Texas was signed by President Tyler on March 1, 1845, serious trouble with Mexico began. Before Texas became an integral part of the United States, territorial disputes were always resolved, sometimes by ignoring the problem as in the early days of the Louisiana Territory. But the acquisition of Texas required fixed precise boundaries and put salt into the wounds of Mexican pride.

In September, 1845, Mexico indicated a willingness to negotiate a reestablishment of diplomatic relations with the United States. John Slidell, a New Orleanian went to Mexico City as President Polk's personal emissary to ascertain whether Mexico would settle for the boundaries of the Rio Grande and the sale of Upper California and New Mexico for a sum of $40 million.

Upon reaching the capital, Slidell was refused an audience with President Jose Herrera. While Slidell attempted to negotiate with Manuel de la Pena y Pena, the Mexican foreign minister, Herrera resigned, and Slidell was forced to begin anew with Joaquin Castille y Lanzas, the new Mexican foreign minister. When Slidell attempted to set up a meeting with Lanza, he received an inflamatory note castigating the United States for its territorial intrusion. Slidell returned a note citing his presence as evidence of the United States's good intentions and added that he could not let Lanza's accusations go unchallenged. To emphasize his point, Slidell left for New Orleans, and en route he composed a fateful letter to President Polk.

The Mexican War, declared on May 12, 1846, was to consist mainly of offensive campaigns by the Americans. To the three main movements first decided upon—Matamoros to Monterrey, San Antonio to Chihuahua, and Fort Leavenworth to New Mexico—were added the advance from Vera Cruz to Mexico City and the expedition from New Mexico to California.

General Zachary Taylor had been ordered to station his army at the Sabine River, as early as May, 1845, in preparation for an advance upon the Rio Grande. In July he advanced as far as Corpus

Prelude to Peace 67

Christi, where he remained until Slidell's mission failed. He then moved to Point Isabel, at the mouth of the Rio Grande. Since Mexico considered the Neuces River the Texas boundary, Taylor's army was deemed an aggressor. A Mexican army, under General Mariano Arista, crossed the river and gave battle in April, 1846. The United States then called Arista's action an invasion of American soil, and after a plea from President Polk, Congress declared war on Mexico.

Soon after the declaration of war, General Taylor, in the battles of Palo Alto and Resaca de la Palma, forced the Mexicans back across the Rio Grande. He then took Matamoros and invested Monterrey which fell after five days in September, 1846. General Santa Anna, in exile in Havana, was allowed passage through Vera Cruz and soon became president of Mexico. Assuming command of the armies, he met head on with Taylor's army at Buena Vista, but was forced to give up the battle, and he retreated in confusion. A New Mexico expedition led by Colonel Stephen Kearny took possession of that area in August, 1846, and after organizing a provisional government pushed on to California. The Missouri Volunteers, led by Colonel Alexander Doniphan, moved on to northern New Mexico in December, 1846, and defeated the Mexicans at El Paso. They later took possession of Chihuahua. In March, 1847, General Winfield Scott, leading an army of twelve thousand, reached Vera Cruz. After a three-day bombardment, the Mexican troops surrendered, and Scott began his advance on Mexico City. He defeated Santa Anna's army at Cerro Gordo, occupied Jalapa, and pushed on to Mexico City. At Churubusco, the Mexicans put up a heroic fight until their ammunition ran out.

An armistice was offered the Mexicans in August, 1847, and peace negotiations were begun, but fighting resumed the following month. General Worth led an assault on Casa Mata and Molino del Rey outposts of the castle-fortress Chapultepec. As soon as these forts were taken, the hill of Chapultepec, believed by the Mexicans to be impregnable, was stormed. Despite heroic resistance, the American army occupied Mexico City where it remained until peace was restored.

A treaty was ratified by the United States Senate on March 10, 1848, and Mexico, by the Treaty of Guadalupe Hidalgo, ceded to the United States two-fifths of her territory and received $15 million and the assumption of claims by the United States. The boundary between the two countries was to follow the Rio Grande from its mouth to the New Mexico line, then west to the Gila River, and with that stream to the Colorado River and then following the boundary between upper and lower California to the Pacific. The Gadsden Purchase in 1853 in terms of cash—$10 million—finally defined the boundaries where they remain today.

Louisiana's role in the Mexican War was noteworthy because it not only provided troops for the immediate needs of General Zachary Taylor's army, but New Orleans was the departure point for troops going to Vera Cruz and other points in Mexico. Taylor's army initially had about eighteen hundred troops as he advanced into Texas. Immediately a call went to General Edmund P. Gaines, commander of the Department of the South at New Orleans. Two batteries of the New Orleans Artillery, commanded by Captain Forno and Captain Bercier, left New Orleans on August 22, 1845, on the *Alabama* headed for Corpus Christi. These two units were Louisiana's first contribution to the Mexican War—militiamen. By April, 1846, Taylor asked the governors of Louisiana and Texas for five thousand volunteers. During this period Isaac Johnson was governor of Louisiana; Charles N. Rowly adjutant general; Major General John L. Lewis commanded the First Division of the Louisiana militia; Brigadier General Horatio Davis the First Brigade; Brigadier General Augustin the Louisiana Legion; Colonel Persifor F. Smith the Washington Regiment; Colonel James A. Dakin the Louisiana Volunteers; Major Isaac F. Stockton the Native Americans and Major Louis Gally, the Orleans Artillery.

To facilitate the quick mobilization and dispatch of these troops the Louisiana legislature appropriated $100,000. In addition, a banker, Ben Story, president of the Bank of Louisiana, pledged a half million dollars from his personal account to Taylor for whatever he needed, plus whatever he could procure from other banks and merchants. The state of Louisiana with its admixture of races responded with even more eagerness than in the War of 1812.

The steamers *Galveston, Telegraph,* and *James L. Day* departed from New Orleans laden with over one thousand Louisiana men. In the meantime, another call went out for more troops, and soon four more companies from the Andrew Jackson Regiment sailed on the *Alabama* for Mexico. Volunteers were formed into companies to serve as a homeguard. And the city of New Orleans became the scene of encampments of troops from the North, awaiting embarkation

Prelude to Peace 69

for Mexico. From boats along the Missouri, Ohio, Cumberland, and Tennessee rivers, they entered the Mississippi and came to New Orleans and made camp.

A total of forty-five hundred men of the Louisiana militia were soon ready, and some were on the scene of action with Taylor's troops. The legislature again responded with an appropriation of $300,000; the state was geared for war and its soldiers eager for the fray.

The First Louisiana Brigade, under Persifor F. Smith, concentrated at Lake Buena Vista about thirty miles above Matamoros on the Mexican side of the Rio Grande; they were part of Taylor's army. While there their duration of enlistment expired, and they returned to New Orleans with the exception of the Phoenix Company of Donaldsonville which remained for the duration of the war. Company A of the Washington Regiment was also mustered out but retained its batteries under the name Washington Artillery beginning— officially—its great continuity of readiness for war service which prevails today.

By December, 1846, a regiment of infantry from New Orleans, commanded by Colonel Lewis G. De Russy was sent to Tampier, and in May, 1847, another battalion which consisted of five companies, in command of Lieutenant Colonel Charles Fiesca was ordered to Vera Cruz where it served under General Winfield Scott. A battalion of cavalry, under Lieutenant Colonel Walter F. Briscoe, reached Vera Cruz did scout and reconnaisance duty, and patrolled Mexico City after it fell to the Americans. General Persifor F. Smith with General Winfield Scott's army with distinction and was brevetted brigadier general.

In all, Louisiana furnished about ten thousand men to serve in the Mexican War. The command of some of the military units changed at first to men more suited to command. General Smith responded immediately by joining General Zachary Taylor on the Rio Grande. Eventually the following Louisiana units were mobilized: the First Regiment (Washington Regiment), commanded by Colonel J. B. Walton and Lieutenant Colonel Henry Forno; Second Regiment (Louisiana Volunteers), under Colonel James H. Dakin and Lieutenant Colonel Emerson; Third Regiment (Jackson Regiment), under Colonel Samuel F. Marks and Lieutenant Colonel Theodore G. Hunt; Fourth Regiment (Montezuma Regiment), under Colonel Horatio Davis and Lieutenant Colonel Charles K. Johnson; Fifth Regiment (National Guard regiment), under Colonel Baillie Peyton and Lieutenant Colonel Hugh W. Dunlap; Sixth Regiment (Gaines's regiment), under Colonel Edward Featherstone and Lieutenant Colonel Samuel

H. Peck; the Independent Company of Louisiana Volunteers which later became known as the Phoenix Company; regiment of Louisiana Volunteers under Colonel Lewis G. DeRussy; regiment of Louisiana Volunteers under Lieutenant Colonel Charles Fiesca and the battalion of Louisiana Mounted Volunteers, under Lieutenant Colonel Walter F. Boscoe. The Orleans Artillery Battalion under the former French army officer, Major Louis Gally, relieved the regulars at Forts St. Phillip and Jackson.

When General Zachary Taylor was encamped at Brownsville, opposed by a Mexican army far larger than his, he wondered where his reinforcements would come from. On May 10, 1846, Colonel Walton and his regiment landed at Point Isabel, and on May 17 Colonel Marks and his regiment arrived to join the desperate Taylor. The Americans and Mexicans were soon engaged in the successive battles of Palo Alto and Resaca de la Palma; the Americans were victors each time and drove the Mexicans from the Rio Grande.

A misinterpretation of the enlistment regulations caused a temporary stall to the eagerness of the Louisiana men. General Gaines, in a stupid interpretation of his own, decided the enlistments were only for three months and caused many of the men to return to Louisiana. But many of the returned officers and men immediately formed two regiments of infantry under Colonel DeRussy and Colonel W. Briscoe, and three battalions under Major Fiesca, Major Girault, and Major Besancon. Others such as Colonel Marks, Major Duperu, Captain Copeland S. Hunt, and men of the First Louisiana brigade returned to Mexico to serve throughout the war. Colonel Walton accepted a staff position with Winfield Scott and was with him at the peace negotiations. But the Phoenix Company under Captain A. G. Blanchard never returned home; it was formed on the spot when Gaines ordered the Louisianian home.

General Gaines is responsible for interrupting the continuity of the Louisiana militia by his high-handed personal definition of the enlistment requirements. The men in question wanted to remain and serve the duration of war. It was an unfortunate incident, but it did not detract from the devotion of their service or the valor of their actions. The Washington Artillery went back to Mexico in 1846 as Infantry Company A of the Washington or First Louisiana Regiment.

An outstanding military figure is Pierre Gustave Toutant Beauregard, the central figure of this chapter. At lower left is the first Episcopal bishop of Louisiana, Leonidas K. Polk, who was killed at Pine Mountain, Georgia, in June, 1864. Louisiana's first flag as a sovereign state is drawn at bottom center. The young lady at the bottom right depicts the *vivandiere*, a female nurse who attended the soldiers, named after the dedicated French women who served in Napoleon's armies.

CHAPTER 7

Rehearsal and the Battle of Brothers

The Mexican War has been called a dress rehearsal for the American Civil War by many historians because of the many Civil War officers who served in Mexico. Among the West Point graduates alone, 166 who fought as youthful officers in Mexico became Confederate or Union generals. This, of course, does not include those from the state militias who later distinguished themselves as officers in blue or gray.

The Civil War was a most unequal struggle between industrial and agrarian sections. The South had only two foundaries capable of producing armaments: the Tredegar Iron Works at Richmond and the Leeds Foundry in New Orleans. These two ironworks were capable of producing only 5 percent of the nation's entire output. The North had over 22,000 miles of organized railroads; the South only 8,541, and they were of three different gauges, which necessitated unloading and reloading as the width of the rails and train axles varied. The North had a navy of ninety ships; the Confederacy had none. The North was able to build ships at a rapid pace and also had 90 percent of the commercial shipping vessels. Although the Confederate did acquire a navy by using nondescript ships that were available and by building some, it never did reach a proportion to effectively run the blockades established by northern vessels.

Even the population presented a wide disparity of numbers. The North had over 20 million people from which to draw armies, while the South had barely 6 million whites. The South had a potential of over 1 million to put on the field of battle while the North had over 4,500,000. The closest estimates of men actually armed for action were 1,550,000 to 2,200,000 in the North and about 750,000 in South. The Union navy had 105,963 men to the Confederacy's 3,674. About the only equal element in the Civil War was valor.

Although slavery was called the main issue of the war the Confederate states contended that antislavery forces had violated the "Constitutional Compact"; as a result, the southern states felt they were relieved of their obligations and asserted their rights to self-determination. The threat made by the New England states to secede, at the time of the purchase of the Territory of Louisiana and again when the southern portion became a state had been festering in the minds of many who tried to resolve sectional differences. The issues were complex, to say the least and had portended trouble as early as the Missouri Compromise of 1820.

The demise of such giants as Calhoun, Clay, and Webster, who could reach the hearts of Americans and heal sectional differences, left the country without a national leader of stature. It took the Civil War and the division of people and principles to produce a Lincoln. In the meantime, the nation reeled in a perplexity of emotions. Where once there was reason, there was now doubt; where once there were compromises, there were now adamant stands on individual principles.

Louisiana did not give one vote to Abraham Lincoln for the presidency. But it did cast a combined majority for the other two pro-Union candidates, Stephen A. Douglas, who, like Lincoln, was from Illinois, and John Bell of Tennessee. John C. Breckinridge received a plurality, however, and garnered 22,681 votes to carry Louisiana, since the candidate with the most votes won without additional primaries.

Governor Thomas O. Moore, called a special session of the Louisiana legislature on December 10, 1860. Just ten days later this same legislature called for a convention to determine the question of secession, and on that same date, December 20, South Carolina seceded from the Union. When the delegates to the secession convention were elected (January 7, 1861), the body contained eighty secessionists, four cooperationists, six undecided, with twenty-nine of the forty-four parishes for secession and nineteen opposed. One can readily see that despite an emotional agreement on the problem, there was much disunity among the people.

Rehearsal and the Battle of Brothers

On January 10, 1861, the Washington Artillery, Louisiana Grays, Louisiana Cadets, Sarsfield Rifles, Orleans Cadets, and Crescent Rifles of the First Brigade, First Division of the militia were ordered to assemble at the foot of Canal Street to embark for Baton Rouge. Upon their arrival at Baton Rouge, they surrounded the U.S. Arsenal and demanded its surrender. On January 11, the U.S. commander, Major Joseph A. Haskins gave up the arsenal and marched his troops out. Coincidental with this action Forts St. Phillip and Jackson on the Mississippi River in Plaquemines Parish were also seized by the state militia.

While in New Orleans on that fateful day, January 11, Captain Charles M. Bradford, New Orleans district attorney and commander of the First Company, Louisiana Infantry, was ordered to seize Jackson Barracks, which housed the patients who had been cared for in the U.S. Marine Hospital. The regular hospital on the west bank of the river at McDonoghville had been evacuated because of a break in the levee during May, 1858, and the patients removed to Jackson Barracks. So the militia seized Jackson Barracks but assured Federal authorities that the patients there would be cared for. This action nevertheless caused bitter recriminations by word and letters between Washington and local military authorities in New Orleans.[1]

An interesting sidelight concerning the U.S. Marine Hospital is the fact that it was established upon an order by President Thomas Jefferson in 1802, and before the Louisiana Purchase. This was a most unusual arrangement since the Marine Hospital became a United States function before Louisiana was part of the nation.

These concerted actions: the seizure of the U.S. Arsenal at Baton Rouge, the capture of Fort St. Phillip and Fort Jackson, and the occupation of Jackson Barracks were the first overt actions of Civil War in Louisiana.

The secession convention, to make matters complete, adopted a state flag. The flag had thirteen stripes—six white, four blue, and three red. In the upper left-hand corner was a red field with a yellow five-point star; the flag represented the thirteen states of the original Union, the tricolor of France and the red and yellow of Spain. Although Louisiana's culture by now was predominantly French in the south and Anglo-Saxon in the north, the Spanish influence upon the territory was still felt.

[1] William E. Rooney, "The New Orleans Marine Hospital, 1802-1861" (M.A. thesis, Tulane University, 1950).

Another example of the lingering European influence was a *vivandiere* in the Phoenix Company of Donaldsonville. *Vivandiere* in this case was French for a female nurse who attended the soldiers. Such women served the armies of Napoleon. Lawrence Drake Nicholls, who captained the Phoenix Company until his death at Gaines Mill, mentioned the vivandieres many times in letters to his wife, and possibly other units from dominant French areas also had these nurses.

Jefferson Davis had, on February 18, 1861, been inaugurated president of the Confederate States of America. Thus, in a brief time, the United States was split into two nations posed for war.

By the time of the Civil War, Louisiana's population exceeded 700,000, of which almost half were black slaves or freedmen. And the population through the years continued to be cosmopolitan. The sugar and cotton boom with the added convenience of war transportation drew investors from all over the United States and Europe. A review of the census during the period immediately prior to the Civil War reveals some interesting facts.

There were 13,500 plantations and farms owned by Anglo-Saxon Protestants, French and Spanish Catholics, Jews, and Negroes. There were approximately 1,640 large slaveholders who tilled 10 percent of the total acreage planted. A large slaveholder was one who owned 50 or more slaves. Therefore, 90 percent of the planted acreage in Louisiana was farmed by small slaveholders, nonslaveholders, and free blacks. There were Negro slaveholders throughout the South but more in Louisiana than any other state. In 1830 there were 10 Negroes in Louisiana who had 50 or more slaves. By 1860, only 6, who together owned 493 slaves or an average of 82 each. There were a considerable number of Negro slaveowners who were not classed as large slaveholders; Natchitoches Parish for instance had 14 Negro slaveholders. Many northerners and Europeans who had money to invest settled Louisiana to enjoy its prosperity. The census reveals that in 1850 among the large slaveholders were 9 from Connecticut; 9 from Massachusetts; 7 from Ohio; 6 from Missouri; 6 from New Hampshire; 5 from Maine; 4 from Indiana; 4 from New Jersey; 3 from Vermont; 1 from Delaware; 2 from Rhode Island; 2 from the District of Columbia; 17 from Pennsylvania; 20 from New York; 33 from Maryland; 12 from Ireland; 6 from Scotland; 5 from England; 2 from Germany; 2 from Santo Domingo; 1 from Canada; 1 from Austria; 1 from Wales; 1 from Jamaica; and 17 from France. Of course, many who owned fewer than 50 slaves and who were not considered large owners also came from out of state or from foreign lands. The attraction to Louisiana was the same then as it is today—prosperity. The sugar and cotton boom offered great wealth for anyone with enterprise and enough money for the initial investment. The ancient plantation system, pattern after the English manorial system, found its ultimate fruition in the South and especially in Louisiana.

Fewer than one-third of the men who fought for the South in the Civil War came of families who had slaves. Therefore, one can readily dismiss the idea that every Confederate was a planter sipping bourbon or gin on his spacious veranda while his minions in the field brought in his wealth. The majority of southern people were hard-working small farmers, carving a niche in the wilderness, intent upon attaining some security in a troublesome world. The response to the call to arms by the states of the Confederacy was motivated more by the desire to protect their investments than anything else. The wealth of the citizens varied with their stations in life, but surely the motives were the same—to protect what they had and their earning potential. Emotional northerners, upon the death of Lincoln, reflected the claim that the war was fought solely for slavery. But Lincoln himself stated that if it would save the union, he would rather see the United States all-slave, part-slave or slave-free, depending upon the recipe needed for the preservation of the United States. Even the Emancipation Proclamation clearly exempted those southern states held by Union forces. To quote that document, slaves were to be "for the present left precisely as if this proclamation were not issued."

As in other conflicts, Louisiana sent a more diverse ethnic group into the Civil War. About 350,000 white inhabitants provided 56,000 men to the Confederate ranks, plus an additional 9,000 who served in home defense units or posts. There were 77 infantry regiments, 40 regiments, 40 artillery units, 12 cavalry regiments, and 11 cavalry battalions, all formed from the nucleus of Louisiana militia units. Of the 982 companies raised during the war, 400 were militia units.

The Civil War was the last of the romantic wars where masses of men filed out on the open field without cover, to take their chances against firepower. But it was also the first of the modern wars; the first use of the telegraph, rifled artillery, observation balloons, trenches, land mines, ironclad battleships, and extensive use of railroads for mass troop movements.[2]

---

[2]Railroads were used in the Crimean War (1854-56) but were very limited and occasional.

It has been called the War of Rebellion; the War of Secession; the War for Southern Independence; the War for the Union; the Confederate War; and the War Between the States. But the term Civil War is more definitive; such a division within a nation is certainly a civil war.

Louisiana had many prominent men in the military and in the Confederate government. Judah P. Benjamin, who was called the brains of the Confederacy, held the offices of attorney general, secretary of war, and secretary of state. John Slidell, a United States senator, who had negotiated with Mexico prior to the Mexican War, represented the Confederacy diplomatically in France. Pierre Rost was on the first diplomatic mission sent to Europe. A. B. Roman, a former governor, was sent by Jefferson Davis in 1861 to Washington to bargain for a settlement with the United States. The most powerful member of the Confederate Congress was Duncan F. Kenner (brother of Minor for whom Kenner, Louisiana, is named), who was chairman of the important Ways and Means Committee. Kenner also acted as plentipotentiary minister for Jefferson Davis and the Confederate government to negotiate with England and France for recognition of the Confederacy, assuring them that the slaves would be freed as the primary condition. Others who served in the Confederate Congress were Edward Sparrow, Henry Marshall, John Perkins, Jr., Lucius J. Dupre, Thomas J. Semmes, Charles J. Villere, and C. M. Conrad who had been secretary of war under President Fillmore.

Two capable and dedicated men served Louisiana as governor during the war: Thomas Overton Moore, who served until 1864, and Henry Watkins Allen, who served when the capitol was at Shreveport. Alexander Mouton was president of Louisiana's secession convention.

Pierre Gustave Toutant Beauregard was the most important Louisiana military figure. He was in command at Fort Sumter when that fort was fired upon, officially opening the war. He was also in command at the Battle of First Manassas (Bull Run); later, he was in command at Shiloh, when Albert Sidney Johnston met death early in the battle. He served in the West and East with distinction and was one of only eight full generals of the Confederacy. Braxton Bragg, though a North Carolinian by birth, had married a Louisiana widow in Terrebonne Parish and lived in Louisiana at the time of the outbreak. John B. Hood, a tragic figure of the Army of Tennessee, resided in Louisiana after the war and is buried in Metairie Cemetery at New Orleans. Edmund Kirby Smith was in command of the Trans-Mississippi Department and signed the document surrendering his army in Houston where he had retreated from Louisiana, thus ending the last organized resistance.

General Richard Taylor, son of the Mexican War hero, and onetime president Zachary Taylor, lived in Louisiana and owned Fashion Plantation near Hahnville. He served under Stonewall Jackson. And Leonidas K. Polk called the "Fighting Bishop" was the first Episcopalian bishop of Louisiana. A graduate of West Point, he became a minister but changed vestments when war broke out. A cannonball tore his head off at Pine Mountain, Georgia, in June, 1864. He is buried in New Orleans.

Louisianians fought all over the South; some in Lee's fabled Army of Northern Virginia. Of about 566 military actions in Louisiana, including, battles, raids, skirmishes, and scouting reconnaissances, the most important was the fall of New Orleans on May 1, 1862. When Farragut's ships passed Forts St. Phillip and Jackson, the Confederacy lost its largest city and greatest banking center, and even worse the Mississippi was shut off as a port for foreign goods. Except for a trickle of boats using the difficult to patrol bayous entering Louisiana waterways, no vessel could enter the New Orleans port.

When New Orleans fell, Farragut's fleet went up river, bombarded Donaldsonville on August 9, 1862, and soon thereafter the town, was occupied which effectively controlled Bayou Lafourche, then an outlet to the Gulf of Mexico from the Mississippi. Baton Rouge, the capitol, lay ahead. In the meantime, Vicksburg had surrendered on July 4, 1863, which meant the garrison of 20,000 men of Port Hudson, just above Baton Rouge, lay in the path of Union forces. After a bitter siege, Port Hudson surrendered on July 8, 1863, cutting the Confederacy in two. The jubilant Abraham Lincoln said on this occasion, "The father of waters again goes unvexed to the sea."

In 1864 General Banks made a move against Shreveport on the Red River. A Federal force was to advance from Arkansas in an attempt to press out the Confederate forces. But General Richard Taylor, with far fewer troops at his command, repulsed Banks near Mansfield. The following day, at Pleasant Hill, Taylor again hit Banks, and after an indecisive battle Banks retreated. Taylor than went back toward Shreveport to head off the forces coming from Arkansas, but news of Banks's defeat and retreat made them turn back. Banks's army never was effective after meeting head on with Taylor's.

South Louisiana was occupied in time to be exempt from the provisions of the Emancipation Proclamation, for by the time of its issuance, January 1, 1863, the parishes of St. Bernard, Plaquemines, New Orleans, Jefferson, St. John, St. Charles, St. James, Terrebonne, Lafourche, St. Mary, St. Martin, Assumption, and Ascension were already occupied and under Federal control.

General M. Grivot was adjutant general of the state of Louisiana at the outbreak of the Civil War, and so anxious was he to mobilize his militia that he began by censuring the legislature for not appropriating sufficient funds for volunteer troops. But the naturally enthusiastic Louisianians did not let monetary considerations interfere with their individual preparations for war. Many made their own uniforms and furnished their own guns; there was little uniformity among the troops at the beginning of the war. Toward the end there was still a wide assortment of guns, pistols, and cannons.

Volunteer companies sprang up like daisies in the field. Among the first were the Opelousas Rifles, East Baton Rouge Pelican Rifle Company, the Phoenix Company of Donaldsonville, St. Mary Parish Teche Guards, St. James Parish Chasseurs de St. Michel, and the Orleans Parish Fort Rifles. A battalion of the Louisiana Legion of the First Division formed a unit of Zouaves, named after the *Zouaoua* tribe in Kabyle, Algeria, whose uniforms were similarly bright, colorful, and distinctive.

The older units of the militia went about "getting ready," and their efforts were directed toward acquiring sufficient arms and uniforms. Confederate Gray had not, at this early date, become the offical color; consequently many colors and styles of dress were worn as the military units swelled in number.

The Washington Artillery, commanded by Colonel J. B. Walton, was considered the epitome of military efficiency and decorum as were the Donaldsonville Cannoneers of the First Brigade, Second Division, led by Captain Victor Maurin. These two companies vied with each other for *esprit de corps* and were considered by many to be the best batteries, Union or Confederate.

Metairie Race Track (now Metairie Cemetery) was established as Camp Walker to receive the large groups of soldiers who were assembling in New Orleans from all parts of the state. This camp, under

Rehearsal and the Battle of Brothers   81

the command of General E. L. Tracy, was later moved to Tangipahoa Parish, along the railroad, and named Camp Moore.

To fully impress upon the minds of militiamen that they were entering an entirely new army—the Confederate—they were mustered *out* of state service and *into* Confederate service. Instead of such traditional names as Crescent Rifles and the Phoenix Company, they were given a letter, as Company A, or B, or K causing some loss of pride and identity. Then the secretary of war of the Confederacy announced that no more volunteer one-year enlistments would be accepted; the only terms would be for the entire war. This caused such a controversy that the secretary had to reverse his directive. Of course, few who left for the fighting front returned at the end of their enlistment.

In May, 1861, the elite of the Louisiana contingents left for Virginia. In the forefront was the Washington Artillery—the Sixth, Seventh, Eighth, and Ninth regiments, the latter under Richard Taylor. They left amid a frenzy of excitement, band-playing, cheering, and wild displays of affection from the women. The first to march off, they joined with the immortal Stonewall Jackson and became "Jackson's Foot Cavalry"—so-called because of their long forced, rapid marches, sometimes at night over the roughest areas of Virginia. Jackson marched his ragged troops straight onto the pages of military history with brilliant victories in "David and Goliath" style as he turned his numerically inferior forces against all that the Union could set against them. They arrived in time to engage in the first great battle of the Civil War, First Manassas, on July 21, 1861.

More and more troops were sent to be assimilated into the Confederate Army. By November 22, 1861, there were 25,592 Louisiana troops on the potential battle fields. They were as follow:

The Washington Artillery	320
Four Companies or Orleans Artillery	304
One Company of Orleans Chasseurs	95
Crescent Blues	80
Jackson Regiment	450
Zouaves	650
Donaldsonville Artillery (the Cannoneers)	85
Watson's Artillery	100
Pointe Coupee Light Artillery	90
Soulakouski's Regiment (14 companies)	850
Breaux's Battalion	480
Lt. Colonel Bradford's Regiments (15 companies)	450

Marion Infantry	129
Carroll Guards	76
Fourteen companies transferred to Confederate service from state service	1,231
Thirteen companies for service within the state at Camp Lewis	1.050
Number of troops already in service of the Confederate states	19,152*
Total	25,592

This number included companies who lost identity by being mustered out of state service and into Confederate service, such as the Phoenix Company of Donaldsonville, as mentioned above.

The Washington Artillery, from First Manassas in 1861 to Appomattox in 1865, was constantly in the vanguard of the Confederate forces and participated in campaigns in Virginia, Maryland, and Pennsylvania. One battery was assigned to the Army of Tennessee to fight General William T. Sherman and his troops as he marched to the sea. The Washington Artillery represented the broad spectrum of New Orleans society; from the richest to the poorest, it reflected the permanence of the early colonists.

The Reverend Dr. Benjamin M. Palmer, a Presbyterian, and one of the city's most distinguished clergymen, said, in a farewell to the Washington Artillery as they marched off to Virginia, "And should the fate of the soldier befall you in a soldier's death, you shall find your graves in thousands of hearts and the pen of history shall write your martyrdom." They found death in proportionately large numbers.

Brigadier General Allison Owen related a vivid account of some of the Washington Artillery activities:

> During the Civil War the organization had a long and interesting period of service, opening with the seizure of the United States Arsenal at Baton Rouge on January 10, 1861. The rush to arms at this time is shown in the expansion of the battery into two batteries on January 28, followed further expansion into a battalion of four batteries on March 3; on Washington's birthday the Confederate Secretary of War, Judah P. Benjamin, on behalf of the ladies of New Orleans presented the battalion with an embroidered silk standard, and on May 13, the command volunteered "for the war" was accepted and mustered in on May 26, as part of the regular army of the Confederate States. The day after it was mustered in it entrained for Richmond, under the command of Major James B. Walton [of Mexican War fame] with W. Miller Owen as adjutant.

They brought their own equipment of 9 guns to Virginia and one 8-pounder rifle.

The batteries were known as First, Second, Third and Fourth Companies and were commanded by Captain H. M. Isaacson, First Lt. C. C. Lewis, Captain M. Buck Miller, and Captain Benjamin Franklin Eshelman, respectively. The battalion arrived in Richmond on June 4th, was supplied with horses and placed under the instructions of Lieutenants T. L. Rosser, James Dearing, and J. J. Garnet, who were fresh from West Point and who later rose to high rank in the Confederate Army.

The command went into the trenches at Petersburg on June 18, 1864, and there remained until April 2, 1865, making the last stand at Fort Gregg under Lt. F. McElroy. During the retreat at Appomattox, the Second Company, under Captain Richardson, served with the rear guard and was engaged up to 11 p.m. at night before the surrender.

At Gettysburg, the Battalion reached the field at 8:00 A.M., on the 2nd of July and on the morning of the 3rd was placed on the left of the peach orchard under the command of Major B. F. Eshelman. The two signal guns for the great cannonade which preceded Pickett's charge were fired by the right platoon of the First Company under Lt. C. H. Brown, the right gun under Sgt. W. T. Hardie, the second under Sgt. P. O. Fazende, each exploding a caisson of opposing batteries.

Colonel Walton and the old officers again assumed command but the reduced numbers formed with 3 batteries known as A, B and C, successors to the Third, Fifth and First Companies, respectively.

As soon as a sufficient number of its members had returned to New Orleans after the surrender, two attempts were made to organize the Battalion but the Federal commander dispersed both meetings and Confederate military organizations were prohibited, so the Washington Artillery took a civil and benevolent character to care for its impoverished members and their families and the families of the dead.

Although emphasis has been placed on hardships in Virginia, Georgia, and South Carolina, other sectors were experiencing the trauma of certain defeat. Louisiana's situation was particularly bad because from the time that General Benjamin F. Butler and his troops came to New Orleans on May 1, 1862, south Louisiana was lost to the Confederacy. The loss of control of the Mississippi River isolated most of Louisiana and Texas. And while the war was going on in other places the Federal government was already experimenting with the "redemption" of Louisianians.

By January, 1864, Federal forces occupying Louisiana were intent upon effecting a civil government through which they could enact laws and render conditions amicable to their interests. On January 11, General N. P. Banks issued a proclamation ordering an election of state officials in federally occupied Louisiana. By *federally occupied*, he acknowledged the division within the state. In the meantime, Governor Moore delivered his farewell address, and on January 25 Henry Watkins Allen was inaugurated Confederate governor of Louisiana. On March 4, Michael Hahn was inaugurated governor of Federal Louisiana. Although Louisianians had been politically divided early in the war, the reality of two state administrations was a source of despair.

The Union Army captured Fort DeRussy and the interior towns of Alexandria and Natchitoches in March of 1864. A convention was meeting in New Orleans on April 6 to draft a constitution for federally occupied Louisiana while General Banks was marching on Shreveport. But two days later General Richard Taylor defeated him near Mansfield and stymied him at Pleasant Hill. A brief flicker of hope was rekindled, but these were the last two victories for the Confederates in Louisiana, and on May 13, 1864, Alexandria was set afire by the Federals, who until then were occupying the town. Almost the entire settlement was left in ashes.

On July 23, 1864, a Republican convention revised the constitution of the state of Louisiana and abolished slavery. It was this act and not the Emancipation Proclamation that freed the slaves in federally occupied Louisiana, and it occurred one year, six months and twenty-three days after Lincoln's issuance of his proclamation.

On September 5, a new constitution was adopted, and five representatives were sent to the national congress in Washington, D.C. On October 12, a resolution of that same Congress ordered the attorney general to institute criminal proceedings against all members of the 1860 Louisiana legislature who had voted for the Convention of Secession.

While all these events were taking place, the Confederates were still intent upon fighting for the rest of Louisiana. General Edmund Kirby Smith ordered all the cotton in Confederate Louisiana to be burned over the objection of Governor Allen. Lincoln was reinaugurated on March 4, 1865, and the once proud and efficient Army of Northern Virginia, commanded by General Robert E. Lee, and which included so many Louisianians, was gradually becoming encircled by General U. S. Grant's troops. But Lee, in his retreat, was exacting a terrible toll, for Grant lost the horrendous number of 56,000 men within twenty-nine days from the Wilderness to Cold Harbor. In quick succession, nevertheless, Richmond and Petersburg were evacuated by Lee and his army, and just one week later, on

Rehearsal and the Battle of Brothers

April 9, 1865, the South's greatest single figure, Robert E. Lee, surrendered his worn and decimated army at Appomattox, Virginia.

General William T. Sherman (earlier the first president of Louisiana State University) had marched through Georgia, wreaking destruction and death. As a result of his march to the sea the Confederacy was now in three segments. Yet, there were Confederate armies willing to fight on, even after Appomattox, and Governor Allen called a public meeting in Shreveport to consider "the wants and conditions of the country and suggesting such measures as may be necessary to encourage our people and to promote the success of our glorious cause." Later, General Kirby Smith requested a meeting of governors of Louisiana, Texas, Missouri, and Arkansas to take action for the common defense and welfare of the states mentioned. Kirby Smith, hoping to fight on, was forced to move the headquarters of the Trans-Mississippi to Houston, giving the Federals complete control, geographically, of Louisiana, with the seat of government in New Orleans.

On June 2, 1865, Governor Allen delivered a farewell proclamation to the people of Louisiana and went into exile in Mexico; on the same day, General Kirby Smith signed an official document surrendering his army in Houston, ending the last organized resistance. The next day, southern naval forces on the Red River surrendered. The first precipitous action of the Civil War had taken place in Louisiana with the militia seizing the U.S. Arsenal at Baton Rouge, the Forts St. Phillip and Jackson and the U.S. Marine Hospital; the final action was the surrender of the small naval force on the Red River.

The Confederacy held out as long as it did because of the excellent condition of the southern states' militias. At the beginning of the war, the northern state militias were not equal to those of the South. The advent of the Copperheads (southern sympathizers) created much dissension in Union ranks. Cash bonuses were offered as inducements and short-term enlistments—3 months and a bonus —were also a means of attracting men into the Union forces. The draft riots in New York City were partly caused by some naturalized citizens who had immigrated in recent decades and did not want to serve in the army. These people had sought refuge in the United States but were disinclined to defend it.

It took the North a long time to get organized, to quiet dissident groups, and to find ingenious leadership for its armies. But when these problems were resolved, it was only a matter of time before the

South would be defeated. Grant and Sherman, emerged from the wealth of military figures in the North and became a superb team. They coordinated a grand scheme by which they defeated Confederacy.

The South, on the other hand, had inadequate leadership in Jefferson Davis who could neither envision the scope of the war nor the objectives in attaining victory. The adulation he received in later years was more a tribute to the cause than it was to the man. His judgment of the men he placed in responsible positions was based more on personal friendship than on their ability. Unlike Lincoln he could not see beyond his own circle of admirers. Limited resources, want of materiel, and often times the lack of necessary manpower, railroads, and even horses and mules retarded the efforts and hastened the defeat. Ironically, both Lincoln and Davis were born in Kentucky within a hundred miles of each other. But Davis, who moved to Mississippi as a child, was from a distinguished, landed family; he was educated at West Point and served in the Mexican War and in the House and Senate and as U.S. secretary of war. Lincoln was poor, roughhewn, and self-educated. Lincoln was a man of the people and Davis was proud and shy. Both men suffered great personal tragedies. History proved Lincoln to be by far the greatest leader.

There were many capable leaders in the South who had the confidence of their men and performed ably, some brilliantly, and some like Stonewall Jackson and Nathan Bedford Forrest exhibited genius. Lee, Longstreet, Richard Taylor, Wade Hampton, John B. Gordon, Albert Sidney Johnston, A. P. Hill Joe Wheeler, Jeb Stuart, Patrick Cleburne, E. P. Alexander, P. G. T. Beauregard, and many others were great, dedicated leaders. But from Richmond they never received cohesive plans for all fronts in all sections of the Confederacy. The loss of New Orleans and the control of the Mississippi River early in the war foredoomed their efforts.

Lee realized, but too late, the urgency of taking the offensive and went on to Gettysburg, but the usual indecision, and lack of concerted effort made the tremendous loss of life and the tragic loss of battle a nightmare. Lee and his Grays marched back southward and left behind what little chance of victory the South had.

The losses of the Confederate armies were monstrous; 258,000 southern men died. The North lost 360,000, proportionately fewer considering its population. Louisiana lost 15,000 men or 27 percent of its Confederate force.

Rehearsal and the Battle of Brothers

Perhaps, now, with the advantage of hindsight, we may view all that they fought, bled, suffered, and died for as a terrible waste of life and energy. But I am certain that if some of us had seen that battle flag unfurl, heard the bugle call, the drums beat, the rattle of muskets, and the tread of marching feet, we would have raced to join their ranks, never looking back, except to wave goodbye. We would have marched with them to destiny and death.

> Gallant Grays! Forward! Forward!
> Duty Calls! Onward! Onward!
> March! March! Mud . . . mud!
> In cadence! Thud! Thud!
> Rain. . . . rain! Snow. . . .snow!
> A soldier's lot! Woe! Woe!
> Reposed in death! Sleep. . . . sleep!
> Sweethearts, widows! Weep. . . . Weep!

The dejected couple, center, signifies this depressing chapter in Louisiana's history. With their land wasted, their homesteads destroyed, and little optimism for their future, they saw little happiness in the newborn liberation of the slave with his banjo. And the freed blacks quickly learned that the carpetbaggers from the North had no intention of giving them a mule and forty acres of land to start anew. Two inflictors of this woe are drawn in the personages of General Shepley, the Union adjutant general of Louisiana, 1862-1864, and the governor, Henry Clay Warmoth, drawn at the bottom right.

CHAPTER 8

Conquerors, Carpetbaggers, and Home Rule

The end of the Civil War found the state of Louisiana and the entire South in economic chaos, and the political situation was even worse. The Republican radicals who dominated the government of Louisiana split into two factions; one segment advocated the abolition of slavery and a new state constitution; and the other, the Conservative Union Party, wanted to keep the state constitution of 1852 and to retain slavery. This seemed to contradict the moralistic cause of the Yankees' war. Eventually, both Republican groups collapsed in their bitter rivalry for the spoils. The resulting vacuum was soon filled by yet another faction with a political pipeline to the national administration.

However, by December 18, 1865, Secretary of State William H. Seward declared that the Thirteenth Amendment to the U.S. Constitution abolishing slavery to be in effect because of its ratification by twenty-seven states. This act and declaration further ridiculed the Emancipation Proclamation.

The great post-Civil War problem was the reconstruction of the southern states and their restitution to the Union, but the constitutional significance was much less important than the social issues. The conservatives of the north favored a compassionate reconstruction, but the radicals were anxious to insure Negroes the benefits of the war, and to make sure that former Confederates would be punished. The radicals prevailed and the Reconstruction era proved to be sordid and vengeful.

On April 9, 1866, barely a year after the surrender at Appomattox, the Civil Rights Bill was passed. On July 16 the Freedmen's Bureau Bill was passed. Both bills were vetoed on constitutional grounds by Andrew Johnson who had succeeded Lincoln to the presidency. However, the Congress promptly passed the two bills over his veto, and its Joint Committee on Reconstruction declared that the states of the Confederacy were not entitled to representation in the national Congress. It further stated that reconstruction of the Union was beyond the realm of the authority of the president of the United States—a move to divest Johnson of his veto power.

Unhappily, the radicals won by substantial majorities in the northern elections in 1866, and on March 2nd and 23rd, 1867, Congress passed the Reconstruction Act which, in effect, made the southern states subservient to the whims of the radicals. Under the provisions of this Act the southern states were divided into five military districts, each under the command of a military governor. The constitutional status of the southern states was argued, with theories ranging from the doctrine that the states still retained their sovereignty to the other extreme that they were conquered provinces. All former Confederates were disenfranchised and the Negroes enfranchised. The power of administrating these acts was solely in the hands of the military governors. An Army appropriation bill was passed on March 2, 1867, with a rider attached that ordered the disbanding of all southern state militia units and specifically forbade the forming of any such forces, whatever the size, until Congress authorized their restoration. This effectively suppressed state militias for the entire Reconstruction period.

From the time that Benjamin F. Butler's troops marched into New Orleans on May 1, 1862, until the inauguration of Francis T. Nicholls in 1877, Louisiana was under the heel of an oppressive radical regime. Self-government ceased; only the Negroes, white scalawags, and carpetbaggers had voting rights. Military rule was, in effect, martial law, and whatever could not be gained politically was accomplished with the bayonet. Black votes were manipulated, and the state legislature soon comprised a great number of illiterate Negroes who did the bidding of their new masters.

U.S. Grant, a great soldier, was a weak president, and willingly or not, he became the tool of the radical Congress. He associated himself with a group of disreputable financiers and politicians. His administration brought ruin and anarchy by overturning a society and offering no substitute for social groundwork. The Reconstruction policy of the Radical Republicans, to which Grant gave his full support, assured the supremacy of the northern mercantile and industrial classes in the councils of the nation. But it also created a defensive unity among the people of the South, and it kept alive the hatred between the two sections of the country.

A climate of hate, vindictiveness, and class distinction raged, with Negroes as the political pawns. On July 30, 1866, a procession of blacks on its way to a noontime political meeting at Mechanics Hall (now the Fairmont Hotel) became involved in a fight with white men; 38 persons were killed and 146 wounded.

General Absalom Baird, the Federal subordinate to General Phil Sheridan, who was absent, had consented to send his troops from Jackson Barracks to the area of the meeting. Unfortunately, Baird was confused about the time and thought the convention was at 6:00 P.M. He and his troops arrived after most of the bloodshed had occurred. Governor Wells, upon first learning of the trouble, fled and locked himself in his residence.

The Republican-dominated legislature passed an act making service in the "Louisiana Native Guard" compulsory for all able-bodied citizens between the ages of eighteen and forty-five. Since the organization excluded disenfranchised whites, it was a black militia. In some instances these troops were used to terrorize white communities. Meanwhile, the average black farmer, who had been promised forty acres and a mule, received nothing. Most relied upon their former masters for succor or advice, and often the freed slaves and their former masters weathered this troubled era together.

General George F. Shepley had been appointed military governor of Louisiana within Union lines and served in this capacity from 1862 until 1864. He was followed by Michael Hahn—also within the Union lines—who served until 1865. Lieutenant Governor James Madison Wells followed, when Hahn resigned to become a United States senator, and served until 1867. Two military appointments followed, with Benjamin F. Flanders (1867-1868) and Joshua Baker (1868) serving as governors.

Then followed the remarkable carpetbagger Henry Clay Warmoth, a native of Illinois who had spent some time in Missouri. One of Warmoth's utterances during the height of his influence in politics was: "I don't pretend to be honest . . . . I only pretend as honest as anybody in politics. . . . Why, damn it, everybody is demoralized down here. Corruption is the fashion."[1]

A power struggle developed between whites and blacks for the control of the Radical Party. Oscar J. Dunn, a Negro house painter, had been elected lieutenant governor with Warmoth. In the meantime, Louisiana was readmitted to the Union on June 25, 1868, no doubt because of the influence of the Louisiana Radical Republican Party in Congress. General Grant had ordered the military authorities in Louisiana to install Warmoth and Dunn in the state Capitol. Yet within the alliance of whites and blacks in the Radical Party there were undercurrents of jealousy and hostility. The average freed Negro still waited for his forty acres and his mule promised by the Freedmen's Bureau and those evangelistic northern missionaries. To the sadly gullible blacks, the Radicals promised a $300 bonus in addition to those forty acres and the mule if the black would vote for their convention. Of course, the blacks got neither.

The minority Democrats, despite the disenfranchisement of so many of their former members, were making inroads into the Radical strength. The Radicals had charged that no Negro became a Democrat unless coerced. Many blacks, disgusted with Radical corruption and the dissension in the state, stayed away from the polls in the presidential election of 1868; so many did so that Horatio Seymour, the Democratic nominee for president, carried the state. This was at a point in history when far more blacks were registered voters than whites.

It has been averred that Warmoth amassed a million dollars while he served as governor on a salary of $8,000 a year. Corruption was such that even the Radicals, Negro supporters, and their allies began to talk of impeaching Warmoth. When Oscar Dunn, the lieutenant governor died, Pickney Benton Stewart Pinchback, another black, succeeded him. And when Warmoth was later impeached for fraud in the 1872 election Pinchback succeeded him, thus becoming the first and only black governor of the state of Louisiana.

Warmoth, now incensed at his former colleagues and at his impeachment, created another party and again ran for governor. John McEnery was the choice of the Democrats with D. B. Penn the candidate for lieutenant governor. McEnery polled 65,579 to Kellogg's 55,973, but it took more than a majority of votes to win an election in Louisiana during this period of history.

---

[1]Charles L. Dufour, *Ten Flags In The Wind* (New York, Evanston, and London: Harper & Harper), 180.

The Returning Board, which had been set up by the Radicals to validate returns, declared William Pitt Kellogg, the Radical candidate, the winner. The McEnery forces set up a Returning Board of their own and declared McEnery the winner. Consequently, Louisiana had two governors, two lieutenant governors, and two state legislatures. President Grant reorganized Kellogg and his ticket. Historians have reconciled this dispute by listing John McEnery "elected, but ruled out," 1873, and William Pitt Kellogg "governor de facto," 1873-1877.

McEnery, assuming to be the duly elected, legitimate governor, called his own militia into action and attacked Kellogg's police station then housed in the Cabildo. Sixty-five attackers threw themselves at the Kellogg policemen, resulting in three deaths; among the eight wounded, was General Frederick N. Ogden who commanded McEnery's militia. Like a Hollywood Western, the United States troops arrived and quelled the disturbance.

In Colfax, Grant Parish, a race riot broke out on Easter Sunday, 1873. The casualties were enormous; some have estimated the Negro dead as high as six hundred but sixty-five to seventy, would be more accurate. Appeals had been made to Kellogg to send troops when trouble was brewing in this area, but there had been no response. Tragedies such as the Colfax riot served to keep the U.S. military forces in Louisiana. Their presence and power insured the election of Radical candidates; for whenever there was a scarcity of votes for the Radical candidate, Federal troops could always tip the balance in their favor.

A Reform Party, composed of many prominent Louisianians among whom were General P. G. T. Beauregard, General Randall L. Gibson, and others who fought for the Confederacy, endeavored to unify the people of the states, irrespective of race or party. They pledged equal civil rights and political freedom to all. This party was a forerunner to other solidifying movements that were forming in the minds of Louisiana citizens, white and black, as they saw bankruptcy, anarchy, and bloodshed ahead.

Because of rumors that some Negroes were organizing "Black Leagues" to counteract the "White League," there was fear of a general black uprising. Eventually, Louisiana soon became an armed camp.

General Frederick N. Ogden, who had recovered from his wounds, organized the Crescent City White League, a semimilitary unit. This encouraged more such leagues, and soon there were nearly fifteen thousand armed White Leaguers in the state. Such military organizations were in direct violation of the terms of the Reconstruction Act, but the citizens had reached the limits of their patience with the conduct of local and state government. An incident at Coushatta portended further terrors to come. In August, 1874, the White League forced six Republicans to resign and they were killed en route to Shreveport under armed guard.

The steamer *Mississippi*, docked at New Orleans, was found to contain a great quantity of guns and ammunition. Governor Kellogg, suspecting it was designated for the White League, ordered it confiscated. The White League in turn called for an assembly of citizens on Monday, September 14, near the foot of Canal Street, near the statue of Henry Clay. D. B. Penn, a former Confederate officer, in the absence of the contesting Governor McEnery, was in command. His forces drew a line of defense, roughly, from Poydras Street and from St. Charles Street to the river. Each intersection and all the areas between Front Street and the river were barricaded.

A crowd in excess of five thousand people assembled to hear orations and to hear two proclamations from acting governor Penn. The purpose of the assembly was to urge Kellogg to resign, to guarantee the Negroes their civil rights and to formulate plans "for the purpose of driving the usurpers from power." An appeal was made to enlist all males from the ages of eighteen to forty-five, irrespective of color to arm and assemble.

Kellogg infuriated the crowd by refusing to sign the petition for his resignation. They were hell-bent on getting something done that day. The Metropolitan Police, directed by Kellogg from their headquarters in the Customhouse, prepared to move against the White Leaguers. General James Longstreet, former Confederate commander, confidant of Lee, and former corps commander of a segment of Lee's Army of Northern Virginia, commanded the Metropolitan Police. At about four o'clock in the afternoon, Longstreet and his immediate subordinate, General Algernon Badger, moved five hundred Metropolitan Police and six cannons to a position opposite the White Leaguers on a line between the Customhouse and the river. Cannonfire from Longstreet's force opened battle, and legend says the Rebel yell from the White Leaguers caused Longstreet to pale as he recalled the fabled battlecry. The White League responded with a vicious volley from behind their barricade. A force, under the cover of sugar hogsheads and cotton bales, outflanked Longstreet's left and charged.

Immediate panic enveloped the Metropolitan Police; they scattered, seeking the protection of the Customhouse; some even discarded various parts of their uniforms to escape identity. General Badger, despite his wounds, tried in vain to rally his frenzied troops; Longstreet at the head of reinforcements was forced back toward Jackson Square.

The battle lasted one quarter hour. There were some troops of the United States in the Customhouse, but they did not enter the fray; some witnesses said they actually cheered the victorious White Leaguers. There were eleven killed and sixty wounded among the Metropolitan Police while the White League lost sixteen killed and forty-five wounded. The very next morning the White League still under arms forced the Negro militia and the Metropolitan Police to surrender.

The McEnery and Penn supporters were placed in state and city offices that had been denied them upon their election. Penn was put into office pending the return of Governor McEnery. The barricades were torn down, the White League had a grand march, and all became quiet.

But the victory was short-lived; although the Kellogg regime was discredited, President Grant, nevertheless, issued a proclamation of September 15, barely a month after the battle, ordering, "the turbulent persons to disperse in five days and submit to the laws and constituted authorities of the State." To add emphasis and force, Grant then sent more Federal troops and three warships. Two days later Governor McEnery surrendered arms and state property to the Federal forces. And things became just as they were before the conflict: an entrenched rather than a duly elected government existed with Kellogg back in his governor's seat.

It did not help matters when General Phillip Sheridan was sent to Louisiana by Grant to "report on conditions." Sheridan, after a cursory tour reported, "I think that the terrorism . . . could be entirely removed and confidence and fair dealing established by the arrest and trial of the ringleaders of the armed White Leagues." He referred to the insurgents as "banditti" and recommended they be tried by a military court.

A subcommittee sent by Congress to investigate conditions in Louisiana stated that McEnery and his people would be immediately installed in office were it not for the Federal troops and that the conservatives did not intend to fight the U.S. government. A compromise was reached whereby it was agreed that Kellogg would serve as governor until the end of his term in 1877, and the seats in dispute would be resolved by this congressional subcommittee. The stage was set for one of the momentous and monumental events in Louisiana's colorful history, the end of the Reconstruction era.

By 1876 three southern states were still under carpetbag rule—Louisiana, South Carolina, and Florida. The national Democratic Party was determined to restore home rule and the Republicans, now conscious of the scandals in the Grant administration and the continuing discredit of their "alien" rule in the "unredeemed" states; were actually not very confident concerning the impending presidential election.

In Baton Rouge, on July 24, 1876, the Democrats' nomination for governor began, and Francis T. Nicholls was persuaded to run for office. Nicholls had risen to brigadier general during the Civil War and had lost an arm and a leg. In a dramatic speech, State Senator F. S. Goode, of Terrebonne Parish, said: "I nominate all that is left of General Nicholls!"

Nicholls' greatest appeal besides his war record was that he was not a professional politician. His name was new, the spirit of deliverance from oppressors was born anew, and a heretofore unheard-of alliance of whites and blacks joined to rid the state of carpetbaggers, scalawags, and their camp-followers.

The Republicans used every trick imaginable to disqualify the white voters in the election. But when the returns came in, Nicholls seemed to have a clear majority by eight thousand votes. He then declared himself and his ticket elected and proceeded to establish all three branches of government—executive, judicial, and legislative—into a de facto position and purposely avoided conflicts that might provoke Federal intervention. Five hundred volunteer policemen were sworn in to maintain order in New Orleans, then the capital. His militia, drawn from Longstreet's opponents, seized the supreme court building, the police station, and the arsenal. He could not enter the St. Louis Hotel (now the site of the Royal Orleans) in the Vieux Carre, where the Republicans had barricaded themselves to keep Nicholls out. Isolated at the St. Louis, the Republicans could not keep in touch with Nicholls while he was establishing his government in St. Patrick's Hall on Camp Street.

The Louisiana situation attracted national publicity which did

Conquerors, Carpetbaggers, and Home Rule 97

not help the cause of Rutherford B. Hayes, the Republican presidential aspirant. It also damaged the image of the Republican Party. The Republicans in Louisiana, attempting to retain the governorship and other state offices, appealed as usual for Federal troops. This time, however, Grant hestitated to use armed force to reseat Radical Republicans in Louisiana.

The worse blow befell the Radical Republicans in Louisiana when former governor Pickney Pinchback, transferred his allegiance to Nicholls. He took with him three other prominent black politicians—George B. Hamlett, former sheriff of Ouachita Parish; Henry Demas; and C. B. Wheeler. Pinchback defended his switch by saying: "Though I am Republican at heart, I am likewise familiar with the workings of the Republican Party in Louisiana and would say without hesitation that for corruption and dishonesty, it has not it's equal on the face of God's earth." He also charged that each member of the legislature received $250 for electing Kellogg to a senatorial seat. As president of the State Central Committee, Pinchback even wired President Grant that he acknowledged the Nicholls government.

Nicholls sent three emissaries to the National Democratic Party to keep him advised on activities of Congress. An initial count clearly showed that Samuel J. Tilden had defeated Hayes for the presidency. But a question arose concerning the electoral votes in Louisiana, Florida, South Carolina; and one of the Oregon vote gave Hayes the opportunity to ask for a recount. It became imperative therefore that the Louisiana electoral votes go to Hayes. Nicholls needed time to maneuver Hayes into recognizing his government. Therefore his emissaries in Washington urged a Democratic filibuster to delay the electoral count until the Louisiana issue was resolved. Backed into a corner, Hayes agreed to recognized Nicholls' election in Louisiana provided the state's electoral votes were conceded to the Republicans to insure his election to the presidency.

In April, in order to give the outward appearance of impartial observation, Hayes, now president-elect, sent a commission of five men to investigate the legitimacy of the Louisiana gubernatorial election. They soon validated the election of Nicholls much to the anger of the Radical candidate, Stephen B. Packard. Packard wanted to know how he the Republican candidate could have lost an election that could give the electoral votes to the Republican president of the same ticket. Hayes quieted Packard by giving him a consulate post in England.

Nicholls had managed to rid Louisiana of the carpetbag government and gain the confidence and admiration of the people at large, white and black; he had emerged as the one man who could be trusted, and he fulfilled the faith the Louisianians had in him. A former militia captain of the Phoenix Company of Donaldsonville, Nicholls, like a latter-day Moses, had delivered his people.

On April 24, 1877, President Rutherford B. Hayes ordered all Federal troops out of Louisiana. The blue-clad soldiers marched to Jackson Barracks to gather up their gear, preparatory to entraining for the north. The Washington Artillery, federally restricted from organizing since the end of the Civil War, hastily assembled and gave a one-hundred-gun salute. Packard gave up the state Capitol; Nicholls and his fellow elected officials assumed their rightful places, and thus ended the epoch of Reconstruction.

A personification of courage and strength is symbolized in the central figure of this chapter—Governor Francis T. Nicholls. Outstanding for similar dedication were the men of the Washington Artillery, shown with their many decorations, upper left. On the governor's mind was the new war with Spain and the annual threats from Mississippi River flooding, like the flood of 1890. A man with the know-how to build a better state militia, a better flood control, and a people with greater pride.

CHAPTER 9

Rebuilding and a New Rehearsal

During the administration of Henry C. Warmoth an amendment to an Act, approved on April 5, 1870, was formulated "to organize, arm and equip a uniform militia." The amendment carried use of the term *National Guard*, as follows:

> Section 1. Be it enacted by the Senate and House of Representatives of the State of Louisiana in General Assembly convened, that the uniformed militia of the State shall constitute and be known as the National Guard of the State of Louisiana, and shall consist of the present uniformed militia and such volunteers as shall enroll themselves or enlist therein.
> Section 2. Be it further enacted, etc., that thirty-five non-commissioned officers, musicians and privates shall be in minimum and one hundred the maximum of the troop and organization and company, of cavalry and infantry, and sixty non-commissioned officers, musicians, and privates, the minimum and one hundred and twenty the maximum of the battery organization of Artillery, and all troop battery and company organization shall always exceed the minimum herein specified.
> Section 3. Be it further enacted, etc., that whenever any troop or battery or company shall fall below the minimum established by the preceding section such troop, battery or company may be consolidated or disbanded by the order of the Commander-in-chief in which case the officers, non-commissioned officers, musicians, and privates shall have allowed to them as part of their term of service, the time already.
> Section 4. Be it further enacted, etc., that any officer or non-commissioned officer who shall enlist, or muster in his company any

person belonging to another company, or who may have been dismissed in disgrace from the *National Guard* of the State under the provisions of the military laws of the State, shall be liable to be tried by court martial for conduct prejudicial to good order and military discipline and punished at the discretion of the court, but any member deserving transfer, and applying therefore in writing to the Adjutant General of the State, may be transferred from one Company to another upon obtaining the written consent of the Captain of his own company, and the Captain of the company to which he deserves to be transferred and also the written consent of the commandants of the regiment or battalion to which companies may belong.

This Act and the amendments were formally approved by the state legislature on April 4, 1873. If Governor Warmoth did nothing else worthy of commendation, the Louisiana National Guard did obtain its present name under his administration. However, the Guard was not necessarily representative of Louisiana since most white citizens were rendered ineligible at that time by disfranchisement.

The salute from the Washington Artillery to the departing Federal troops at New Orleans also announced the re-forming of a truly representative Louisiana National Guard. High on the list of priorities of Governor Francis T. Nicholls was the restoration of the militia. He had tacitly done as much when he organized the police force to keep the peace pending the outcome of the election in 1876. Being a former militiaman, Nicholls realized the importance of the home soldier. Immediately after his inauguration, he urged the legislature to repeal all the abortive laws passed by the Radical Republicans. This was speedily done. And on March 31, 1878, the state legislature passed an act with an appropriation of $10,000 to revive the militia.

The Washington Artillery was one of the few units to emerge from the Civil War with its name intact. Most other militia groups identified with their Civil War deeds and lost their historic connections with earlier military actions.

No man in Louisiana's history so well personified the courage and resiliency of its people as did Francis T. Nicholls. Of a distinguished family, he represented the pioneer element that had helped nurture the state during its earliest years. On the battlefield he had shared the common miseries of the ordinary soldier. He lost an arm and was soon taken prisoner by Union forces; upon his recuperation in a prison camp, he was exchanged. He then lost his leg while in action at Chancellorsville; a cannonball severed his foot just above the ankle and by a near miracle it also cauterized the wound, thereby keeping him from bleeding to death on the battleground.

Giving further attention to the militia, Nicholls had the assessors enroll the names of all males between the ages of eighteen and forty-five and report to the governor, who was the commander in chief of all state forces. The infantry companies would contain no fewer than 60 men or more than 100 privates. Cavalry companies were limited to 90 privates but no fewer than 40 men including officers. For artillery companies the maximum was 120 men.

The Louisiana State National Guard constituted a part of the state forces, and the rest of the militia was to be known as the Militia of the State of Louisiana. As commander in chief the governor was empowered to reorganize the militia and to remove any officer he deemed unsuited.

Historians have stated that during Reconstruction the National Guard undertook the enormous chore of cataloging the names of all the men who were killed or wounded in the War of 1812. If this was done, it had to be an independent action since under the terms of the Reconstruction Act, any organization of former militiamen was forbidden. And if the cataloging was done by the Radicals' Louisiana Native Guard, the project had nothing to do with what is now called the Louisiana State National Guard. Without question, the Louisiana National Guard did catalog the names of the casualties in the Mexican and Civil wars.

The military forces of the state merged into the National Guard as a result of an Act of April 10, 1880. Enlistment of noncommissioned officers and men was for four years, and officers' terms were for two years. The shorter term for officers allowed the governor to replace them if they proved unsuited for command. The governor's staff was to consist of the adjutant, inspector (a tradition from Spanish colonial times), quartermaster, and surgeon-general, each of whom would be rated brigadier generals. Also included were the necessary aides-de-camp with ranks of colonel, lieutenant colonel and major, according to the needs of the commands.

By 1882 the Guard had again reached the degree of efficiency and discipline of pre–Civil War times. Nicholls had by now been succeeded by Louis A. Wiltz who died in office and who was followed by Samuel D. McEnery. With each change of governor progress of the Guard was accelerated, and the Washington Artillery was chosen to go to various cities in the United States to compete in drills against the finest of other state National Guards. The proud unit brought back prizes, and the plaudits of the press.

Francis T. Nicholls again became governor in 1888, and during the catastrophic flood of 1890, he mobilized the National Guard to patrol the areas in danger and aid civilian evacuation. This service became a regular chore when the swollen Mississippi overflowed the low levees. Prior to 1882 there was no uniform system of levees; individual landowners along the waterways had the responsibility of protecting their own property. The states in the Mississippi Valley, with limited resources, endeavored to build levees of sufficient heights to withstand floods; but they were not enough and floods became annual occurrences. In some instances of emergency, members of the Guard filled sandbags to bolster the levees. This and other work, though lacking in military glamour, were heroic services that saved many lives. It was not until the cataclysmic flood of 1927 that the federal government began to assume responsibility for flood control. Today, the U.S. Corps of Engineers has that responsibility. But the National Guard still performs the patrol and evacuation services imperative to maintaining peace, order and the saving of lives.

By an Act of July 5, 1894, a naval battalion was organized and attached to the Louisiana National Guard. Commanded by a lieutenant commander, this force was organized along regulations generally applied by the United States Navy. The governor was authorized to take all necessary action for the procurement of a vessel, its armament, and provisions. The history of the naval force is obscure, but no doubt it was created to render patrol and evacuation services in flood areas.

By the time of the Spanish-American War, the Louisiana State National Guard was superbly organized, equipped, and ready for any contingency. Two distinct and memorable facts resulted from this war: The United States became a world power, and the nation was reunited in a common cause, distracted from the recriminations that lingered among the veterans of opposing sides of the Civil War. Some officers, Blue and Gray, found themselves allied in command of expeditionary forces.

The cause of the Spanish-American war was twofold, economic and humanitarian, with its objective the liberation of Cuba. After the Mexican War, because of the proposed canal routes across the

Rebuilding and a New Rehearsal

Isthmus of Tehuantepec, the Island of Cuba became of primary strategic importance. Spain's exploitation of the island's wealth in the latter part of the nineteenth century brought about a popular party seeking self-government, while a second party, the royalists, made up of wealthy and influential people, favored the status quo. The revolution called the Ten Years' War (1868-1878) was an attempt by the liberals to force concessions from Spain. Some concessions were made and hostilities ceased. But the aristocratic party opposed most reforms, and Spain's promises went unfilled. In 1895 an insurrection occurred with continued guerilla activity for the next two years. In vicious, vindictive actions on the part of the government, all inhabitants of rural areas were garrisoned into towns, where without adequate food and water, they died in great numbers. These incidents and the huge threat to American capital won sympathy for the insurrectionists from the citizens of the United States, and talk of intervention began. But two incidents enraged the people of the United States. A letter written by a Spanish minister in Washington to a Cuban friend, expressing great contempt for President William McKinley, was published in a New York newspaper. Soon after, the battleship *Main* was sunk in Havana harbor. The slogan "Remember the Maine" became the battle cry as McKinley, in an attempt at peace, negotiated for an armistice to which he received unsatisfactory replies from the Spanish government. While negotiations went on, Spain declared war on the United States, and on the following day Congress declared that war had existed since April 21, 1898, three days before Spain's declaration.

A naval squadron, under Rear Admiral Sampson, had as its objective the blockade of Cuba and the interception of the Spanish fleet which had sailed for the West Indies from the Cape Verde Islands on April 29. Admiral Cervera and his Spanish fleet entered Santiago de Cuba harbor on May 19, and on May 28 the American commodore, Schley, established a blockade of the harbor. He was soon joined by Sampson who took command of the blockading fleet on June 1. Cervera, in a desperate attempt to run the blockade, began moving his fleet on July 3, but within four hours his fleet was destroyed.

Meanwhile, about seventeen hundred officers and men under the command of General Shafter were landed without opposition at Daiquiri. On July 1 General Lawton and his forces attacked and entered El Caney while Generals Wheeler and Kent made a successful attack on San Juan Hill with the famous Rough Riders led by Colonel

Leonard Wood and Lieutenant Colonel Theodore Roosevelt. Santiago soon fell, and an expedition was rushed to Puerto Rico which was entirely successful. Admiral George Dewey, in a concerted action, bombarded the city of Manila in the Philippines which fell without great resistance after a combined attack by the U.S. navy and army. This action in the Philippines actually occurred after the signing of a peace agreement with Spain.

On December 10, 1898, with the capitulation of Spanish forces in the New World, a peace settlement was agreed upon in Paris and ratified by the U.S. Senate on February 6, 1899. Spain relinquished all sovereignty over Cuba and ceded to the United States, under terms of indemnity, the islands of Puerto Rico and Guam and sold to the United States the Philippine Islands for $20 million.

The role of the Louisiana National Guard in the Spanish-American War was significant and offered the first test of its reorganization. When war was declared on April 23, 1898, President William McKinley's call for 125,000 volunteers met with immediate response in Louisiana. Two full regiments of infantry, three batteries of artillery, and 250 men from the state naval reserve assembled for duty. As many as five thousand Louisiana National Guardsmen were equipped and sent out of state for duty in the war. Not all engaged in the conflict but they were on the ready! The Immune Regiment with Colonel Duncan N. Wood, commanding, was organized in New Orleans. It was followed by the First Regiment, composed of north Louisianians, commanded by Rufus G. Pleasant of Shreveport, who was later to become governor. By January 1, 1899, the Louisiana Guardsmen were among the first of the American troops to march on the streets of Havana, following the peace. Many Guardsmen from all over the United States served on patrol duty in the Philippines after the war and until an autonomous government was set up. It was the home soldier of the American people who kept peace in the Philippines following the ouster of the Spanish government until their home rule was established.

An inspection in June, 1900, revealed that the Louisiana National Guard contained seventeen companies of infantrymen, ten companies of artillery and cavalry, and five divisions of naval militia. The grass roots interest in the National Guard continued in Louisiana, and pride in its Louisiana traditions was born anew. The quick victories in Cuba, Puerto Rico, and the Philippines helped to perpetuate the American legend of invincibility.

The central figure of this chapter begins to make his mark in history by striking out after Francisco "Pancho" Villa in Mexico. His name is General John J. Pershing. With the sinking of the *Lusitania*, the general faced more than a bandit. Facing the same way with him are the men of the Second Louisiana Cavalry, depicted at bottom right, with trench warfare and the Jennings Cavalry shown at bottom left.

CHAPTER 10

Blood on the Horizon

The early twentieth century introduced global conflict, surpassing anything ever experienced by human beings. It emanated from the political and economic conditions of Europe, buts its origins can be traced to the Middle Ages when repeated invasions by the Slavs created the geographic complexities of western Europe. The natural growth of Pan-Slavism and Pan-Germanism was of course a dormant but potent factor in the struggle. The conflict of minorities became more and more violent as they sought identities in direct opposition of their imperialist overlords.

After the formation of the German Empire in 1871, Europe divided into two hostile alliances, the Triple Alliance and the Triple Entente. Germany began expanding its European colonial empire in the face of increasing resentment. Its commerce and navy began to rival that of Great Britain, and France, still seething over defeat in the Franco-Prussian War, watched Germany with growing anger. Austria's desire to expand her empire to the east and to control the Slavs of the Balkans ran counter to the desires of those minorities who hoped to attain their national independence and political autonomy. Europe, therefore, went from one crisis to another in a fomentation of restless minorities and ambitious empires.

On June 28, 1914, Austrian Archduke Francis Ferdinand, heir to the thrones of Austria and Hungary was assassinated by a Serbian nationalist at Sarajevo. Austria sent an ultimatum to Serbia on July

24 demanding the suspension of Serbia's sovereignty as a state. On July 28, despite frantic efforts of diplomats of most major countries. Austria marched on Serbia over the Tsar's protests which forced Russia to mobilize. On August 1 Germany declared war on Russia. France entered the conflict on August 3, and at midnight of August 4, Great Britain declared war because of Germany's violation of Belgium's neutrality.

The declaration of war in Europe affected the United States's commerce and freedom of movement on the high seas. The sinking of the Lusitania, a large Cunard liner under British registry with 114 American citizens among the 1,153 who perished, caused many Americans to call for war. Woodrow Wilson, who had campaigned for the presidency under the slogan, "He kept us out of war," chose a course of temperate diplomacy. When a torpedo sank the unarmed French ship *Sussex* injuring Americans aboard, Wilson threatened to break off diplomatic relations with Germany, but then settled for Germany's promise of no more such offenses.

In January, 1917, British Naval Intelligence intercepted and deciphered a code from the German foreign secretary, Zimmerman, to the German minister in Mexico informing him of unrestricted submarine warfare. The message also instructed him to suggest to Mexico in the event of war, it should ally itself with Germany, try to persuade Japan to join, and fight, with one of the objectives being to recover the territory in New Mexico, Texas, and Arizona that Mexico had lost to the United States.

The revelation of such a proposition came when conditions between the United States and Mexico were already unstable. As early as 1913 when General Victoriano Huerta coldly arranged the assassination of Francisco Madero, a liberal idealist who had succeeded the dictator Porfiro Diaz in the revolution of 1911, Wilson, idealistic and uncompromising, refused to recognize the Heurta regime despite the urgings of large American business interests. When the Huerta government failed to collapse, Wilson offered help to the anti-Huerta Constitutionalist forces under Venustiano Carranza. Carranza wanted no support from the unpopular Yankees across the border. However, an incident that occurred on April 9, 1914, gave cause for Wilson to intervene.

One of Huerta's officers detained and arrested the crew of an American vessel at Tampico. The Mexicans released the prisoners immediately with expressions of regret, but the American commander of the squadron demanded a more formal apology, which was refused. Wilson took this as an insult and asked Congress to empower him to use arms in order to win redress. But before the Congress could act, Wilson learned of a German ship destined for Vera Cruz with arms for Huerta which he feared would be used against the United States. On April 21, he ordered the United States Navy to occupy the port of Vera Cruz. There was resistance with 126 Mexican lives lost which even American sympathizers resented. Argentina, Brazil, and Chile offered to mediate the differences between United States and Mexico which prompted Wilson to "walk away" from the affair. But mediation failed, Huerta's government collapsed, and Carranza took over the presidency in August, 1914.

One year later a bandit named Francisco "Pancho" Villa began his opposition to Carranza by creating general unrest and marauding border territory belonging to the United States. Wilson ordered General John J. Pershing across the Mexican border on a punitive expedition against Villa. This border incident caused the mobilization of the National Guard, and Louisiana was among the first states to be affected because of its proximity and because its units were well trained. Four units consisting of 1,619 men assembled at Camp Stafford near Alexandria. (The site of old Camp Stafford is now occupied by the Veterans Administration Hospital in Alexandria.)

Mustered into service were the following units: First Regiment of Infantry, commanded by Colonel Frank P. Stubbs, Jr., which was mustered in on July 8, 1916, and out on September 25, 1916; First Separate Troop of Cavalry (the Jennings Unit), commanded by Captain Fred R. Phillips, mustered in on June 28, 1916, and out on October 6, 1916; Washington Artillery, commanded by Major Allison Owens, mustered in June 28, 1916, and out on February 28, 1917; First Field Hospital, mustered in on June 28, 1916, and out on February 28, 1917.

From Camp Stafford the units were sent to various places to join the forces of General Pershing. The First Regiment of Infantry was sent to San Benito, Texas; the First Separate Troop Cavalry and the Washington Artillery to Donna, Texas; and the Field Hospital to Brownsville, Texas. Raymond H. Fleming, who later became adjutant general of Louisiana and the leading luminary of the National Guard for a generation, served as a private in the Mexican border affair.

When the Pershing expedition began, President Carranza immediately mobilized his armies. Wilson, in the meantime, became occupied with the fast-developing events in Europe and finally realized that whatever the United States did, Mexico would continue on a course of instability. He withdrew Pershing and his troops from the area, recognized the Carranza government, and gave his full attention to Europe, thus closing the whole Mexican border affair.

On April 2, 1917, Wilson said before Congress, "The world must be made safe for democracry." And on April 4, the Senate adopted a war resolution by a vote of 86 to 6; the House voted 373 to 6 in favor of war against Germany.

Immediately after declaration of war, the Louisiana National Guard poured into Camp Stafford. As happened in the days immediately before the Civil War, the Guardsmen decided to mobilize the Washington Artillery and other local units for the protection of the port facilities. The levees, water purification plants, and other public utilities were patrolled by the Guard. These safety precautions were actually begun on March 28, 1917, at 2 P.M., one week before the declaration of war.

The National Defense Act of June 3, 1916, had become law before war was declared. By its terms, "The Militia of the United States shall consist of all able-bodied citizens of the United States and all other able-bodied males who have or shall have declared their intentions to become citizens of the United States, who shall be more than 18 years of age and younger than 45, and said Militia shall be divided into three classes: The National Guard, the Naval Militia, and the Unorganized Militia." It also made the National Guard for the first time, a component of the army of the United States when in active military service. This of course included the National Guard of the several states, territories, and the District of Columbia.

The Dick Act of 1903 became the basis for the draft law of World War I and of the selective service legislation for World War II. Each of the major powers engaged in the European war, with the exception of England, had entered the conflict with conscripted standing armies and trained reserves numbering in the millions. The United States began to build a commensurate force of its own by the slow and tedious method of drafting and training its armies around the nucleus of the National Guard. In 1914 little Belgium, with an army as big as that of the United States, had fought hopelessly against the Germans. Some U.S. leaders wanted compulsory military service; National Guardsmen thought in terms of individual responsibility to one's country. Under the draft, manpower would be acquired, organized, and motivated. The National Guard units, throughout the United States, already had these requisites plus a tradition of continued service since the founding of the nation.

The Selective Draft Law, passed on May 18, 1917, provided manpower for the Regular Army and determined that the National Guard and National Guard Reserves were to be called into Federal service automatically and immediately on the same terms as the draftees. They were to retain, when practicable, their own state units and designations. The law also provided for the drafting of 500,000 men between the ages of twenty-one and thirty and at the discretion of the president another 500,000 would be drafted in similar fashion. Further, the president was authorized to accept into the army enough men for four divisions of volunteers composed of men over twenty-five. This part of the draft act was in deference to the wishes of the Guardsmen who considered themselves free citizens willingly and voluntarily accepting service to defend their country. Unlike Civil War practices, bounties or bonuses were strictly forbidden as means of attracting men into the service, as were substitutes. After five generations the military system proposed by George Washington in 1792 had become a reality.

The first American troops arrived in France in June, 1917, and hastened to the front to bolster the thin, fatigued lines of the Allies. At home haste was made to draft, organize, train, and equip more troops for European assignments. Louisiana Guardsmen and citizens at large responded patriotically; men gave up their jobs, lucrative and otherwise, to answer the call to arms.

The state was able to (theoretically) recruit 392,658 men, of which 9,942 were aliens. Among the aliens were 1,021 German subjects who technically were not answerable to the draft. Of Louisiana's total registrations, there were 233,185 white and 158,479 blacks eligibles for service in the armed forces. Louisiana ranked second only to Wyoming in having 45.88 percent fit for service among all its registrants. Of 66,142 examined, only 13.94 percent were physically disqualified; at the camps only 10.38 percent were rejected. On a national scale Louisiana's eligibles for the draft were highly rated, and the cost of inducting each man was seventh in terms of state ratio. Louisiana was also the first to complete and send in its records for the draft. Among all eligibles there were only fifty draft evaders. The records indicate that in all branches of the service there were 65,988 men from Louisiana in the army—1,004 with the

Marine Corps; 3,845 in the Regular Navy; 3,155 in the Naval Reserve, in which were 131 women who served as yeomen, making a grand total of 74,203.

Despite the assurances that they would retain their unit and state identifications, most of the Guardsmen were assimilated into various national units which were hastily drawn up and filled with the men who were handy at the moment. Nevertheless, history records the great contributions of the National Guard.

FIRST SEPARATE TROOP OF CAVALRY

The Jennings Cavalry or the First Separate Troop of Cavalry, got into the army virtually intact. They quickly reached the front where a dramatic victory was imminent, and they came home amid wild welcomes and congratulations. The people in the Jennings area are said to have celebrated the World War I valour of their unit for the duration of a generation.

Known as the 108th Cavalry, the troop entered Federal service on April 19, 1917, and after training at Camp Nicholls in New Orleans and Camp Beauregard, at Alexandria, were assigned to the Forty-second Division on August 5, 1917. They became the headquarters troops of that division and were composed principally of men from Jennings and the surrounding area. They demonstrated in a spectacular way the value of National Guardsmen who were able to mobilize, depart, and be at the front in a few months. It has been said that "luck favored them"; it would be more accurate to say that they made their own luck by being prepared. The declaration of war excited Americans and filled them with patriotic fervor that hastened the nation to prepare for action. The Guardsmen traditionally stand so prepared for defense throughout history.

The Jennings cavalry, with 105 men and officers, had an enviable record in the brief Mexican border encounter. They were mustered out in October, 1916, and were permitted to take home twenty-two of the horses assigned to them. When war broke out with Germany, they quickly reassembled with Louis J. Taylor, of Norwood Plantation, as captain, Roy S. Miller, of Jennings, as first lieutenant, and Robert B. Ricker, also of Jennings, as second lieutenant. Most of its men were the descendants of the early Acadian settlers.

Major General Flaglar, the Forty-second Division commander, recorded the Jennings cavalry's achievements. He stated that this group contained two of three principal means of liaison, motorcycle

THE LOUISIANA NATIONAL GUARD
THROUGH HISTORY

Color Paintings

By

ROBERT M. RUCKER

Page 117:
    Federal troops landing at Baton Rouge, December 17, 1862, with Old State Capitol in background.

Page 118:
    Washington Artillery at Fredericksburg during the Civil War.

Page 119:
    American troopers, Spanish-American War.

Page 120:
    122nd National Guard Fighter Training Squadron, P-39 over the Saraha Desert, Africa, 1943.

Page 121:
    National Guardsman giving succor to victims of Hurricane Camille, 1969.

Page 122:
    The adjutant general's residence, Jackson Barracks.

couriers and mounted orderlies. The ability of the men in the company to speak fluent French no doubt made their value inestimable in France. They continuously maintained lines of communications over shell-pocked roads, often under small-arms fire or artillery. At Chateau de Fere, at Essey, at St. Benoit, Camp Drachen, or at Hill 272, they kept that vital link with the overall command. Many were grandsons of France in American uniforms whose forefathers had gone to the New World two and one-half centuries before. Now their language link was renewed and was still spiced with the patois of Louis XIV.

Part of General Flaglar's order read, "The Headquarters troop may well feel pride in its excellent record of fidelity, efficiency and devotion to duty, and its home state, Louisiana, may well be proud of her contributions to the "Rainbow Division." They began fighting in February, and with the French held the Baccarat sector until June. After this, they were removed to the region east of Rheims where they met the enemy in hand-to-hand combat, repulsing them and inflicting heavy losses. During the last week of July they crossed the Ourcq and resisted a vicious German counterattack. In August they took Hill 272 and crushed the concentration at St. Mihiel. October found them at the Meuse-Argonne where blood flowed like creeks at springtime; they captured Cote de Chattillion, continued the advance, and on November 7 scaled and conquered the heights of Sedan encroaching upon the suburbs of that city on the Meuse. They entered Germany and were facing the enemy when the Armistice was signed.

The French cheered and kissed them as they marched back through scarred villages and towns on their way towards the coast and waiting ships that would take them home. New York was the first city to welcome doughboys home, showering them with affection in many forms as the soldiers marched down the streets. But the Jennings boys chose to go directly to New Orleans where they received a tumultuous welcome. Stories of their exploits preceded their arrival, bringing great personal pride to Louisianians. They had again taken the French language onto the battlefield to fight for the United States.

THE WASHINGTON ARTILLERY

The Washington Artillery, which had served in every war since its official organization in 1838, was accepted into the Federal service on June 19, 1916, for the Mexican War and had virtually a continued record of service from this time until it entered World War I. It had been stationed at Donna, Texas, under the command of James Parker and formed part of the provisional Thirteenth Division. The battalion, designated as the First Louisiana Field Artillery, was under the direct command of General E. M. Lewis, commandant at Llano Grande. While there they trained, maneuvered, and engaged in target practice with their three-inch guns at such places as Palo Alto and Resaca de la Palma. In competition with fifteen other batteries from Indiana, Iowa, and Minnesota, they scored four wins out of five and were second in the other; as a result, their fame spread far beyond Louisiana. By January 9, 1917, they transferred to McAllen, Texas, where they became attached to the New York Division in the artillery brigade under command of General W. S. McNair. They served eight months on the border and arrived back in New Orleans on Mardi Gras Day, 1917. Encamped at the Fair Grounds, they were honored with a huge reception on Washington's birthday. Plaudits and honors were accorded their commander, Major Allison Owen, and other officers and men, notably Captain Stanley Lemarie, Lieutenant Lloyd Posey, Lieutenant John Vigliero its chaplain, and Lieutenant W. J. Ratigan. Recognition was also given Battery A and its officers, Captain Schaumberg McGehee, First Lieutenants W. W. Hobson and A. Caron Ball, Second Lieutenants Cyril Baccich and James Mason; Battery B, Captain James E. Edmonds, First Lieutenants Peter Hamilton and Harold Nathan; Second Lieutenants Garish Gassoway and Meigs O. Frost; Battery C, First Lieutenant Guy R. Maloney, First Lieutenant Walter Stauffer, Second Lieutenants George Clark and Louis Goldstein, and all its noncommissioned officers and men.

Barely a month after being mustered out of the service, the Washington Artillery was reactivated to serve in World War I. By such a narrow margin they missed being in continuous service for two consecutive war actions. They went to Camp Nicholls, remaining there until October 17, when they were transferred to Camp Beauregard at Alexandria. By then the unit had expanded into a regiment with the following officers: Colonel Allison Owen; Lieutenant Colonel Bryan Black; Captain Stanley Lemarie, adjutant; Captain Louis Goldstein, supply officer; Lieutenant Frederick B. Freeland, assistant supply officer; Captain McHugh, surgeon; Major McGehee, commanding the First Battalion; Major Edmonds, commanding the Second Battalion; Captain Gassoway, headquarters company; Captain W. W. Hobson,

Battery A; Captain Hamilton, Battery B; Captain Stauffer, Battery C; Captain George Clarke, Battery D; Captain Nathan, Battery E; and Captain Maloney, Battery F. They became part of the 141st Field Artillery and reported to Brigadier General Ira Haynes, commander of the Sixty-fourth Field Artillery Brigade, which was part of the Thirty-ninth Division under Major General Henry C. Hodges.

The officers were sent to a field officers' school at Fort Sam Houston, and later to gas, signal, and deciphering classes. In November, 1917, 120 men and 3 officers were chosen from the ranks of the Washington Artillery to form the Fourteenth Trench Mortar Battery. Men who spoke French fluently were sent to France in the spring of 1918; 75 men qualified for this assignment. And by June 1918, 400 privates were transferred to the American Expeditionary Forces to fill the places of casualties; some of these men also served in the Rainbow Division. Some were sent to other divisions thus losing their identity with the Washington Artillery but, nevertheless, demonstrating fitness and versatility.

The officers of the Washington Artillery were rapidly advanced in rank. Captain Lemarie became a brigade adjutant; Colonel Black was assigned to the 140th; Captain Maloney became a Lieutenant Colonel with the 142nd. Major Edmonds became an instructor at Fort Sill and later a Lieutenant Colonel in command of a new brigade formed at Camp McClellan. Gus Tolson rose from a lieutenant to a major in the field artillery and was also an instructor at Fort Sill. Captains Gassoway and Clarke were promoted to major and a number of officers were also promoted as time went on and the war progressed. More than 160 men of that command who had served along the border were commissioned at various training schools; one private became a major, some gained the rank of captain and the rest became lieutenants.

The regiment, much overhauled by the departure of men who gained promotion and by the arrival of new men in its ranks, left Beauregard on August 13, was fitted at Camp Mills, New York, and embarked for France on August 26 aboard the *Agamemnon*. They reached Brest on September 3 and camped at Pointe Nazen Barracks. By September 9 they had moved to a village called Guipry, and sixteen days later began training anew at Coetquedan about eighteen miles south of Rennes. When their artillery unlimbered and began their demonstrations of repeated fire power it amazed but brought smiles to their French instructors who stated they were superior to any American volunteer unit.

They completed their training on November 8, but three days later the war was over. To relieve the boredom during the tedious wait for reassignment, the regimental band, under the direction of Hypolite Landry, performed frequently. A glee club was organized which also provided amusement for men far away from home. This glee club gained such popularity that it made a tour of some French areas, particularly hospitals. Major Gassoway and Corporal Fulham directed and arranged the music.

The regiment suffered forty cases of influenza, which in some cases developed into pneumonia and meningitis.

On April 9, 1919, the regiment sailed for home aboard the *Kaiserin Augusta Victoria* and landed in New York amid the wild demonstrations of welcome that the city was daily giving the returning doughboys. Upon arriving in New Orleans, on April 21, they were again received by thousands. They were mustered out on May 3, 1919. A complete list of the Washington Artillery's World War I leaders follows:

> Colonel Allison Owen; Captain Harry E. McCord; Captain Elmer E. Wood; First Lieutenant John Vigliero, chaplain. Headquarters Company: First Lieutenant A. C. Ball; Second Lieutenant Edward P. Benezech, Second Lieutenant Gervais Favrot. Supply Company: Captain Harold P. Nathan; First Lieutenant Raymond Sherrard. Battery A: Captain Peter O'Donnell, Second Lieutenant Adrien Bodet; Second Lieutenant Lawrence J. Currier. Battery B: Captain Peter Hamilton; First Lieutenant William L. Hoskins; First Lieutenant Lucien J. Moret; Second Lieutenant Eugene Mogabgab. Battery C: First Lieutenant Harvey Green. Battery D: Captain Raymond H. Fleming; First Lieutenant M. W. Wilkinson; Second Lieutenant Snyder Morgan. Battery E: Captain Jean Mason Smith. Battery F: Captain Louis S. Goldstein; Second Lieutenant Joseph F. Robinson. Medical Detachment: Captain Thomas H. McHugh. Headquarters Sixty-fourth Field Artillery Brigade: Major Stanley M. Lemarie, brigade adjutant; First Lieutenant Thomas B. Denegre, aide; First Lieutenant Charles E. Black.

Many of these men had availed themselves of special schools in France and England. Some studied at the Sorbonne and other schools in France; some studied law in London. A few served in the army of occupation immediately following the Armistice.

Immediately upon demobilization the Washington Artillery was disengaged from the United States Army and returned to the adjutant general of Louisiana as it has in generations past.

THE FIRST LOUISIANA REGIMENT

The First Louisiana Regiment was commanded by Colonel Frank P. Stubbs of Monroe. Stubbs had served in the Spanish-American War and in the action of the Mexican border. He took personal pride in the regiment's tradition and also in being its titular leader. The Regiment mobilized for World War I on April 1, 1917, and remained at Camp Nicholls until August, when it was transferred to Camp Beauregard. Before its departure it had two thousand men and officers. In October six of its companies were detached to form the nucleus of another regiment. In the meantime, other qualified men were drawn away to be placed in engineer and signal units. The remaining six companies were then divided into twos and then filled out by new recruits, bringing the regiment up to three thousand men; one-third over its normal complement.

In May, 1918, half of the men in the First Louisiana Regiment were detached and sent overseas as replacements for first line casualties. In June two thousand more men were added to the regiment and on August 9 the entire unit was finally ordered overseas. Its officers were as follow:

Colonel Frank P. Stubbs, Lieutenant Colonel Bret W. Eddy, Major Louis E. Duval, Major Louis F. Guerre, Major Richard A. Young, Jr., battalion commanders; Major Herbert C. Cole, commanding sanitary troops; Captain Joseph A. Redding, regimental adjutant; Captain Walter B. Kendall, personnel adjutant; Captain Elisha S. Brien, operations officer. The chaplains were J. Gilmore Buskie and Francis H. Cassidy. Company commanders: Headquarters Company, Captain E. L. Irvin; Machine Gun Company, Captain John B. Johnson; Supply Company, Captain Percy S. Prince; Company A, Captain H. S. Ford; Company B, Captain B. F. Edmondson; Company C, Lt. E. W. Warren; Company D, Captain J. H. Kuttner; Company E, Captain G. B. Buchel; Company F, Lt. Abe B. Harris; Company G, Captain J. H. Lowley; Company H, Captain Phillip H. Pugh, Jr.; Company I, Captain Tom B. Martin; Company K, Captain W. S. Rutter; Company L, Captain Frank B. Mays; Company M, Captain T. E. Utley.

After a short stay at Camp Mills, the regiment sailed on the U.S. transport *President Grant* and landed at Brest on September 3. It became part of the Thirty-ninth Division which also constituted the Fifth Depot Division. Officially titled the 156th Infantry, they were finally assigned to a training camp near Saint Florient. The regiment again became depleted as men from the unit were assigned to other detachments that had suffered casualties. By November there were only seven hundred men left in the regiment. It was finally dissolved in France. Although the regiment did not actively engage the enemy, many of its former members did earn that distinction. It was one of those instances where the "mother regiment" supplied the men to earn the glory for other units. This has frequently been the role of Guardsmen throughout their history.

THE LOUISIANA NAVAL BATTALION

World War I found the Louisiana Naval Battalion with four hundred men, divided into five divisions of sailors and one of marines. Most of the men were immediately assigned to the base at Charleston, South Carolina. Battalion commander G. W. Robotham was attached to headquarters of the Eighth Naval District in Louisiana.

Lieutenant Commander C. W. J. Neville was in charge of the Charleston contingent but later was assigned to patrol with a base at Burrwood at the mouth of the Mississippi River; later he was transferred to Galveston, Texas. Other officers of the battalion who served in the war were: Lt. Commander W. H. Henderson, the battalion surgeon, in charge of the naval hospital at Charleston; Lieutenants Carey, Lucy, and Mulvey served on scout duty on the Atlantic Ocean escorting transports and chasing submarines; Captain Sidney Simpson, commander of a marine unit, trained men in New Orleans and served in Florida.

The Louisiana Naval Battalion did not participate in any battles against the enemy, though officers Carey, Lucy, and Mulvey did see some submarine action.

THE SECOND LOUISIANA CAVALRY

Captain Albert de St. Aubin organized the Second Louisiana Cavalry in New Orleans. The troop was composed entirely of residents of Orleans Parish with First Lieutenant Charles R. Railey and Second Lieutenant James D. Douglas as second and third in command. Volunteers with ragtail equipment, they had much difficulty getting recognized since the National Guard equipment had been allotted to other units who entered the war before them. They were forced to raise funds for the regiment by holding a benefit at a local theater, but they were finally accepted at Camp Nicholls and were sent to Camp Beauregard where they became the headquarters company of the Thirty-ninth Division.

They eventually got to France and went as far as St. Florient where they were absorbed by the Ninth Army Corps at Mihiel and the Eighth Army Corps at Montigny. Collectively there is not much to relate about them, but as individuals they served their country nobly, especially during the last days of the war, and they had the satisfaction of being at the front. They suffered the rigors of trench warfare, participated in the victory, and came home to receive riotous welcomes.

The role of the American troops in World War I was fortuitous, vital, and climactic. When the sagging Allied lines were reaching their breaking point, American troops poured in to strengthen them. The National Guardsmen taken into Federal service during World War I numbered 12,115 officers and 366,956 men. This was actually less than their authorized strength but represented 32 percent of the men in action, since virtually all men in the National Guard saw action. As early as August 5, 1917, nearly two-thirds of the Guardsmen were in Federal service when the entire National Guard was federalized.

Casualties on both sides were horrendous. In deaths alone, Germany lost 1,800,000; Austria-Hungary 1,200,000; Britain 947,000; France 1,385,000; Russia 1,700,000. Americans losses were 48,000 killed; 2,900 missing in action; 56,000 dead of disease; and over 57,000 wounded. Of the total casualties suffered by the United States, National Guard casualties came to 103,731, and those of the Regular Army totaled 61,817. No accurate figure is available on the Louisiana National Guardsmen since so many of its men were absorbed in Regular Army detachments, but it was proportionately as great as the national average.

A peace was made after much discussion by President Wilson of the United States, Pierre Clemenceau of France, Lloyd George of Britain, and Vittorio Orlando of Italy. Called the Treaty of Versailles it contained fourteen idealistic but impractical points. Germany and her allies were chastened and deprived of equality within the European order; some of their territories were declared autonomous enclaves determined by the location of ethnic minorities indigenous to the locale. Clemenceau of France refused to sign the peace treaty unless a provision was included in which the United States promised to come to the aid of France in the event of a future attack. Wilson sensing that the United States Congress would quickly reject such a proposal, countered with his proposed League of Nations. Congress ratified neither the Treaty of Versailles nor the League of Nations. The war officially ended when Congress, on July 2, 1921, passed a joint resolution which declared the end of hostilities and reserved the rights and privileges of a victorious power. They had washed their hands of Europe and hoped that they had seen the "war to end all wars."

So dedicated was this particular central figure, General Raymond H. Fleming, that he served for seven terms as adjutant general of Louisiana. Depicted at the left are two Guardsmen overlooking the swollen waters of the Mississippi and their efforts in 1922 and 1927 to contain it. Adjutant General L.A. Toombs is drawn at the bottom and beside him is the floor plan of Jackson Barracks, which had for one hundred years before 1921 been the possession of the U.S. War Department.

CHAPTER 11

Reorganization and Natural Disasters

Prior to World War I the National Guard alone had maintained any semblance of military preparedness. Within a span of thirty-seven years the Guard had been "ordered" or "called" into emergency service, and it may well have made the difference in World War I's result or duration. Whatever the case, the affair in Europe, which necessitated the quick mobilization of men into capable fighting units, brought into focus the sobering danger of unpreparedness.

The National Defense Act of 1920 brought about, for the first time, troop allotments, and though there may have been much inconsistency between what was intended and what resulted, at least the legislators had good intentions. By the Act of June 2, 1920, the states, territories, and the District of Columbia were allotted troops on the basis of 800 per congressional district, which theoretically provided an aggregate of 464,000 men. The Regular Army was to be maintained at a consistent 280,000. But each of these objectives failed; Congress, in an economy move, made it impossible. The Regular Army shrank to a mere 118,000 men, and the National Guard was reduced to 210,531. The Guard eventually suffered even more because appropriations limited personnel to 190,000.

By 1920 Louisiana began reorganizing its National Guard with Adjutant General L. A. Toombs as its propelling force. General Toombs, in a typical description of those times said, "Upon assuming my duties as Adjutant General of the State July 1, 1920, I found myself the only existing member of the National Guard of this State." An interpretation of the terms of the National Defense Act had caused the immediate discharge from service of all men who had served in the army during World War I. This left the state without a militia since the Guard had overwhelmingly served in the conflict.

When Federal funds were allotted, the reenlistment of men into the state National Guard was soon underway. Battery A, Field Artillery, from the New Orleans area was the first unit to be reorganized after World War I. Raymond H. Fleming, captain of Battery A, was among the leaders, and from this point on until his retirement, he played a primary role in the affairs of the National Guard. Bogalusa's Troop A Cavalry was the second unit to be reorganized, with others following.

In 1920 the adjutant general's office was moved from the State Capitol in Baton Rouge to the second floor of Washington Artillery Hall in New Orleans. And in 1921 the U.S. War Department gave up the ancient hallowed Jackson Barracks in New Orleans, which had been a United States Army post for eighty-eight years. Since October, 1922, the Louisiana National Guard has occupied the old barracks.

On January 15, 1921, Major Norman P. Morrow of the Regular Army was named instructor for the Louisiana National Guard. This formally established an intimate peacetime relationship between the Guard and the Regular Army and effected a coordinated effort toward military preparedness. More than seventeen hundred officers and men were instructed under this program from July, 1921, to December, 1923. Coincidental with initiating the teaching program, Camp Beauregard, the centrally located training camp during World War I, was purchased. The camp, containing twenty-three buildings and two hundred acres of land, became the site of annual state encampments.

In 1922 a disastrous flood inundated areas along the Mississippi River. National Guard patrols were stationed at critical points; people were evacuated from flooded or threatened areas, and refugee camps were established to shelter and feed large numbers of the homeless. Even the state penitentiary at Angola came under the surveillance of the Guard. When the prison was flooded, students from Louisiana State University were pressed into service, and under

Reorganization and Natural Disasters 135

the direction of the Guard they prepared a camp for the convicts on the LSU campus. Coordination of these relief activities presented a monumental task which the Louisiana National Guard handled with dispatch and efficiency.

A review of the troops participating in the flood relief program indicates the widespread areas of the state affected. Company A of 156th Infantry was in charge of the Comstock Springs Refugee Camp. Company B performed patrol service along the Atchafalaya River.

When a break in the levee at New Orleans occurred Company D enforced emergency measures and did patrol duty; Jackson Barracks was the headquarters post for this assignment. Company E with headquarters at Ferriday, patrolled the Mississippi River in north Louisiana and maintained a kitchen as well. The Red River levees were guarded by Company F which also kept a food rations station in Avoyelles Parish. Company G established food ration stations at Jonesville and Sicily Island and maintained a refugee camp at Harrisonburg. Company I patrolled the Mississippi River just north of New Orleans, and the 141st Field Artillery (Washington Artillery) did patrol duty with headquarters at Jackson Barracks.

Excerpts from a letter written by Major General Walter H. Gordon, United States Army and acting commander of the Fourth Corps area, to Governor John M. Parker tells the role the Louisiana National Guard played during the 1922 flood. "At the time of my inspection and visit to you at Baton Rouge the crisis of the flood was on, and [the reason] that I did not turn out the Federal troops was because my inspection showed me the State of Louisiana, through its Guard, was doing everything possible in the way of patrolling levees, establishing camps and caring for refugees, and in preparing for the worst should the main levees break and submerge a part of the state, which, however, was happily avoided."

In a letter to the governor, Major General C. C. Hammond, chief of the Militia Bureau, said, among other things, "Your wonderful work during the flood conditions has not only brought your Guard the highest commendations of the people of Louisiana but has gained the praise of the people and the National Guard of the entire country. It seems to me that Louisiana owes you and your Guard a very deep debt of gratitude, when I note that the records show that you have 1,758 men out of 2,100 on flood duty saving lives, property and guarding the levees and also handling refugee camps with some

250,000 people, all of which was done without the loss of life of a soldier or a refugee. A most remarkable service."

The 1922 flood was bad but the one in 1927 was even worse. A quick Spring thaw in the north plus unseasonal rains caused floodwaters to race into the relatively narrow confines of the Mississippi and its tributaries. Levees were topped or broken, and water reached into low levels with sudden fury. The swift flooding spread over about 1,300,000 acres of land, and 300,000 persons found themselves homeless. The task of providing shelter, food, and medical attention to these people presented huge problems.

Human efforts were pressed to match the speed of developing events. The city of New Orleans lay below the level of the swollen river at its doors. Authorities decided to dynamite the levee below New Orleans in order to save the city, which meant that all livestock and people had to be evacuated from the lower reaches of the Parishes of Orleans, St. Bernard, and Plaquemines within forty-eight hours. The National Guard went in, organized the operations, and beat the deadline.

For six weeks approximately 1,780 men of the National Guard performed various arduous duties attendant to the flood crisis. People were evacuated; refugee camps were established; sanitation methods were also initiated to avoid disease, especially typhus; levees were patrolled; and discipline was sustained through the entire trying period. The worst flood in the state's history had been combatted with a minimal loss of life and property.

The legendary Raymond H. Fleming became the National Guard's adjutant general in 1928 and began an unprecedented program. He expanded the Guard, accelerated its training program, improved its armories throughout the state, and with the aid of a grant from the War Department, Camp Beauregard was expanded and refurbished. A target range was built, twelve new mess halls were constructed, new roads were laid giving access to all areas by motor vehicle, and part of the area was reforested.

In the summer of 1935 a record peacetime assembly of troops was gathered at Beauregard for general training and maneuvers. In addition, the military records of more than eighty thousand men who served in World War I were compiled and indexed. Records were also made of the Mexican, Civil, and Spanish-American wars. These records aided immeasurably in ascertaining the eligibility of widows for pensions. Under General Fleming the Louisiana National

Reorganization and Natural Disasters 137

Guard made advances theretofore unreached either in scope or detail. Broad and innovative measures were taken to assure quick mobilization, complete with equipment and conveyances, in wartime or peacetime. By the time Hitler invaded Poland to begin the events that culminated in World War II, Louisiana's National Guard's strength was at two thousand men and officers. It was also the nucleus upon which to build forces of far larger numbers as was in the case in World War I.

During the years of the Second World War, the adjutant general of Louisiana who contributed outstandingly to the military welfare was Major General Raymond F. Hufft. He is surrounded by many of the battalion insignia of units that served gallantly during that period. At the bottom of the drawing are G.I.s, servicemen of Louisiana.

CHAPTER 12

World War II, Lineages, and Heroism

Adolph Hitler came into power in Germany in 1933 and within fifteen months renounced the Treaty of Versailles. He solidified his position with the German people by appealing to their inherent sense of national pride, demanding the return of German territory lost in World War I and launching an economic program that brought—during the depression years—a measure of prosperity.

Sensing the indecisiveness of British and French leaders, who did not want to bring their country into armed conflict barely a generation after World War I, Hitler moved in and occupied the Rhineland abutting France. In September, 1938, he threatened to take the Sudetenland of Czechoslovakia where other German nationals lived. Representatives of England and France met with Hitler in Munich, where they capitulated to Der Fuher's demands, by letting him occupy the Sedentenland, and Neveille Chamberlain, of Britain, explained the concession by calling it "Peace with honor . . . peace in our time." In March, 1939, the German army occupied all of Czechoslovakia.

In the meantime, Italy's Mussolini had, in 1936, attacked Ethiopia, and after Germany's occupation of Czechoslovakia, moved in and took all of Albania. Franklin Roosevelt, president of the United States, in an attempt to arrest the aggressive actions of Germany and Italy, asked Hitler and Mussolini to pledge for ten years that they would not attack thirty-one nations which Roosevelt listed. Hitler made fun of the proposal. The Congress of the United States lent its encouragement unwittingly to the dictators in May, 1939, by turning down an administration request to repeal or revise the post-World War I neutrality laws in order to send economic aid to England and France. Since the United States was committed by law to neutrality, the two dictators became emboldened.

Hitler, in an about-face, signed a nonaggression pact with his avowed enemy Russia in August, 1939. This action freed his army for an attack upon Poland; Russia's reward was a territorial concession sliced from Poland. On September 1, 1939, Hitler's army invaded Poland while his air force rained bombs on helpless cities. England and France, in a courageous move considering that at this time they were without the help of the United States, declared war on Germany, honoring their treaty guarantee. It was the first truly noble gesture made during those terrible days of power politics, blatant violation of the Versailles Treaty, and aggression. Roosevelt was powerless and had to abide by the neutrality laws enacted by Congress.

Hitler moved on Germany's western front in April, 1940, with an attack that brought France to its knees in a *Blitzkrieg*, taking, too, the neutral countries of Holland, Belgium, and Luxembourg within seven weeks. And when Belgium fell England almost lost its army on the continent. Between May 28 and June 4, England managed to evacuate more than 335,000 men from Dunkirk, France, in one of the heroic events of the war. On June 10 Mussolini attacked France, and by June 22 France, completely under Axis control, signed an armistice. England now stood alone without a major ally.

President Roosevelt, by an executive agreement which did not need Senate confirmation, transferred fifty U.S. destroyers to help England fight German submarines. In return, the United States received two North Atlantic naval base sites and six in the Caribbean and South Atlantic. Hitler's air force poured bombs over England in a continual assault to demoralize its people. These massive air strikes and the courageous resiliency of the British people earned the admiration of the world, particularly in the United States.

Congress, in an unprecedented action, created a peacetime draft and appropriated sixteen billion dollars for defense. Soon after, the national elections occurred in which Roosevelt won an unprecedented third term for the presidency. His victory was tantamount to an endorsement of his international policies. He asserted, "There will be no bottlenecks in our determination to aid Great Britain." Soon thereafter a Lend-Lease program was started to supply England with the materiel to wage war, and a defense line was extended as far as Greenland and Iceland. On March 31, 1941, Roosevelt ordered seizure of sixty-five German ships in American ports. On May 15, the American merchant ship *Robin Moor* was torpedoed by a German submarine in the South Atlantic. Roosevelt immediately declared a national emergency and asked the German and Italian consulates to depart. Hitler reciprocated by ordering Americans out of Germany. From that time the United States was drawn closer to war.

In a dramatic gesture of unity Roosevelt met Winston Churchill, the British prime minister, in August aboard an English battleship in the Atlantic. Roosevelt and Churchill delivered their eight-point Atlantic Charter which in effect was a declaration of their common interests in war and politics.

A quick succession of events hastened the entry of the United States into the war. A United States destroyer was fired upon by a German submarine in September. Then, two merchant ships were sunk causing Roosevelt to declare over national radio that the United States would defend itself against German "piracy." Soon after, the American destroyer *Kearney* was damaged in a battle with a German submarine. Roosevelt called this action an attack upon the United States. When the destroyer *Reuben James* was sunk by Germans, Congress immediately lifted the limitations on lend-lease and permitted American ships to sail into war zones. This action also nullified the Neutrality Act of 1939.

Adolph Hitler, in one of the most amazing turn-abouts in history, on June 22, 1941, attacked Russia. But the quick, easy victories he had had in Poland, Belgium, Holland, and France were not repeated, and winter found the German Wehrmacht bogged down on the Russian frontier.

Winston Churchill, an avowed enemy of communism, hailed the Russians as allies and explained the association by saying, "If Hitler invaded Hell, I would make at least a favorable reference to the Devil in the House of Commons." And Britain, battling against the Nazis alone barely six months before found itself allied with the two most powerful nations on earth, the United States and Russia.

Meanwhile, Japan, grown bold and militaristic with successes in Manchuria and fattened by quick acquisition of Indo-China territory and Holland's East Indian colonies, had, as early as September, 1940, joined a Berlin-Rome-Tokyo Axis. The United States had helped the forces in China that had opposed Japan but their relationship had not deteriorated as fast as with Germany and Italy. However, Roosevelt moved the Pacific fleet base from San Diego to Pearl Harbor.

On December 7, 1941, in one of the most surprising attacks ever, a large force of Japanese airplanes borne by carriers, attacked Pearl Harbor. The Americans, despite warnings of possible attack, were caught completely by surprise and unprepared. Five battleships and three cruisers were either sunk or rendered useless. Virtually all planes on the ground were destroyed, 2,335 servicemen and 68 civilians were killed and 1,178 wounded. The shock was demoralizing, but it did awaken the American people from their passiveness and isolationism. The next day Congress issued a declaration of war on Japan. Germany and Italy, in a bold united gesture toward Japan, declared war against the United States on December 11. Congress, in turn, declared war on the two European powers.

The National Guard was inducted into Federal service beginning September 15, 1940, and reached completion on October 1, 1941. For that period, there were 20,918 officers, 221 warrant officers, plus 279,358 enlisted men making a grand total of 280,497. What must be taken into account, however, is that at least every division and many special units became the nucleus upon which larger commands were built.

Since the mobilization of the National Guard occurred before the declaration of war (and during this period there were still hopes of avoiding war), men with dependents and employed in key industry necessary to the ultimate defense of our country were encouraged to resign from the Guard. A two-fold purpose was served: getting eligible men into the expanding army and eliminating, as much as possible during the interim of peace, unnecessary hardships at home. Between August 1 and the date of induction, 51,216 were discharged from the National Guard of the states, District of Columbia, and territories. An additional 19,544 were released on account of a twenty-eight-year-old age limit. But when war was actually declared, many of these men were inducted into service.

The mobilization of the National Guard in that period immediately prior to the declaration of war by the United States was a delicate but well-organized operation. Statistics on a national scale

World War II, Lineages, and Heroism 143

are most revealing and impressive. Of all officers from the National Guard, 91 percent remained the entire war; the 9 percent who did not were discharged due to statutory age, retirement, and general disability. More commissioned officers rose from the ranks of the National Guard. Exact figures are not readily available, but a careful estimate indicates that eighty-two thousand officers were commissioned or appointed from the ranks. There was a preponderance of second lieutenants from the Guard.

In proper terms, the National Guard was *called* by the president or *ordered* by Congress into active Federal service as the provisions call for in a national emergency. As previously stated, the governor may *order* into the active service of the *state* any part of the military forces necessary in the event of insurrection, invasion, riot, imminent danger thereof, or natural or man-made disaster. Further, the president of the United States takes all precedence over the governors of the respective states.

Proponents of the National Guard were concerned with the preservation of the organization and the integrity of the individual units. The experience of World War I prompted an appeal to Congress to make an expression of policy. This brought the following statement from Congress which was included in the Selective Service Act of 1940:

> The Congress further declares in accordance with our traditional military policy, as expressed in the National Defense Act of 1916, as amended, it is essential that the strength and organization of the National Guard, as an integral part of the first line of defense, be at all times maintained and assured to this end, it is the intent of Congress that whenever the Congress shall determine *that troops are needed in excess of those of the Regular Army* and those in training under Section 3 (b) (Of this Act), the National Guard of the United States or so much thereof as may be necessary, shall be ordered into the active Federal service and continue therein so long as the necessity exists.

This statement of policy by Congress was reinstated in the Selective Service Act of 1948 and in the Universal Military Training and Service Act of 1951. Louisiana responded with its mobilization by drawing manpower from every section of the state as early as November 25, 1940.

Organizations and units of the Louisiana National Guard inducted into Federal service were the following (all inductions effective November 25, 1940):

All elements of the 31st Division and specifically:

Hq. & GSS Hq. Det. 31st Division (La. Components), Col. Oswald W. McNeese

Hq. 61st Brigade (La. Components), Brig. Gen. Louis F. Guerre

156th Infantry, Col. James H. Kuttner

106th Medical Regiment (La. Components), Col. Anees Mogabgab

106th Quartermaster Regiment (La. Components)

Med. Dept Det., 156th Infantry, Cpt. James A. White, Jr., at Pineville

Band, 156th Infantry, WO Frank J. Rosato, at New Orleans

Hq. Co., 156th Infantry, Cpt. Ralph H. Stephens, at New Orleans

Staff Section, Service Company, 156th Infantry, Cpt. Frank C. Blackburn, at Lake Charles

Service Company, 156th Infantry, Cpt. Cecil C. Belgard, at Alexandria

Antitank Company, 156th Infantry, Cpt. Herman J. Huber, at Jennings

Hq. Det., 1st Bn., 156th Infantry, 1st Lt. Hilary J. Boh, at New Orleans

Company A, 156th Infantry, Cpt. Joseph A. Holliday, at Baton Rouge

Company B, 156th Infantry, Cpt. Paul J. Citrano, at Morgan City

Company C, 156th Infantry, Cpt. Christian L. Olivier, Jr., at Houma

Company D, 156th Infantry, Cpt. Mires C. Gehr, at New Orleans

Hq. Det., 2nd Bn., 156th Infantry, 1st Lt. Alfred G. Francis, at New Orleans

Company E, 156th Infantry, Cpt. Roland P. Desonier, at Jeanerette

Company F, 156th Infantry, Cpt. Simon Castille, at Breaux Bridge

Company G, 156th Infantry, Cpt. Howard O. Roy, at New Iberia

Company H, 156th Infantry, 1st Lt. Levi Jordan, at Lafayette

Hq. Det. 3rd Bn., 156th Infantry, 1st Lt. Edward A. Becker, at New Orleans

Company I, 156th Infantry, 1st Lt. Erwin C. Andrus, at Crowley

Company K, 156th Infantry, Cpt. Henry W. McGowan, at Lake Charles

Company L, 156th Infantry, Cpt. William J. B. Kuttner, at Lake Charles

Company M, 156th Infantry, Cpt. Stanley O. Whitehouse at Alexandria

Division Surgeon's Office, 31st Div., Col. A. Mogabgab, at New Orleans

106th Medical Regiment, Headquarters, Col. A. Mogabgab, at New Orleans

Company A, 106th Med Regiment, Cpt. Zachary J. Romeo, at New Orleans

World War II, Lineages, and Heroism

Company D, 106th Med Regiment, Cpt. Clarence A. Bishop, at New Orleans

Company G, 106th Medical Regiment, Cpt. James W. Vaudry, at New Orleans

Hq. 1st Bn., 106th Q. M. Regiment, Cpt. Dewitt H. Clark, at Alexandria

Company B, 106th Q. M. Regiment, Cpt. Beuford A. Pittman, at Alexandria

Organizations of the Louisiana National Guard inducted into Federal service (World War II):

6 January 1941, 204th Coast Artillery (AA), Col. Joseph A. Redding

6 January 1941, 105th Sep. Bn. Coast Artillery (AA), Lt. Col. Frederick H. Fox

13 January 1941, 141st Field Artillery, Col. Henry B. Curtis

141st FIELD ARTILLERY (155mm. How.) at New Orleans, 13 January 1941

    Commander Col. Henry B. Curtis
    Medical Dept. Detachment, Maj. Paul S. Parrino
    Band, Cpt. Thomas F. Bienvenu
    Headquarters Battery, Cpt. Bernard J. Rauch
    Headquarters Battery, 1st Bn., Cpt. Duncan Gillis
    Service Battery, 1st Bn., Cpt. L. G. Duke, Jr.
    Antitank Battery, 1st Bn., Cpt. Jonas C. Sporl
    Battery A, Cpt. George E. Dickey
    Battery B, Cpt. Demetrio D. Diaz
    Battery C, Cpt. C. C. Apffel
    Hq. Battery 2nd Bn., Cpt. Walter D. Ledig, Jr.
    Service Battery 2nd Bn., Cpt. Frederic W. Delamain
    Antitank Battery 2nd Bn., Cpt. Frank G. Spiess
    Battery D, Cpt. William B. Harvey
    Battery E, Cpt. Numa P. Avendano
    Battery F, Cpt. Minter A. Bliss

204th COAST ARTILLERY (AA), 6 January 1941

    Roster of Officers, Shreveport, Col. Joseph A. Redding
    Medical Dept. Det., Monroe, 1st Lt. Wood H. Scott
    Band, Shreveport, Cpt. Olin T. Conner
    Hq. Battery, Shreveport, 1st Lt. Dorsey W. McDonald
    Hq. Battery 1st Bn., Shreveport, 1st Lt. Hugh A. King
    Battery A, Shreveport, Cpt. Henry H. Breazeale
    Battery B, Shreveport, Cpt. Erin E. Rentz
    Battery C, Shreveport, Cpt. Frank M. Crow
    Battery D, Shreveport, Cpt. Wilbur H. Funderburk

Hq. Battery 2nd Bn., Monroe, 1st Lt. Francis X. Shaughnessy
Battery E, Minden, Cpt. Arthur R. Life
Battery F, Ruston, Cpt. Lawrence J. Fox
Battery G, Monroe, Cpt. Joseph G. Elliott
Battery H, Natchitoches, Cpt. Thomas A. Baker

105th SEP. BN. COAST ARTILLERY (AA), 6 January 1975

Roster of Officers, New Orleans, Commander Lt. Col. Frederick Fox
Medical Dept. Det., New Orleans, Cpt. G. K. Rogers
Hq. Battery, New Orleans, Cpt. Stuart E. Smith
Battery A, New Orleans, Cpt. Fred A. Wulff, Jr.
Battery B, New Orleans, Cpt. John Barkley
Battery C, Bogalusa, Cpt. Karl L. Starns
Battery D, Franklinton, Cpt. Thomas A. Pedneau
122nd Observation Sqdn., New Orleans, Maj. Glynne M. Jones 9Sep41

Interestingly, many Louisianians, particularly those from the southwestern part of the state, still spoke the French language, a legacy from early colonial times.

HEADQUARTERS AND HEADQUARTERS DETACHMENT of the Louisiana National Guard was inducted into Federal service on October 8, 1940, though its staff was previously called as individuals. Its heritage dates to 1770 when Don Carlos Luis Boucher de Grand pre became the first major of the militia of the Spanish Province of Louisiana.

Over the years the detachment has been and continues to be the indispensable element in the entire structure of the Louisiana National Guard and is never considered separate from the office of the adjutant general. The mission of the detachment was basically that which was set up in World War I, but provisions were added to meet the exigencies of World War II.

The detachment operated Selective Service until October, 1941, when it was released from active military service of the United States and reverted to state control "to protect the interest of National Guard Personnel by continuing their service under state control in order to permit their records to show the number of years in Federal and State service necessary to meet requirements of Sec. 3 (c) of the Selective Training and Service Act of September 16, 1940 as amended and to furnish the State a means of maintaining a trained and classified nucleus from which the National Guard may be rebuilt as circumstances may require."

On January 10, 1942, an administrative staff was organized for the Louisiana State National Guard. By July 2, 1945, the Louisiana State Guard, formerly known as the Louisiana State National Guard, was reorganized with a state staff and state detachment supplanting the administrative staff. Through all transitional periods the state Headquarters and Headquarters Detachment has served as a unit employed in the adjutant general's office with duties related to mobilization, Selective Service, state security, and all matters pertaining to civilian peace.

THE THIRTY-NINTH INFANTRY DIVISION (LA. PART):

In 1913 the Division of Militia Affairs first advocated the organization of National Guard tactical divisions, "that made it easier . . . to prepare the National Guard . . . for call and draft into the Federal service" for World War I. One of these divisions was the Thirty-ninth Infantry.

Designated as a tactical organization of the National Guard, the Thirty-ninth was constituted July 18, 1917, and allocated to the states of Louisiana, Mississippi, and Arkansas as the Eighteenth Division. The table of organization, under which the Division was organized, proved to be cumbersome and was changed in August of the same year.

Pursuant to a War Department order of August 3, 1917, the component units of the unorganized Eighteenth were directed to organize and concentrate for training at Camp Beauregard at Alexandria, Louisiana. On August 5 the National Guards of the three states were inducted into Federal service. It was at this time, that the Eighteenth was noted as having been redesignated the Thirty-ninth Division. Though the units were inducted in August and had been called in the early summer of 1917, it was not until induction that the division began assembling, and it was not until August 25 that it was formally organized under Major General Henry C. Hodges, Jr.

Following its stateside training at Camps Beauregard, Merrit, Mills, and Stuart, it sailed for overseas duty. When it arrived in France it was understrength by 1,396 men. This factor, *viz.*, the lack of full strength, was shared to some extent by all the divisions arriving for service in the American Expeditionary Forces. By virtue of same "and the fact that replacements had not been furnished in the amounts requested, the A.E.F. faced a serious shortage." The critical situation existing on the Western Front in addition to the previous conditions caused the replacement system to be changed. The new policy utilized one base depot division in a group of six divisions. As a result the Thirty-ninth, on August 14, 1918, was redesignated and reassigned from a tactical to a depot division, *viz.*, the Fifth Depot Division. From September through October, 1918, it functioned in this capacity.

It was demobilized at Camp Beauregard on January 23, 1919, and Headquarters Sixty-fourth Field Artillery Brigade at Camp Shelby on May 1, 1919.

In a report dated January 23, 1923, a joint board of general staff officers recommended that the Thirty-ninth be redesignated the Thirty-first; reasons for this change were probably (1) the Thirty-first was not on the Army divisional list at that time; (2) two of the four states comprising the Thirty-ninth were formerly of the Thirty-first Division, and (3) the redesignation would retain the popular name with its World War I divisional number. The recommendation of the joint board was agreed to though there were questions relative to the organized unit numbers within the states.

On July 1, 1923, the Thirty-ninth Division was redesignated the Thirty-first, the designation change in Louisiana being made effective by GO No. 2 AGO La. dated January 31, 1924.

In plans prior to the World War II the entire National Guard was summoned for a year's duty. It was done (1) for the "betterment of the Guard itself"; (2) "for training a large percentage of the prospective draftees"; and (3) "for release of certain Regular Army units for possible use in emergency." The quick and easy victories of Hitler on the European continent made this action imperative—even though the United States was not at this time in the war—because the extent of the dictator's ambitions and his (then) ally Russia could not be predicted. The combination of Germany, Japan, Italy, and Russia portended ominous signs for the future.

A mobilization order for the Thirty-first Division brought the National Guardsmen to Camp Blanding, Florida. By December, 1940, the units were assembled and training begun. During August and September, 1941, the division maneuvered in Louisiana with the Third Army and in November went to the Carolinas where it participated in more training action for four weeks. The division comprised National Guard units from Louisiana, Mississippi, Alabama, and Florida and was known as the Dixie Division since it represented four of the southernmost states.

In February, 1942, the Thirty-first made a change of station from Blanding to Camp Bowie, near Brownwood, Texas. By midsummer it came back to Louisiana for more maneuvers and at conclusion went to Camp Shelby, near Hattiesburg, Mississippi. It continued maneuvers from September, 1942, until June, 1943. From Louisiana the division went to Camp Pickett, Virginia, and then moved by regimental combat teams to West Virginia for mountain maneuvers near Elkins. It underwent amphibious exercises at Camp Bradford in Virginia and ended at Chespeake Bay in 1943.

By February, 1944, the Thirty-first started its overseas movement through Camp Patrick Henry, Virginia, and embarked at Hampton Roads for active service against the Japanese in New Guinea, Mortai, and the Philippines.

By this time the only unit from the Louisiana National Guard with the Thirty-first in the Pacific Theater of Operations was the 106th Medical Battalion. It arrived at Oro Bay, New Guinea, on February 9, 1944, set up its facilities, and immediately began operating in the combat zone. The Medical Battalion campaigned at Oro Bay and Aitape, New Guinea, in the Wake-Sarmi area from March 21, 1944, to January 31, 1945. One of the highlights of the battalion's war service was the participation in the Mindanao campaign. The close of the war found it in the Del Monte area. In December, 1945, it was deactivated at Camp Stoneman, California.

After World War II, Louisiana and Arkansas were allocated the divisional number Thirty-nine, and divisional headquarters was reconstituted, organized, and federally recognized on September 30, 1946, for the Louisiana part, and on August 26, 1947, for the Arkansas part.

Of the Louisiana units that were inducted into Federal service with the Thirty-first Division, *viz.*, Headquarters, GSS Headquarters Detachment, Headquarters, Sixty-first Infantry Brigade, the 156th Infantry Regiment, the 106th Medical Regiment (part), and the 106th Quartermaster Regiment (part), all are represented either in whole or part in present-day units of the Thirty-ninth Infantry Division.

UNITS OF THE THIRTY-NINTH INFANTRY DIVISION (part, Louisiana)

Unit	Station/Area
Hq., 39th Inf. Div. (part)	Louisiana

Headquarters Company	Louisiana
Medical Detachment	New Orleans
Signal Company	New Orleans
Quartermaster Company	Alexandria
Reconnaissance Company	New Roads
Band	New Orleans
156th Infantry Regiment	Southern Louisiana
199th Infantry Regiment	Northern Louisiana
39th Div. Arty., Hq. & Hq. Btry. (part)	New Orleans
935th Field Arty. Bn. (105mm. How.)	New Orleans
141st Field Arty. Bn. (105mm. How.)	New Orleans
105th Anti-Aircraft Arty. (AW) (SP)	Southeast Louisiana

THE 105TH ANTIAIRCRAFT ARTILLERY BATTALION drew its strength from the West Florida Parishes of Washington, St. Tammany, and Tangipahoa. The parent unit of the organization began in 1913 and is steeped in the traditions of state history. Long before the modern era of advanced weaponry, men from this tri-parish area had participated as soldiers in the West Florida rebellion of 1810; the British campaign in Louisiana, 1814-1815 (War of 1812); the Mexican War, 1845-1846; the Civil War, 1861-1865; the Spanish-American War, 1898; and World War I.

The militiamen of this locale had served as sentinels when it was feared the Choctaw Indians would join the Creeks who were a threat to the Alabama frontier and posed as danger to the early settlements on the west bank of the Pearl River. They stood guard at the Tchefuncta Navy Yard in 1814 when the British invested Louisiana while their counterparts from St. Tammany manned the Dupre line behind Jackson at Chalmette. Soldiers from St. Helena and St. Tammany, known as Laughlin and Goff's companies, were in DeClouet's Regiment which opposed the British on the west bank of the Mississippi River at the Battle of New Orleans.

The St. Helena Riflemen of General Gaines's regiment and the Staples Company from St. Tammany in the Montezuma regiment served in the Mexican War.

In the Civil War the parishes of Washington, St. Tammany, and St. Helena (Tangipahoa in 1861 was part of St. Helena) and their regiments of twenty-nine companies in the First Brigade, Third Division, of the Louisiana militia continued their legends. Such groups as the St. Tammany Grays, the St. Tammany Artillery, and the Pumpkin Studs, though not active on the field, served as a home guard. Such units as the Beaver Creek Rifles, the St. Helena Rifles, the Louisiana Swamp Rangers, and the Rebels of St. Helena, the Edward Guards of St. Tammany, and the Washington Rifles, Slocum's Company, and Turner's Company of Washington Parish served with distinction in the Army of Tennessee and in the Army of Northern Virginia.

In 1895 Thomas W. Cate formed the Fourth Separate Company of Infantry at Hammond which became, in 1896, Company H of the First Infantry Regiment. They were among the first to answer President McKinley's call for volunteers in the Spanish-American War. They reached Mobile, then Miami and Jacksonville, but the war was over before they saw action; they then disbanded.

They reestablished the lineage in 1904 with T. M. Bankston's Company of Amite. O. J. Toujan's Fourth Troop of Cavalry of Covington followed in 1905 and existed until 1910. Then on January 22, 1913, it was organized again in Bogalusa under Captain Louis F. Guerre as an infantry company which eventually mustered into the National Guard as Company G, First Infantry, and actually became the parent unit of the 105th Antiaircraft Artillery Battalion. The Bogalusa and Amite companies were mobilized as units of the First Regiment when the United States became embroiled in that border action with Mexico. They got as far as San Benito, saw no action, but experienced valuable training which conditioned them for the approaching World War I.

In World War I they became part of the First Regiment which became the 156th Infantry Regiment in the new Thirty-ninth Infantry Division. In a reorganization shuffle they lost their identity when their members were assigned to the 154th Regiment and the 114th Engineers. The men from the Florida Parishes area did see service in World War I, most on battle fronts, particularly in the Meuse-Argonne operations. They were demobilized in 1919.

After World War I, in Bogalusa, P. W. Lindsley formed Troop A, Cavalry. In 1921 M. J. Sylvest organized Troop C. These two troops were renamed Troops E and G in 1922 and assigned to the 108th Cavalry Regiment. By 1927 Troop E was expanded by the organization of Headquarters and Headquarters Detachment of the Second Squadron, but after two years it was disbanded and Troop G at Franklinton was redesignated as Troop F. In 1940 the two cavalry squadrons were converted and redesignated as Batteries C and D when the 108th Cavalry was converted to Coast Artillery, equipped with 37mm guns and redesignated the 105th Separate Battalion

Coast Artillery (AA). Headquarters of the Second Troop became Headquarters (part) of the 105th, commanded by Lieutenant Colonel Frederick H. Fox.

As early as January 6, 1941, eleven months before Pearl Harbor, Batteries C and D (commanded by Captain Karl L. Starns and Captain Thomas A. Pedneau respectively) were ordered into Federal service. The battalion was at Camp Hulen when the Japanese attacked Pearl Harbor. From here Batteries A and B (commanded by Captains Fred A. Wulff, Jr., and John Barkley at the time of their order into active service) departed in January, 1942, for California, leaving the echelon of the 105th. They served in the Pacific operations on Canton and Christmas Islands throughout the war.

Batteries C and D increased their size and trained at the Desert Training Center at Indio, California. They were redesignated the 105th Coast Artillery Battalion (AA) (AW) and by August, 1942, were sent overseas. In England and Scotland they began intensive amphibious training preparatory to action in the campaigns of North Africa, Sicily, and Italy.

In the Allies' Operation Torch, which carried the war to the Axis in North Africa, the battalion (minus Batteries C & D) equipped with 40mm Bofors guns was in the Amphibious Assault Landings at Arzew with Batteries C & D landing at Andelousee, Algeria, November 8-11, 1943. They immediately set up their antiaircraft positions to protect the beaches. When France surrendered, the Battalion maintained stations to protect dock installations at Oran and Mers-el-kebir and for two airports in the vicinity. Two weeks later two machine-gun platoons took up positions at Faid Pass and Thelepte Airport after being flown to Tunisia. On December 10, the remainder of the battalion left the Oran area to furnish protection at the airports and docks of Bougie, Djidjelli, and Phillipeville.

In January of 1943, one battery was left at Phillipeville, and the remainder of the battalion was stationed at airports near Telergma Youks-les-Baine and Thelepte. When the enemy advanced along the Gafsa-Feriana route, the Battalion gave protection to the First U.S. Infantry Division at Feriana and the critical Kasserine Pass. They also furnished protection for the Ninth Division in the area of the Kasserine Pass and Sidi-bou-Zid until the attack on Gafsa when it returned to the First Division. They were again engaged in action at Gafsa, Guettar, Seja, Mateur, and Bizerte areas and were in the Bizerte locale at the close of the Tunisian Campaign with the Third

Division upon the return of the First to Algeria.

The U.S. II Corps through the foregoing action were able to join with the British 8th Army thus bringing an end to Erwin Rommel's Afrika Corps. Their service in the Tunisian campaign was spectacular for on two occasions they were pressed into service as infantrymen, when their section was overrun by Germans in their counterattacks. At Kasserine Pass in late February and early March they converted the gun pits into foxholes and fought it out as foot soldiers. At the Battle of El Guettar, Battery A's gun position was overrun by units of the Tenth German Panzar Division at Djebel Berda. They fought back a vicious attack and with enforcement from "real" infantry drove back the enemy. For these exemplary and extraordinary actions they received the Presidential Unit Citation. After the close of the African Campaign the Battalion returned to Oran where they were reequipped with self-propelled antiaircraft guns and were assigned to the First Division for Operation Husky.

When the Americans landed at Gela, Sicily, to begin the campaign on the island and Italian peninsula, the 105th positioned its guns on the decks of assault LSTs to furnish cover for the First Division (July 8-10, 1943). Thus began a thirty-eight-day campaign against the Italian Sixth Army and the German Fifteenth, First Parachute, Twenty-ninth Panzer Grenadier, and the Goring Panzer Division. Being part of the four field artillery battalions of the First Division Artillery, the 105th drew the artillery commander's "appreciation, respect and admiration for the manner in which the 105th Battalion ... performed its duties."

In Operation Avalanche with its initial landing at Salerno, the 105th arrived at "Red Beach" at Paestum on the Italian coast south of Salerno. Their guns afforded protection for troops and installations of the Forty-fifth, Thirty-sixth, and Third divisions. In late September they were attached to the Thirty-fourth Division, and when the division went on to the Volturno River, Venefro, and Cassino, the battalion gave protection from air attacks. When the British brought in relief, the 105th was sent back to Benevento and once again was up front in support of the Eighty-fifth Division during the remainder of the Naples-Foggia campaign, September 9, 1943–January 21, 1944, which brought about the liberation of Rome.

In the Rome-Arno campaign (January to September, 1944) the battalion continued their support as protection to the Eighty-fifth, Eighty-eighth, Ninety-first and Thirty-fourth divisions. And in the

North Appennines Campaign (September 10, 1944-April 4, 1945) they were in the Thirty-fourth and Eighty-fifth, and when German air power faded, the battalion began a new role in 1944 and 1945 by undertaking infantry ground support.

When the Fifth Army entered the Po Valley in the campaign (April 5-May 8, 1945), the 105th was in that rapid advance as they guarded vital river crossings. When the campaign ended, the battalion was at the foot of the Alps and 790 combat days beyond that first landing in North Africa.

They were in six major campaigns which included three amphibious assaults as they fought off more than a thousand German Junkers and Messerschmidts and shot down seventy-five and probably destroyed forty-six others and damaged hundreds more. By late 1944 the men of the battalion had been awarded thirty-seven Silver Stars, two Legion of Merits, four Soldier's Medals, twelve Bronze Stars, while 129 men earned the Purple Heart for wounds in action. The battalion had been redesignated the 105th Antiaircraft Artillery Automatic Weapons Battalion (SP) and was in activated on September 15, 1945, while in the Mediterranean Theater of Operations.

Two years after World War II the battalion reassembled on April 11, 1947, when Battery C of Bogalusa was reorganized and federally recognized as Headquarters and Headquarters Battery and Battery A and Battery D of Franklinton as Battery B. On July 29, 1948, Battery C was organized at Hammond to continue where Battery H in 1898 had left off after the Spanish-American War. On December 16th, 1948, thirty-eight years after the disbanding of Troop C, First Squadron of Cavalry, Battery D was organized in Covington.

As part of the Thirty-ninth Infantry Division, the 105th represents an area of Louisiana whose people have been engaged in making history from Spanish and French Colonial times until today. With devotion and valor, they have participated in crucial activities related to the freedom and protection of this country.

BATTLE HONORS
of the
105th Antiaircraft Artillery Battalion

WORLD WAR I
Streamer Without Inscription

WORLD WAR II
Algeria-French Morocco (with arrowhead)
Tunisia

Sicily (with arrowhead)
Naples-Foggia
Rome-Arno
North Appennines
Po Valley

Unit Decorations

Battery C authorized Distinguished Unit Streamer embroidered *Tunisia*.

THE 141ST FIELD ARTILLERY is the most hallowed segment in the Louisiana National Guard because it is the oldest continuous unit. Its beginning goes back to September 7, 1838, when it was offically organized as the Washington Artillery Company of the Fourth Regiment, Louisiana Militia. There is some credence to the claim that the Washington Artillery had its origin during the British occupation and the Battle of New Orleans (1815). For many years efforts have been made, in vain, to get official recognition of the origin from chief of military history. The Washington Artillery underwent a reorganization in 1841 and was redesignated the First Company, Native American Artillery.

Their first official active service was in the Texas campaign which culminated into the Mexican War, first as a battery of light artillery in 1845, and later as a company of infantry of the Washington Regiment in 1846, indicating its versatility.

In 1848 the First Company Native American Artillery was renamed the Washington Artillery Company, a name they have, with difficulty, managed to keep. During the 1850s, that peaceful and bountiful era immediately preceding the Civil War, they continued their training program with regular periods of drill and instruction preparing to be one of the crack units of that kind to enter the war.

They participated in the earliest action of the Civil War in Louisiana, for on January 9, 1861, the Washington Artillery, upon orders from the governor and in concert with other units, seized the Federal arsenal at Baton Rouge. It was after this action that the company was expanded to battalion strength and called Battalion of Washington Artillery. It was mustered into the service of the Confederate States of America on May 26, 1861, and included four companies.

They were at First Battle of Bull Run July 18-21, 1861, and engaged in an artillery duel with concentrated light artillery of the

Federal army. Firing from a less advantageous position than their adversaries, they nevertheless, held their position and completely routed the Federals. Thus they early established the reputation that increased as the war wore on. Most of their service was with the Army of Northern Virginia commanded by Robert E. Lee. One battery was attached to the Army of Tennessee where they also experienced front line action of long duration.

They did not formally surrender at Appomattox, for early on April 9, 1865, they slipped away unnoticed, buried their cannons, and destroyed their gun carriages. Some even sought President Jefferson Davis and acted as his escort and protectors. Others went into North Carolina and joined up with General Joseph Johnston in that last vestige of resistance through the Atlantic states. They had fought in sixty battles, including First Manassas, Second Manassas, the entire Peninsula campaign, Shiloh, Bull Run, Antietam, Fredericksburg, Chancellorsville, Murfreesboro, Gettysburg, Chickamauga, Petersburg, the Wilderness, Spotsylvania, Appomattox, and virtually every battle of major consequence. Six of its officers were promoted out of the command, several rose to the ranks of major and brigadier general, and of 808 men who served, 139 were killed or died of wounds received in battle. No other military unit from the state of Louisiana participated in as much first-line action nor were there any who came out of the conflict more renowned. They made the name Washington Artillery synonymous with Louisiana gallantry, tradition, and antiquity.

Unable to reorganize after the Civil War because of Federal occupation and restrictive measures by the military governor, the Washington went into a state of limbo, meeting unofficially on social and fraternal levels. But as soon as Francis T. Nicholls established home rule, it quickly reestablished the battalion at a meeting in Hawkins' Club Room, and on July 22, 1875, the members voted to form an independent battalion. In December of 1879 they were mustered into the Louisiana State National Guard but withdrew in 1888 and formed an independent military unit. Then, in April, 1893, the unit was again mustered into the Louisiana State National Guard. The Washington Artillery, with one battery, was mustered into the United States Army on July 6, 1898, during the Spanish-American War but did not see any action.

Following the Spanish-American War the battalion again became independent, but in December, 1909, it returned to the Louisiana

National Guard where it has remained. Between wars the battalion participated in drill and accuracy contests in which it won many honors. It also performed flood relief and riot duties and generally aided in peacetime services where military discipline was necessary.

In June of 1937, between World Wars, the Washington Artillery retired its horses and adopted motor vehicles. The unit was expanded in 1939 to include two battalions and was again redesignated the 141st Field Artillery and equipped with 75mm guns. In December of 1940 these guns were replaced with 155mm Howitzers.

By order of the president, the 141st, under the command of Colonel Henry B. Curtis, was inducted into Federal service on January 13, 1941, when they repaired to Camp Shelby, Mississippi, for training and maneuvers. The success of the German tank attacks brought about a change in the artillery of the 141st. Two antitank batteries were organized as Batteries G and H.

When the Seventy-third Provisional Antitank Battalion was organized, Batteries G and H of the 141st with other units were used to form that unit. In December of 1941 the 773rd Tank Destroyer Battalion was formed from these units.

All field artillery regiments of the United States Army were reconstituted into separate battalions during the early part of World War II. On March 7, 1943, the 141st Field Artillery was divided into two separate battalions, the first known as the 934th Field Artillery Battalion, and the second becoming the 935th Field Artillery Battalion. The Headquarters and Headquarters Battery of the old 141st Field Artillery became the 141st Field Artillery Group; and then redesignated Headquarters and Headquarters Battery, 141st Field Artillery Brigade; and later Headquarters and Headquarters Battery, XIX Corps Artillery.

Major General Raymond H. Fleming, the adjutant general, championed an action whereby the numerical designation of 934 was redesignated the 141st Field Artillery Battalion, which, mainly through his efforts, became effective on July 30, 1943. Fleming, with a strong appreciation for Louisiana's tradition and history was able, through the high respect and influence he enjoyed, to restore the Washington Artillery's continuing identity as the 141st.

The 141st and 935th left New York in August, 1943, reached Oran, and in short time traversed the nine hundred miles to Bizerte. After a short stay the 141st was sent to Bagnoli, Italy, arriving on November 19, and was sent immediately to a combat position on the

Volturno River near Venafro. They fired their first barrage on November 30. Their mobility came to good use as they were dispatched hastily to the Cassino area and then to Anzio Beachhead. In concert with the Allied push north toward Rome, the 141st pursued the German-Italian armies. On June 5, 1944, the 141st became the first American artillery unit to enter the Eternal City.

Meanwhile, the 935th was dispatched from Bizerte by way of Salerno and Naples to Sparanise where it was engaged in its first European combat on October 31st. They were in the thick of the action at Monte Cassino when the Americans dislodged entrenched Germans on the mount. After this they moved toward Rome and entered that city on June 5 several hours after the 141st.

In the invasion of southern France the two battalions were assigned different points of entry; the 141st landed at Ste. Maxime and the 935th entered by way of Marseille. This drive pushed the Germans back beyond the French frontier into their hinterlands. At war's end on May 7 the 141st was near Munich while the 935th was at Hammel near the city of Augsburg near the Italian frontier. By this circuitous route they helped conquer much of Italy, went by way of the Mediterranean to French ports, marched eastward, and ended the war in south Germany (Austria).

In 463 combat days the 141st fired 150,871 rounds during 7,004 missions while occupying 108 positions. The 935th, was in combat 462 days, fired more than 141,000 rounds during 8,845 missions in support of eighteen divisions and six different corps.

The 141st Field Artillery Battalion and Headquarters and Headquarters Battery, XIX Corps Artillery, were consolidated to form the 141st Field Artillery Battalion. It was reactivated into Louisiana National Guard service on November 8, 1946, under command of Lieutenant Colonel Duncan Gillis.

Parenthetically, although the traditional designation *Washington Artillery* has been used by the 141st Field Artillery Battalion since its inception, it was not officially designated as such until February 10, 1971, by certificate issued by Secretary of the Army, Stanley R. Resor.

The Washington Artillery has always had two fights on its hands whenever it has gone into Federal service: fighting the enemy and fighting equally hard to retain the name that it has carried for 137 years—the *Washington Artillery*. Its records in both fights substantiate its battle honors:

BATTLE HONORS

Campaign streamers authorized to be borne
by the 141st Field Artillery Battalion (Washington Artillery).

MEXICAN WAR

Bull Run	Gettysburg
Peninsula	Chickamauga
Manassas	Petersburg
Shiloh	Wilderness
Antietam	Spotsylvania
Fredericksburg	Appomattox
Chancellorsville	Murfreesboro

WORLD WAR I

Streamer without inscription

WORLD WAR II

Rome-Arno	Rhineland
Southern France	Anzio
Central Europe	Normandy
Naples-Foggia	Northern France

Unit Decorations

Distinguished Unit Streamer
embroidered *Colmar*

THE 156th INFANTRY REGIMENT drew its strength from units located in New Orleans, Alexandria, Baton Rouge, Lafayette, Jeanerette, Morgan City, Houma, Breaux Bridge, New Iberia, Lake Charles, Crowley, and Jennings. The original 156th was activated during Civil War times, between April 27 and May 8, 1861. The Second and Third regiments of Louisiana volunteers were chosen as the parent units. Both were in the forefront of Civil War battles. The Second Louisiana Regiment spent the war in the eastern section, mainly Virginia, Maryland, and Pennsylvania, while the Third Regiment was in the midwestern campaigns—Mississippi, Tennessee, and Alabama.

The Second Regiment was at First Manassas (Bull Run); became a part of Stonewall Jackson's foot cavalry in the Shenandoah Valley campaign; fought through Maryland and back to Virginia, and finally retreated from Sharpsburg battlefield (Antietam). On to the Wilderness they marched into more front-line action; then to Gettysburg and Pickett's gallant charge at Cemetery Ridge that carried them within one hundred yards of the enemy's entrenchments only to be driven back in defeat and to the long trudge from Pennsylvania to home base in Virginia.

Victories and defeats alternated like night and day as they marched and countermarched up and down the uneven terrain of Virginia, through Payne's Farm and Mine Run, across the Potomac, and back again, continually on the move with weary monotony. They got close to Washington with Jubal Early's raid in July 1864; they fought more battles at Winchester, Fisher's Hill, and Cedar Creek, and eventually the landscapes of Virginia became as familiar and recognizable as landmarks in Louisiana.

By February, 1865, they were with the remnants of the Louisiana Brigade at Hatcher's Run where they made their last great charge. When they entered the war they numbered in the thousands, but after Hatcher's Run barely 400 answered call. From then on they were always on the defensive and at Appomattox had depleted to 250 men.

The Third Regiment scaled their ladder of exhilaration during the early days of the war with the South's dramatic victories. They were at Oaks Hills, Elkhorn Tavern with Major General Sterling Price, and then with their own colorful Beauregard and the Army of the West, and at Farmington, Corinth, and Iuka where General Price recognized them: "The brunt of the battle at Iuka fell upon Hebert's brigade and nobly did sustain it, and worthily of its accomplished commander and of the brigade which numbered among its forces the everglorious Third Louisiana [Regiment], the Third [Louisiana] and the Third Texas Cavalry Division had already fought under my eyes at Oaks Hill and Elkhorn. No men have ever fought more bravely or more victorious than they."

During the seige of Vicksburg the Third Regiment was entrenched at Snyder's Bluff, the northernmost point of the fortifications. When Forts Jackson and St. Phillip below New Orleans fell to the Federals, only Vicksburg and Port Hudson, north of Baton Rouge, lay in the way of the Union's complete control of the Mississippi Valley. But Vicksburg was the Third's last action, for when the city fell so did the hopes of the men within its defenses. They were parolled by the Federals and went on to Alexandria and Natchitoches where they reorganized, doing mostly duty at Shreveport. They saw no more action in the Civil War. Remnants of the troop east of the Mississippi met at Demopolis, Alabama, and at Enterprise, Mississippi, and became Company H of the Twenty-second, Louisiana Heavy Artillery. In June, 1864, they were at Mobile where they reinforced Tracy in Mobile Bay. When the city fell they retreated to Meridian, Mississippi, saw no more action, and surrendered in May, 1865.

After the Civil War they became inactive as did all the rest of Louisiana's militia units because of the U.S. military governors and the subsequent Reconstruction acts. Finally in 1878, the unit was reconstituted with that new name, Special Militia Force, and by 1890 it contained fifteen companies from all areas of the state. On December 26, 1891, they reorganized as the First and Second battalions of infantry. These two battalions reorganized to form the First Regiment of Infantry on March 17, 1896. This regiment in turn became known as First Louisiana Volunteer Infantry Regiment and was called into Federal service during the Spanish-American War, May 8-18, 1898. They went to Miami and Jacksonville where they suffered from disease. They saw no action and were mustered out on October 3, 1898.

The unit became the First Battalion of Infantry on August 8, 1899, but soon went under another reorganization. On December 6, 1904, it expanded into First Regiment of Infantry, direct predecessor of the 156th. In the Mexican border action it was at San Benito, Texas.

The First Regiment arrived in Brest, France, with yet another name, the 156th Infantry Regiment, the result of a redesignation on September 27, 1917. Most of the men in the regiment were assigned to other units as replacements for the Thirty-ninth Division. They were at St. Aignam when the war ended and were demobilized on June 23, 1919, at Camp Beauregard.

On November 25, 1940, the regiment, commanded by Colonel James H. Kuttner, was ordered into Federal service and, interestingly, was not part of any division but remained a regiment for five years and four months (November 25, 1940-March 22, 1946). They first went to Camp Blanding, Florida, for a two-month stay in the Sabine-area maneuvers. After Pearl Harbor the regiment served as a security guard on the Atlantic seaboard, stationed at Fort Fisher, near Wilmington, North Carolina. From there they went back to Camp Blanding and then on to Camp Bowie, Texas, where they underwent strenuous training for combat. They were then sent overseas and landed in England on October 6, 1942.

The regiment was divided and the Second Battalion was sent to Oran, Algeria. Many members of the battalion spoke French which made them ideal military police. In the fall of 1943 they became the 202nd Infantry Battalion (Sp). But just prior to the Italian campaign the unit was deactivated and its men assigned to the Sixty-sixth through the Seventy-fourth Military Police companies. Most of the companies served in the Rome-Arno, Rhineland, and central Europe campaigns.

Meanwhile, the regiment in England was assigned to the U.S. Assault Training Center, at Woolacombe, staying there from July, 1943, until spring of 1944, training combat units in amphibious landings, securing beachheads and other tactics necessary for the coming Normandy invasion. And when the invasion came, the regiment served as security guard in the areas from which the troops were dispatched to France.

A regimental headquarters echelon and Company L went in with the landing parties and after completing their mission returned to England. But by August 18 the First Battalion, soon to be followed by the Second Battalion on August 23 and the rest of the regiment on September 3, landed at Utah Beach; went on to St. Lo and Coutances to Rennes, Brittany. The Cannon Company followed in December. These piecemeal actions indicate the versatility of the units within the regiment.

In Normandy and Brittany the regiment patrolled the flanks and lifelines of the advancing armies. The Third Battalion was dispatched on a security mission to Brest on September 25 while the First Battalion was assigned the same type of duty in Paris. The 156th guarded the Red Ball highway which was the supply road that fed the huge armies marching against the Germans. On October 15 the Second Battalion was attached to Supreme Headquarters, Allied Expeditionary Force. By mid-November the rest of the 156th became the security guard for the American embassy, U.S. Naval Headquarters and the Headquarters, Seine Section, in Paris. In mid-December, the regiment, minus the Second Battalion, was assigned to a mission of defense on the Normandy coast from Mont St. Michele to Cape de la Hagne (a distance of 200 miles) against the bypassed Germans on the Channel islands of Guernsey, Jersey, Sark, and Aldernay. They remained there until the unconditional surrender of the Germans was announced.

Late May found the First Battalion at Mons, Belgium, and the regimental headquarters and the Third Battalion were also brought up to assist in guarding the Loire D.T.C. The First Battalion rejoined the regiment, and preparations were already underway for their transfer to the Pacific Theater when Japan surrendered, August 15, 1945.

The regiment left Le Havre, France, on March 12, 1946, aboard the *Sea Corporal* and arrived at New York March 21 and was stationed at Camp Kilmer, where they were deactivated the next day.

The regiment was again organized after World War II when Company F at Breaux Bridge was federally recognized on November 4, 1946. Colonel James H. Kuttner was the commander. Other companies soon followed, and by May 6, 1952, the last company was organized at Sulphur to continue their lineage.

BATTLE HONORS

CIVIL WAR
(Confederate)

Virginia, 1861	Gettysburg
Missouri, 1861	Vicksburg
Peninsula	Wilderness
Second Manassas	Spotsylvania
Sharpsburg	Cold Harbor
Arkansas, 1862	Petersburg
Mississippi, 1862	Shenandoah
Fredericksburg	Appomattox
Chancellorsville	

WORLD WAR I

Streamer without inscription

WORLD WAR II

Northern France

Central Europe

Asiactic Pacific Streamer
without inscription

Hq. Co. 3rd Bn. (Lake Charles) additionally entitled to World War II (EAME)—Normandy.

Co. A 3rd Bn. (Breaux Bridge) additionally entitled to World War II (EAME)—Rhineland.

Co. C 3rd Bn. (Jennings) additionally entitled to World War I Champagne-Marne, Aisne-Marne, St. Mihiel, Meuse-Argonne, Lorraine, 1918, Champagne, 1918

THE 199TH INFANTRY REGIMENT, according to the official statement of lineage and the battle honors of the 199th Infantry Regiment, is identical to the 156th Infantry Regiment from 1861 through February of 1940.

About November of 1939 the Second Battalion of the 156th Infantry Regiment had been expanded and reorganized into the 204th Coast Artillery (antiaircraft) Regiment and was inducted into Federal service on January 6, 1941, at Shreveport, under the command of Colonel Joseph A. Redding.

In September, 1943, the regiment was redesignated into three separate battalions. The First Battalion was redesignated the 769th Antiaircraft Gun Battalion: the Second Battalion became the 527th Antiaircraft Artillery Automatic Weapons Battalion; the Third became the 244th Antiaircraft Artillery Searchlight Battalion.

The 199th Infantry Regiment actually came into being on December 11, 1946, during the reorganizational period following World War II with headquarters at Shreveport. During its existence, its home area was northern Louisiana.

Upon return to state control, the Headquarters and Headquarters Battery, 204th Antiaircraft Artillery Group became Headquarters and Headquarters Company of the 199th Infantry, and the Rocket, Searchlight, and Automatic Weapons battalions became the First, Second, and Third battalions with headquarters in Shreveport, Natchitoches, and Monroe respectively. The regiment was organized under the leadership of Colonel James B. Hipple.

The 199th, together with the 156th Infantry Regiment in the southern part of Louisiana and the 153rd Infantry Regiment located in Arkansas, comprised the Thirty-ninth Infantry Division.

BATTLE HONORS

Campaign Streamers

CIVIL WAR
(Confederate)

Virginia, 1861	Gettysburg
Missouri, 1861	Vicksburg
Peninsula	Wilderness
Second Manassas	Spotsylvania
Sharpsburg	Cold Harbor
Arkansas, 1862	Petersburg
Mississippi, 1862	Shenandoah

Fredericksburg   Appomattox
Chancellorsville

WORLD WAR I
Streamer without inscription

WORLD WAR II
Asiatic-Pacific Theater streamer without inscription

HEADQUARTERS AND HEADQUARTERS BATTERY 204TH ANTIAIRCRAFT ARTILLERY GROUP originated in the mounted troops of the 108th Cavalry Regiment.

The 108th had been assigned to Louisiana and Georgia in a reorganization of the National Guard following World War I, with Louisiana being allotted the majority of the regimental units. It also had the largest number of ranking officers; James E. Edmonds became its colonel and commander when it became effective on November 10, 1923. But it was 1929 before it had a regimental organization that could be considered complete. At this time there was a headquarters troop, a machine-gun troop, three squadrons of two troops each, a band, and a medical detachment. All these units were in Louisiana with the exception of Georgia's machine-gun troops A and B of the First Squadron.

The 108th had initially been in the Fifty-fourth Cavalry Brigade, Twenty-second Cavalry Division, which consisted of four regiments and two machine-gun squadrons from seven states. By 1927 the 108th was reassigned to the 55th Cavalry Brigade of the Twenty-third Division, uniting the National Guard cavalry units in the Second and Third Army areas consisting of Louisiana, Georgia, Tennessee, North Carolina, Texas, and Alabama. And in 1938 the Twenty-third Division was reorganized again with Michigan, Wisconsin, and Illinois in place of North Carolina and Texas. But the Twenty-third did not become operational until Brigadier General Edmonds was promoted to major general in 1940.

The 108th had attended sixteen summer encampments as a unit and had participated with other contingents of the Twenty-third. However, on October 6, 1940, the 108th Cavalry minus the band in New Orleans, Troop K in Jennings, headquarters of the Twenty-third Cavalry Division and headquarters of the Fifty-fifth Cavalry ended its service as cavalry. It was converted to the 105th Separate Battalion Coast Artillery (antiaircraft). The Headquarters and Headquarters

Troop became Headquarters and Headquarters Battery and furnished personnel to Batteries A and B.

Inducted into Federal service on January 6, 1941, under command of Lieutenant Colonel Frederick H. Fox, the 105th went into field training at Camp Hulen, Texas, as an antiaircraft coast artillery unit.

Following Pearl Harbor, Batteries A and B were ordered to the Pacific Theater of Operations, to protect, principally, the approaches to Australia and New Zealand. Battery A was stationed at Canton Island and Battery B at the Christmas Islands, while batteries C and D trained at Desert Training Center, Indio, California. At Camp Young the battalion was redesignated as the 105th Coast Artillery Battalion (AA) (AW). In August, 1942, it went to England and Scotland and began intensive amphibious training.

It participated in battle activities of Operations Torch, Husky and Avalanche, and finally the redesignated 105th Antiaircraft Artillery Automatic Weapons Battalion (Sp.) ended its World War II service with inactivation on September 15, 1945.

The heritage of the 108th Cavalry and the Antiaircraft Battalion commands remained static until 1949 when the Headquarters and Headquarters Battery, 204th Antiaircraft Artillery Group and the 527th Gun Battalion were organized from personnel of the 105th Battalion.

On April 26, 1949, Headquarters and Headquarters Battery, 204th AAA Group, under the command of Colonel John Barkley was activated and federally recognized at Jackson Barracks with seven officers and nine enlisted men. Colonel Barkley remained in command until replaced by Colonel Francis C. Grevemberg on February 1, 1951.

BATTLE HONORS

Headquarters and Headquarters Battery
204th Antiaircraft Artillery Group

Campaign Streamers

WORLD WAR II

Algeria-French Morocco (with arrowhead)	Naples-Foggia
Tunisia	North Apennines
Rome-Arno	Po Valley
Sicily (with arrowhead)	

527TH ANTIAIRCRAFT ARTILLERY AW BN also originated in the mounted troops of the 108th Cavalry Regiment. Its heritage is steeped in the history of that parent unit, Headquarters Troop of the 108th Cavalry, then comprising only three officers and fifty-two men under the command of Captain A. J. Carter. It was mustered and federally recognized on August 8, 1923, at the old Washington Artillery Hall on St. Charles Street, New Orleans.

The constitution of the parent cavalry unit in 1923 established an unbroken and vigorous heritage that would mold the aggressiveness and dash of the cavalry with the sobriety and steadfastness of the mobile artillery into a unit that would earn for itself, its artillerymen, and its higher commands during World War II, an enviable record of some 790 combat days and three amphibious operations in the North African, Sicilian, and Italian campaigns.

During the early days it was later stationed at Jackson Barracks where drills were held on Sunday evenings; Friday evening drills continued at the Washington Artillery Hall. Its initial complement comprised fifty-five officers and men with about thirty-two horses. This unit was ordered to Amite to assist the sheriff in maintaining order when six men were hanged upon their conviction for murder during the 1920s. In order to help keep the curious crowds off the courthouse grounds, a wide ditch was filled with water and guards patrolled the bridges across it.

In a reorganization of the National Gaurd Cavalry in March, 1929, in order to conform to the Regular Army Cavalry the service troop was converted to a rifle troop and redesignated Troop I, which, with Troop K of Jennings, was assigned to the Third Squadron. During early September of 1934 the cavalry troops were placed on state duty during a controversial election in New Orleans.

The 527th AAA AW Bn and the Headquarters and Headquarters Battery 204th Antiaircraft Artillery Group emerged from the same parent unit, namely, Headquarters Troop of the 108th Cavalry. The 527th AAA Gun Bn (Mbl) (Type C) was activated and federally recognized after World War II on May 23, 1949 at Jackson Barracks under command of Major Joseph H. Cunningham. Of the three officers, one warrant officer, and fourteen enlisted men who comprised the original rolls, all the officers and two enlisted men had been members of the 105th Antiaircraft Artillery Battalion. Hence, the 527th was entitled to inherit the lineage of the 108th and 105th; it was redesignated the 527th AAA AW Battalion on October 1, 1949.

BATTLE HONORS
WORLD WAR II

Algeria-French Morocco (with arrowhead)
Tunisia
Sicily (with arrowhead)
Naples-Foggia

Rome-Arno
North Apennines
Po Valley

THE 769TH ANTIAIRCRAFT ARTILLERY BATTALION (AW) (MBL) had an illustrious background, having historical origin in the six *Spanish* colonial militia companies of the German, Acadian, and Iberville coasts organized in 1770. These militia companies of settlements along the Mississippi were the forerunners of the present National Guard, as indicated earlier in this book. In 1792 they were expanded into two Grenadier and eight Fuselier companies of the Trained Provincial Regiment des Allemands and one Dragoon, one Grenadier, and four Fuselier companies of the Legion Real Mixta de Milicias Disciplinades del Mississippi (Royal Legion of Mixed Trained Militia of the Mississippi). Their heritage evolved under many flags: Spain, France, the Confederacy, and the United States. They have served in seven wars and one rebellion, *viz*., the conquest of English West Florida by Spain 1779-1781; the West Florida Rebellion of 1810; the Louisiana campaign of England, 1814-1815; the Mexican War, 1846-1848; the Civil War 1861-1865; The Spanish-American War, 1898; World War I and World War II.

Although the 769th had its historical origin in the Spanish colonial milita, its official heritage as an organized Louisiana milita force, known as the Baton Rouge Fencibles, established its origin as May 30, 1861, as shown by the Official Lineage and Honors Certificate granted by the chief of military history, Department of the Army.

It was the Civil War that gave the battalion's home parishes their greatest military heritage. The parishes of St. Charles, St. John, St. James, Ascension, Assumption, Iberville, West and East Baton Rouge, West and East Feliciana, St. Helena, and Livingston had so many military commands fighting in so many different Confederate armies, and on so many battlefields that all cannot be noted.

From the first campaigns in Virginia and Missouri in 1861 till the surrender of the last Confederate army at Citronelle, Alabama, in May of 1865, the parishes were consistently represented by some of the battalion's antecedent military commands in the South's heroic struggle for the Lost Cause.

It was not until 1877 that the battalion's military lineage was reestablished with the formation of the Zouaves and Pelican Rifles of Baton Rouge in Louisiana's Special Militia Force. By 1898 Company E, First Regiment, Louisiana State National Guard, continued the heritage of Baton Rouge.

During the Spanish-American War it was in Federal service from May 10, to October 3, 1898. Its tour terminated at Camp Cuba Libre, Jacksonville, Florida.

Companies E and H and the band detachment, First Regiment, Louisiana National Guard, were mustered into Federal service July 28, 1916, at Camp Beauregard, Louisiana.

Following the war the military lineage of the 769th was reestablished on July 6, 1922, by the organization of Headquarters Company, 156th Infantry at Baton Rouge, redesignated the Howitzer Company, 156th Infantry in 1923, then Company A, 156th Infantry in 1926, the unit carried on the military heritage inaugurated in 1792 by the First Company of the Spanish "Legion."

In World War I, it served as part of the 156th Infantry of the Thirty-ninth Division, and in World War II it was again part of the 156th as a battalion. Military lineage was reestablished after World War II on June 3, 1947, in Baton Rouge, when Company A, under Captain Henry LeRoy Riser, was reactivated as an infantry rifle unit of the 156th Infantry Regiment. On November 4, 1947, a medical detachment was activated and assigned to the First Battalion, but on June 1, 1948, it was converted to antiaircraft and redesignated Headquarters Battery and Medical Detachment of the 769th AAA Gun Battalion, Mobile Type C. Captain Riser was commanding officer.

On June 18, 1948, Battery D was activated at Donaldsonville in Ascension Parish and for the first time in fifty years a military unit was in existence in a town known for its famous and renowned Civil War Artillery Battery—the Donaldsonville Cannoneers.

On October 1, 1949, the 769th was converted and redesignated as the 769th AAA AW BN, Mbl, with Lieutenant Colonel Wylie Abercrombie as its commander; until replaced by Major Robert G. Dunn on 27 March 1950. Major Dunn was replaced by Major O'Neil J. Daigle, Jr., on March 14, 1951.

CAMPAIGN PARTICIPATION CREDIT

CIVIL WAR
(Confederate)

Virginia, 1861	Wilderness
Peninsula	Spotsylvania
Second Manassas	Cold Harbor
Sharpsburg	Petersburg
Fredericksburg	Shenandoah
Chancellorsville	Appomattox
Gettysburg	

WORLD WAR I

Without inscription

WORLD WAR II

Northern France

THE 773RD TANK BATTALION's official lineage begins with that of the Washington Artillery, which, at that time, was the 141st Field Artillery Regiment with 155mm Howitzers. When Hitler's legions were overrunning Belgium, France, and Poland with armored units during the latter part of 1939 and early in 1940, the United States Army directed that one antitank battery be organized and activated within each field artillery battalion. Two such batteries were organized within the 141st Field Artillery Regiment of New Orleans.

In anticipation of the Louisiana maneuvers immediately before the entry of the United States into World War II, the antitank batteries of the 141st of Louisiana and the 166th of Pennsylvania were combined and supplemented with the antitank platoons of the battalion headquarters of the 141st and 166th regiments and with antitank personnel of the Regimental Headquarters Battery of the 190th of Pennsylvania, to form the 73rd Provisional Antitank Battalion.

On December 15, 1941, eight days after the Pearl Harbor attack by the Japanese, and at the end of four months of field maneuvers in Louisiana and North Carolina, the 73rd Provisional Antitank Battalion was reorganized and redesignated the 773rd Tank Destroyer Battalion.

The battalion left for Europe in January of 1944 after having been on three field maneuvers, spending ten months in the field, and covering fourteen states. They were equipped with full-track M-10 tank destroyers mounted with three-inch guns. After landing in England and continuing its training, the 773rd boarded two LSTs

(Landing Ship, Tanks) and four LCIs (Land Craft, Infantry), at Portland Harbor, crossed the English Channel, and landed on the coast of Normandy.

Under command of Lieutenant Colonel Frank G. Spiess, the battalion, minus C Company and part of B Company, landed at Utah Beach near St. Germain De Varreville on August 7. The remainder of the battalion landed the same day on Omaha Beach near St. Laurent Sur Mer. Assembling at La Haye Du Puits, the battalion marched ninety-one miles to St. Elliers Du Maine. By August 14 the unit had gotten within a few miles of the enemy who held Argentan, where they relieved the Fifth Armored Division. On the seventeenth a concerted offensive action began in the memorable Argentan-Falaise pocket.

In the hills southeast of Argentan the 773rd destroyers took up a position on the southern tip of the "pincers" around the estimated 75,000-100,000 Germans who were trapped within an army of armor. The battalion was located near LeBourg, St. Leonard, and for one day until the Nineteenth Infantry Division arrived, all personnel of the battalion, including Headquarters Company, served on the line as infantrymen. In the furious action the battalion held and counterattacked against great odds. As a result of this exemplary action the 773rd was awarded the Presidential Unit Citation.

On August 17, Companies A and C moved north to cover the main roads into Le Bourg, St. Leonard. Despite heavy enemy artillery fire two platoons of C Company, in support of the Second Battalion of the 359th Infantry Regiment, attacked Le Bourg from the West as A Company with the First Battalion of the 359th moved into town from the south. The town fell and a German counterattack was effectively repulsed. Passing through the town the Third Battalion of the 359th, with the Third Platoon of C Company in support, moved northwest of Foughy with Hill 129 as one of the objectives.

On Sunday, August 20, the enemy failed in a desperate attempt to escape southwest of Chambois near Hill 129. When C Company's platoon ran out of ammunition, the First Platoon of A Company relieved them.

Nearing Hill 129, the First Platoon unexpectedly came face to face with a mixed column of enemy tanks and vehicles. At point-blank range and under a hail of fire, they fought for three hours. While farther north, the Second Platoon of C Company made a stand at Chambois. After a pause at Chailloue the battalion moved to the

Seine River at Mantes-Gassicourt where Company B and the Second Platoon of Reconnaissance Company were attached to the Seventy-ninth Infantry Division. When the bridgehead was firmly established by the Seventy-ninth and Thirtieth Infantry divisions on the 27, the battalion was relieved and moved near Paris closing in at Bernay-En-Brie on August 30.

The battalion joined the Seventy-ninth Division on September 10 at Thonnance-LesJoinville on the Marne River in support of the XV Corps effort on the Moselle River. A Company was with Combat Team 3 (313th Infantry), B Company with Combat Team 4 (314th Infantry). Company C supported Combat Team 5 (315th Infantry) as it swept through the towns of Neufchateau, Chatenois, Oellville to Poussay which they had secured by the thirteenth of September. Combat Team 4 with B Company headed east to Charmes with the Second Platoon, entering the town on the twentieth. While B Company and C Company were going eastward, A Company with Combat Team 3 took the towns of Puzieux, Poussay, and Ramecourt to secure position overlooking Damvillier and Mirecourt.

When the bridgehead was established over the Moselle at Charmes, Combat Team 4 and B Company made a perilous crossing on the fifteenth while the other tank destroyer companies supported them by direct fire. They were soon relieved and with units crossing to the north at Bayon on the eighteenth, all companies closed in on Luneville by September 22. B Company then crossed the Meurthe River near Houainville and moved into the town of Gerberviller on the twenty-first. After capturing Luneville and clearing Foret de Parroy the battalion moved southwest of Metz.

The historic fortress city of Metz was the next objective. Flanking movements were decided on since frontal attacks would be too costly in lives and time. Two crossings of the Moselle were made, one at Chattenom and the other at Malling. Much difficulty was encountered before the battalion was across safely at Chattenom. The Ninetieth Division, to which the battalion was attached, attacked the line of Maginot forts and was opposed by roadblocks and mines but managed to smash southward. On the nineteenth the Third Platoon of B Company made contact with the Fifth Division troops south of St. Barbe, which closed the last escape corridor of the German garrison at Metz. The division crossed the Nier River near Bouzonville and fought its way to the Saar River and estabished a firm line on the west bank between Merzib on the north and Wallerfangen on the south.

On the tenth of December the first of the antitank destroyers was ferried over the Saar in support of the small bridgehead which had been established by the infantry. They reached the west edge of Dillingen, considered the "Pittsburgh" of the vital Saar region. And on December 15 a coordinated attack by the First and Second battalions of the 358th Infantry crossed the railroad tracks into the town proper; a great objective had been achieved. The Third Platoon of B Company moved up the tracks in advance of the Second Battalion as each destroyer took on previously assigned pill boxes. The infantry advanced from pill box to pill box while the engineers blew up Germans strong points. Company C's Third Platoon and the one remaining gun of the First Platoon of B Company used the same tactics in support of the First Battalion which was on the right of the advancing forces.

The Germans mounted an offensive and broke through in the Ardennes sector which forced the battalion to pull back over the Saar River, a position that had cost them much in effort and men. More troops had to be withdrawn to stem the surge of Von Runstedt's Panzer armies. At first, the 773rd settled and prepared defensive positions in the Saar-Moselle triangle. But about noon on January 6 the battalion moved out making a hazardous day and night march over iced roads to Saeul, Luxembourg. For the rest of the month the 773rd experienced many hardships in the bitterest weather in the mountainous snow-blasted country of the tiny Grand Duchy of Luxembourg.

The battalion launched an attack on January 9 against the south flank of the enemy's "Bulge." On the morning of the twelfth the Second Platoon of Company A took the town of Doncols and moved on to Sonlez and made contact with the 357th Infantry. These towns were along the important east-west road that the enemy planned to use for an escape route. Later during the day C Company was in a position on the right flank, along the road leading southeast into Wiltz when an enemy armored column began to withdraw along this route. In the ensuing fight that lasted all day the enemy was cut up severely by the accurate gunnery of the tank destroyers.

At Oberwampach on the seventeenth, the battalion pushed ahead as the enemy tried to dislodge American troops from this town. Savage counterattacks by the elite SS Panzer troops aimed at the Ninetieth Division positions were repulsed repeatedly by the accuracy of the three-inch guns. Enemy tanks destroyed in these actions brought the battalion total to 102, marking the 773rd as the first American tank destroyer battalion in any theater to exceed a hundred. Four "tank probes" by the Germans failed to be dispersed by Company B guns. The Germans, attacking with ten to twelve tank and supporting infantry, were preceded by an intense artillery barrage. But the Second and Third platoons of B Company knocked out the German tanks while U.S. forces were able to keep strategically important Oberwampach which controlled one escape highway from the vulnerable Ardennes pocket. This action proved to be the turning point in the Battle of the Bulge.

The battalion went on to Biwisch on January 26 and was attached to the VII Corps. In quick succession, they penetrated the Siegfried line to capture Winterspelt, Habschied, Branscheid, and Litenborn. On February 21, Task Force Spiess was again activated, its mission being to protect the Nineteenth Division right flank as it advanced south and east between the Our and Prum rivers. By the twenty-fifth, Task Force Spiess had accomplished its mission and was relieved after taking sixteen towns and much enemy equipment.

By March the Ninetieth and Sixth Armored divisions were preparing to attack along the Kyll River. Small task forces were formed with units of the 773rd as part of each. These probed ahead of the infantry to secure roads and important strategic positions; the advance was rapid despite resistance. They again crossed the Moselle as the Ninetieth tried to establish a bridgehead on uneven terrain. Task Force Spiess was again activated, and on March 16, Colonel Spiess, in command of leading elements of the battalion, reached the Rhine to place and fire its first guns across the river at its confluence with the Moselle. The task force spearheaded the Ninetieth Division up the east bank of the Rhine stopping just outside of Maintz, which was captured later.

The Rhine was again crossed, this time at Nierstein on March 23 and 24, despite the Luftwaffe's attempt to destroy their pontoon bridges. The following day Task Force Spiess captured Darmstadt without too much difficulty. The task force then reconnoitered in front of the Ninetieth Division as it advanced northwestward towards the Main River. Frankfurt and Hanau were captured, after which the division mopped up resistance. In late March the division moved rapidly northward to Hersfeld as the Germans offered less and less resistance.

By April 1 the division reached Hersfeld and then swung east toward Czechoslovakia. The towns of Vacha, Bad Salzungen, Zella Mehlis, and Merkers all fell quickly. Company A remained in Merkers to guard the salt mine wherein most of the wealth of the German Reich was hidden. It is estimated that the cache contained about one hundred tons of gold bullion, plus $400 million in the currency of various nations, and valuable art treasures. On April 12 the Interdefense Command under Colonel Spiess was formed within the Ninetieth Division to protect strategic installations and roads within their zone.

On the eighteenth of April a Ninetieth Division task force and the Second Platoon of Company B entered Czechoslovakia, marking the first penetration of this country by American troops. In late April the division advanced along the Czechoslovakia border clearing the zone and protecting the VII Corp's left flank. Many prisoners of war were gathered in this operation. On May 5 the division attacked south to seize the Regen bridgehead through which the Fourth Armored was to pass. Then, on the sixth, the attack swung northward into Czechoslovakia to the Susice and Petrovice areas where the drive halted. The war in the European Theater of Operations had ended.

The 773rd left Czechoslovakia on May 14 for Tirschenreuth, Bavaria, in Germany, to serve as occupation troops and border guards. They had been in direct fire contact with the enemy for 254 days. The battalion fired 8,219 rounds of fire, knocked out 113 tanks, 25 SP guns, and 105 pill boxes; they also captured 1,970 prisoners. In turn, the 773rd suffered 301 battle and 55 nonbattle casualties. It returned to the United States during the latter part of 1945 and was deactivated at Camp Patrick Henry, Virginia, on October 23 of that same year. The 773rd had written another indelible chapter in the history of Louisiana's National Guard.

With the reorganization of the National Guard following World War II, the 773rd Tank Destroyer Battalion was allotted to Louisiana as the 773rd Heavy Tank Battalion and assigned to the west central part of the state. It received Federal recognition October 18, 1949, under the command of Major C. G. Turner. Its campaign streamers earned in its World War II service were:

BATTLE HONORS

WORLD WAR II

Campaign Streamers:

Northern France

Ardennes-Alsace
Rhineland
Central Europe

Decorations
Distinguished Unit Streamer
embroidered
Argentan-Falaise

Streamer in the colors of the French
Croix de Guerre with Palm,
embroidered
Moselle and Sarre Rivers

THE 935TH FIELD ARTILLERY BATTALION traces its origin to the same famed Washington Artillery Company, Washington Battalion, of the Fourth Regiment, Louisiana Militia, which was organized in New Orleans, September 7, 1838. It did not, however, receive its distinctive appellation until the action of World War II. During the first phases of the war all field artillery regiments of the United States Army were reconstituted into separate battalions. On March 7, 1943, the 141st Field Artillery, while in active federal service, was reorganized to form two separate battalions, the first being designated the 934th Field Artillery Battalion and the second the 935th Field Artillery Battalion.

Upon completion of its training in the United States, the 935th sailed from New York in August of 1943. Landing at Oran in North Africa, it went on to Bizerte and then transported to Salerno where it landed on October 11. From Salerno the battalion moved on to Naples. On October 28 it was attached to the British X Corps and went into a position near Sparanise where the 935th fired its first combat rounds on October 31, 1943. By January, 1944, it became attached to the American II Corps and engaged in a bitter action near the ancient Benedictine monastery near Monte Cassino in attempts to dislodge the Germans farther up the hills. They entered Rome with the advance of the Allied armies on June 5.

Chosen to make the invasion of France, the battalion landed at Marseille and became part of the Allied forces in the drive across France. The 935th breached the Siegfried Line in March of 1945 and advanced into the German interior. At the surrender on May 7 they were at Hammel near Augsburg. After several months of occupation duty they returned to the United States and were deactivated at Camp Patrick Henry, Virginia, on October 26, 1945. Thus closed the 935th's war service; they had served 462 days in actual combat. In Italy they participated in eleven offensives and fired 21,000 rounds of ammunition. In Italy, France, and Germany the 935th supported eighteen divisions and had served in six different army corps.

The 935th Field Artillery Battalion was reorganized in New Orleans and received Federal recognition of November 8, 1946, under the command of Lieutenant Colonel Numa P. Avendano. Its authorized Campaign Streamers were:

BATTLE HONORS

MEXICAN WAR

Streamer without inscription

CIVIL WAR
(Confederate service)

Bull Run	Chickamauga
Peninsula	Petersburg
Manassas	Wilderness
Shiloh	Spotsylvania
Antietam	Appomattox
Fredericksburg	Murfreesboro
Chancellorsville	
Gettysburg	

WORLD WAR I

Streamer without inscription

WORLD WAR II

North Apennines	Rhineland
Naples-Foggia	Ardennes-Alsace
Rome-Arno	Central Europe

Unit Decoration:

Streamer in the colors of the French
Croix de Guerre with Palm
embroidered *Central Italy*.

Thus, through the greatest war fought in the history of the human race were the military units of the Louisiana National Guard able to continue their lineages and service in the defense of this country. They proved adaptable, versatile, devoted, and self-sacrificing. They leave, as did their predecessors, a noble heritage for ensuing generations to protect and secure the American way of life.

THE AIR NATIONAL GUARD evolved in spurts following World War I. There was no great universal interest in creating an air force for the Guard at this time. Only through the efforts of avid, persevering people interested in flying was this dream realized. But during the interim much opposition was met as interested Guardsmen, relying upon their own resources, created the first "wing," which was organized at St. Paul, Minnesota, and federally recognized on January 21, 1921. Called the 109th Observation Squadron, it was an element of the Thirty-fourth Infantry Division.

Louisiana did not begin its Air National Guard until early February in 1941 when the 122nd Observation Squadron was organized with Captain Glynne M. Jones as its first commander. Through recruiting and training at Jackson Barracks, the 122nd reached full strength by September of the same year.

Ordered into Federal service to join the Army Air Corps on October 1, 1941, it was mustered in at the New Orleans Airport. On October 6, the squadron was assigned to the Sixty-eighth Observation Group and transferred to Esler Field, Alexandria, where it underwent further training.

The week following the attack on Pearl Harbor the squadron was ordered back to the New Orleans Airport, the base from which it would perform antisubmarine patrols over the Gulf of Mexico. Four missions were flown each day to a distance of at least one hundred miles offshore, the principal aim being the protection of the shipping lanes emanating from the Port of New Orleans. Using the old 0-47s and BC-1A aircraft, which operate on single engines, these patrols were sometimes performed under extremely adverse weather conditions.

On February 6, 1942, the 122nd was sent to Daniel Field at Augusta, Georgia. The crew underwent a vigorous indoctrination course in order to handle new A-20 Douglas bombers, Republic P-43 fighters and Stinson L-1A liaison aircraft. It was again assigned to submarine patrol duty and as air protection for troop ships at Augusta and Savannah, Georgia, and Charlotte, North Carolina.

By April, 1942, the squadron was ordered to Lawson Field, Fort Benning, Georgia, where it participated in summer maneuvers with the Second Armored Division and the First Infantry. This training period lasted seven weeks after which they were sent back to Daniel Field, then on to Winston-Salem, North Carolina, for the Carolina maneuvers of 1942. From Winston-Salem they were transferred to Morris Field, Charlotte, North Carolina, to begin overseas training. And from Charlotte the squadron was sent to Langley Field, Virginia, for twenty-three days of training in infantry tactics. Prior to leaving the United States it was divided into guard and air echelons.

On October 23, 1942, the unit left Langley and was put to sea in convoy with 150 naval vessels and troop transports to attack the western coast of Africa. At 2200 hours on November 8, 1942, the 122nd joined the infantry who were already fighting on the beach at Fedela, French Morocco. Early on the morning of November 12, the squadron reached the Cazes airport at Casablanca, and there it was assigned the task of refueling all Allied aircraft in the area. The air echelon landed on the Gold Coast of Africa and the two echelons reformed at Oran, Algeria.

The 122nd moved on when the western coast of Africa was secured and arrived at Oujda, French Morocco, on December 10, 1942. Here it again began antisubmarine patrols over the Mediterranean Sea then participated in the Kasserine Pass action as a bombing squadron. It continued these patrol missions until March 22, 1943, when it was transferred to Ber Rechid, French Morocco, where it became part of the Twelfth Training Command. As the need for more bases grew, the 122nd was moved to Sidi Rahal, French Morocco, ten miles from Ber Rechid.

Part of the duty of the 122nd was to train pilots, which necessitated its moving from base to base. Its next stop was Berteaux, Algeria, to train French and American pilots in gunnery and navigation using P-38 and P-39 fighter aircraft.

On November 8, 1943, one year after its initial landing in North Africa, the 122nd Squadron number was retired from active duty with the Army Air Corps. The officers and enlisted men were assigned to other Army Air Corps and went on to fight in Africa, Egypt, the Near East, and, eventually, to Europe to participate in the defeat of Germany.

Its World War II battle credits include antisubmarine duty, December 7, 1941, to September 22, 1942, and North Africa, November 8–10, 1942.

In the latter part of 1946 five air units, comprising over seven hundred officers and men, were allotted to the Louisiana Air National Guard for the purpose of defending the critically important New Orleans area. As a vital link in its "M" Day defensive setup, the Air Force allotted to the 122nd Bombardment Squadron (Light) the 122nd Weather Station, the 122nd Utility Flight, the 211th Air Service Group (Detachment C), and Headquarters of the 135th Radar Control and Warning Squadron (Large Scale). New Orleans was chosen as the site for all units except the two supporting radar organizations of the 135th which were to be activated in Houma and Baton Rouge.

The 122nd Bombardment Squadron and allied units were activated on December 5, 1946, and were among the first air units in the United States to be organized with the former under the command of Lieutenant Colonel Hubbell F. Vincent. Requiring high qualification and performance, combat-trained personnel from the 122nd Observation Squadron, which existed prior to World War II, formed the backbone of the newly authorized units.

Tactical training of the bombardment squadron was limited for a short time in 1947 because the tactically equipped A-26 type aircraft was restricted from operation on the short runways of New Orleans Lakefront Airport where the unit was based. A right of entry to Michoud Airstrip and the adjacent hangar facilities relieved this operational deficiency.

The facilities at Michoud also provided a home for the headquarters of the 135th Radar Control and Warning Squadron with its two radar sites selected at the Naval Air Station in Houma and on the Louisiana State University Campus in Baton Rouge.

The Senior Air Instructor, in his concluding remarks to the adjutant general at the end of the 1946-1947 Biennial, stated, "The transition of the planned but then non-existent Louisiana Air National Guard of November 1946 to the organized, operational Louisiana Air National Guard of today is a big step towards achievement of an 'M' Day Air National Guard capable of defending this critical area against any aggressor air attack."

President Harry S. Truman deserves the limelight in this chapter because his smile never misrepresented him as a pushover. To the left are two prisoners of war, a female Korean and a male American, part of "Operation Switch" in 1953. At bottom center another president, John F. Kennedy deliberates over the Berlin Crisis. And at bottom right a soldier holds a Vietnamese baby.

CHAPTER 13

An Asian Adventure

Following the end of World War II, the National Guard units were mustered out of active service, but their battle flags, guidons, and flags of the individual units were kept by the government as army property. On Armistice Day, November 11, 1946, a national celebration called the "Return Of Colors" was held to honor units and members of the National Guard for meritorious service.

Louisiana units served in many areas of combat and on both sides of the world. They were among the first in the Pacific while their comrades in arms spearheaded invasions in North Africa, Sicily, the Italian peninsula, Normandy, and southern France.

In an impressive ceremony held at Municipal Auditorium in New Orleans, which capped a day of military festivities, the colors of some of the National Guard units were returned to Louisiana. Brigadier General Raymond H. Fleming, adjutant general, presided as master of ceremonies. Colonel Francis A. Woolfley, who represented General Jonathan M. Wainwright, commanding general of the Fourth Army, presented the colors to Jimmie H. Davis, governor of Louisiana and commander in chief of the National Guard.

The colors of the Louisiana National Guard units that had served in World War II were borne by the color guard and bearers of the Regular Army composed of troops of the Fourth Army and presented to the color guard and bearers of the Louisiana National Guard as they met in the center of the stage. An officer of each Louisiana unit received the flag as that detachment's history was recited. On this occasion the return of colors was made to the following units: 156th Infantry Regiment; 141st Field Artillery Battalion (Washington Artillery); 935th Field Artillery Battalion (Washington Artillery); 106th Medical Regiment; 204th Coast Artillery (AA); 527th Coast Artillery (AA); and 105th Separate Battalion Coast Artillery (AA).

Comments were made on the histories of detachments whose colors were not returned at this ceremony. Such units were: State Headquarters; 61st Infantry Brigade; 106th Quartermaster Company; 122nd Observation Squadron; 773rd Tank Destroyer Battalion; and XIX Corps Artillery.

Later, the following year, the home base of the 204th Coast Artillery Regiment (AA) was the site of another ceremony at which the colors of that unit were returned. The 204th had served during the war as an antiaircraft unit at San Diego, California. Held at the Hardin Memorial Armory at Fort Humbug, Shreveport, military and public officials of the state and city participated in honoring the war services of this north Louisiana artillery regiment.

The normalcy that the people of the free world expected following World War II never developed. From May 7, the date of Germany's surrender (Italy had surrendered on September 8, 1943), until the surrender of Japan on August 14, 1945, Russia jockeyed for a position whereby it could lay claim to territories, exert influence in certain areas, and be in a commanding place at the peace table. Russia declared war on Japan on August 8, 1945, only six days before the capitulation.

The wartime alliance of Russia, Great Britain, and the United States was in philosophic and political terms an unnatural association that lasted as long as each had mutual objectives, the defeat of Germany, Italy, and Japan. When the war ended, Russia, intent upon establishing and solidifying a dominant position in the world of nations began negotiating the peace settlements while her troops occupied portions or all of conquered countries. The secret agreements made at Yalta by Churchill and Roosevelt with Stalin sowed the seeds for what was to follow, a continual world crisis that prevails today.

The decline of Great Britain as a major power left the task of maintaining a defense among free nations entirely to the United States. As the years wore on, the situation became more and more critical in an atmosphere described by the news media as the Cold War.

An Asian Adventure

The dropping of the atomic bombs on Hiroshima and Nagasaki hastened the Japanese to the peace table, although the outcome, even before the bombs, had been predictable for some time. Peace feelers had been directed to the United States even before the surrender, but for some reason Roosevelt did not fully appraise the dominance of the United States in the Pacific. Russia moved into Korea while Japan was negotiating with the United States which caused some consternation and calls for immediate reciprocal action by the United States. Upon a suggestion by the U.S. War Department, the Thirty-eighth Parallel of north latitude in Korea became the peremptory division of North and South Korea. On August 14, 1945, the army recommendation of this division was approved by President Harry S. Truman, who had succeeded Franklin D. Roosevelt on April 12, 1945, the Joint Chiefs of Staff, and the State Department. A plan for the division of North and South Korea was presented the following day to Stalin by Truman. On August 16 Stalin agreed to the proposal that Russia would occupy North Korea and the United States the South. Douglas MacArthur, commander-in-chief of the U.S. armed forces in the Pacific, was given the task of arranging the surrender and the provisions of the agreement concerning the 38th Parallel.

When Japan defeated Russia in the Russo-Japanese War (1904-1905), Japan's position in Korea became secure. From this time on, Japan directed all of Korea's internal and foreign affairs from the Japanese foreign office in Tokyo.

With the defeat of Japan and the expulsion of its ruling elite the entire social, economic, and political system of Korea collapsed. Korea had had a desire for independence for many years during the Japanese domination. With that defeat of Japan the spark of hope was ignited. Communism, especially in the North, contested with the nationalists—who leaned toward the western powers—for supremacy; they split along sectional lines creating, in the aftermath, North and South Korea. And with the power of Russia and the United States operating in opposite directions, the dream of Korean unity and complete independence was lost in an incinerator of war. Thus began the Cold War, and the end of the Korean dream.

The first American troops arrived in Seoul in early September of 1945 amid a confusion of political, economic, and social crises, to begin what eventually would be armed conflict between North Korea supported by Russia and South Korea with the support of the United States.

The National Guard, meanwhile on February 6, 1946, was offically released from further Federal service and returned to the states, territories, and the District of Columbia. As was the case after World War I, the National Guard had to start all over again, reorganizing units, recruiting personnel, and generally preparing itself. A troop strength of 5,297 units was established for the army National Guard, and 514 units were projected for the Air National Guard. A total of 678,282, of which 57,287 were the allotment of the Air National Guard, were the long-range quotas, authorized by the War Department.

But based on this number and the needs of the army and air force, the troop allotment following World War II was based, generally on the percentage of the population of the individual states as compared to the overall strength of the nation. With approximately 1.8 percent of the population, the strength of the Louisiana army and air corps approximated that figure. The Thirty-ninth Infantry (Delta) Division was allotted to the states of Louisiana and Arkansas with Louisiana being authorized the following units of that division plus the supporting units and organizations comprising the Air National Guard. An agreement was reached between the two states relative to rotation of certain general officer positions based on attrition. The dates of activation, commanding officers, and unit designations were as follow:

LOUISIANA TROOP STRUCTURE
ALLOTTED BY NATIONAL GUARD BUREAU
FOR ACTIVATION FOLLOWING WORLD WAR II

UNIT	COMMANDER	LOCATION	DATE
Hq. & Hq. Det.	B.G. Raymond H. Fleming	New Orleans	14 Aug. 46
Hq. Det.	Cpt. John H. Boh	New Orleans	14 Aug. 46
Hq. 39th Div.	B.G. Raymond H. Fleming	New Orleans	30 Sep. 46
Hq. Co. 39th Div.	1st Lt. William S. Guill	New Orleans	7 Nov. 46
Hq. Spec. Trps.	Cpt. Frank A. Marino	New Orleans	7 Nov. 46
QM Co.	Lt. Col. Stanley O. Whitehouse	Alexandria	12 Nov. 46
Band	C.W. Robert E. Mittelsteadt	New Orleans	30 Jan. 47
Rcn. Trp.	Cpt. William H. Hogan	New Roads	31 Mar. 48
Signal Co.	Cpt. Henry G. Schopfer, Jr.	New Orleans	5 Feb. 48
156th Inf.			
Hq.	Col. James H. Kuttner	Lafayette	18 Dec. 46
Hq. Co.	1st Lt. Paul C. Short	Lafayette	18 Dec. 46
Svc. Co.	1st Lt. Chester F. Dupont	Lafayette	18 Dec. 46
Cannon Co.	Cpt. Daniel M. Riddle, Jr.	Marksville	12 Nov. 46

An Asian Adventure

UNIT	COMMANDER	LOCATION	DATE
Tank Co.	1st Lt. Nolan Aquillard	Eunice	26 Feb. 48
Med. Sec.	Maj. Wood N. Scott	Lafayette	4 Nov. 47
Hq. 1st Bn.	Lt. Col. Christian L. Olivier, Jr.	Houma	18 Dec. 46
Hq. Co.	Cpt. Edgar L. Chaney	Houma	18 Dec. 46
Co. A	Cpt. Henry L. Riser	Baton Rouge	3 Jun. 47
Co. B	Cpt. Paul J. Citrano	Morgan City	17 Dec. 46
Co. C	Cpt. Sidney A. Pellegrin	Houma	5 Nov. 47
Co. D	Cpt. Woodrow J. Defelice	Thibodaux	17 Dec. 46
Hq. 2d Bn.	Lt. Col. Simon Castille	St. Martinville	5 Nov. 46
Hq. Co.	Cpt. Harry L. Delahoussaye	St. Martinville	5 Nov. 46
Co. E	1st Lt. Harold W. Dunbar	Opelousas	25 Jan. 47
Co. F	Cpt. Samuel S. Broussard	Breaux Bridge	4 Nov. 46
Co. G	1st Lt. Charles Vuillemot	New Iberia	18 Dec. 46
Co. H	1st Lt. Robert J. LeBlanc	Abbeville	29 Jan. 47
Hq. 3d Bn.	Maj. Leonard E. Pauley	Lake Charles	20 Dec. 46
Hq. Co.	1st Lt. Raymond H. Pauley	Lake Charles	20 Dec. 46
Co. I	1st Lt. Hughit J. Boulet	Crowley	19 Dec. 46
Co. K	Cpt. Kamiel Khoury	Lake Charles	2 Apr. 47
Co. L	Cpt. Samuel E. Snider, Jr.	DeQuincy	4 Nov. 47
Co. M	Cpt. Alba S. Haywood	Jennings	28 Jan. 47
199th Inf.			
Hq.	Col. Joseph A. Redding	Shreveport	11 Dec. 46
Hq. Co.	1st Lt. Harry A. Lazarus, Jr.	Shreveport	11 Dec. 46
Svc. Co.	Cpt. George W. Mook	Shreveport	5 Jun. 47
Cannon Co.	1st Lt. Samuel P. Spivey	Shreveport	5 Jun. 47
AT Co.	Cpt. Dan N. Denton	Shreveport	5 Jun. 47
Hq. Sec. Med. Det.	Maj. Wood H. Scott	Monroe	10 Apr. 47
Hq. 1st Bn.	Lt. Col. Frank N. Crow	Shreveport	15 Nov. 46
Hq. Co.	Cpt. Jack C. Wilkerson	Shreveport	15 Nov. 46
Co. A	Cpt. William L. Adams, Jr.	Vivian	11 Dec. 46
Co. B	Cpt. Neill A. Yarborough	Homer	5 Jun. 47
Co. C	Cpt. Van F. Ingram	Jonesboro	10 Apr. 47
Co. D	Cpt. Floyd D. Culberston, Jr.	Minden	9 Apr. 47
Hq. 2d Bn.	Lt. Col. Thomas A. Baker	Natchitoches	13 Nov. 46
Hq. Co.	Cpt. Hampden J. Murrell	Natchitoches	13 Nov. 46
Co. E	1st Lt. Harold W. Andries	Many	14 Nov. 46
Co. F	1st Lt. Joe W. Campbell	Pineville	8 Apr. 47
Co. G	Cpt. Teal C. Calhoun	Winnfield	10 Dec. 46
Co. H	1st Lt. Edwin L. Kelly, Jr.	Natchitoches	8 Apr. 47
Hq. 3d Bn.	Lt. Col. George W. Trousdale	Monroe	12 Dec. 46
Hq. Co.	Cpt. George F. Beckett	Monroe	12 Dec. 46
Co. I	Cpt. Charles M. Womack	Monroe	31 Jan. 47
Co. K	Cpt. Rip D. Pipes	Monroe	31 Jan. 47

UNIT	COMMANDER	LOCATION	DATE
Co. L	Cpt. Earl C. Guillory	Bastrop	7 Nov. 47
Co. M	Cpt. Walter H. Johnson	Ruston	9 Apr. 47
Hq. 141st F.A.	Lt. Col. Duncan Gillis	New Orleans	8 Nov. 46
Hq. Btry.	Cpt. Edward P. Benezech	New Orleans	8 Nov. 46
Svc. Btry.	1st Lt. Reginald G. Booth	New Orleans	16 Dec. 46
Med. Det.	Cpt. Geddes B. Flagg, Jr.	New Orleans	16 Dec. 46
Btry. A	Cpt. Eugene R. Huber	New Orleans	5 Feb. 48
Btry. B	1st Lt. Earl L. J. Pitre	New Orleans	27 Feb. 48
Btry. C	Cpt. Harold I. Holdeman	New Orleans	23 Mar. 48
Hq. 935 F.A.	Lt. Col. Numa P. Avendano	New Orleans	8 Nov. 46
Hq. Btry.	Cpt. Edmond C. Gouaze	New Orleans	8 Nov. 46
Svc. Btry.	1st Lt. Earl J. Wilson	New Orleans	16 Dec. 46
Med. Det.	Cpt. Carlos D. Speck, Jr.	New Orleans	16 Dec. 46
Btry. A	1st Lt. James C. Garrison	New Orleans	16 Dec. 46
Btry. B	1st Lt. Cyril Bassich, Jr.	New Orleans	7 Apr. 47
Btry. C	1st Lt. Earl F. Sword	New Orleans	7 Apr. 47
Hq. 204 AAA Gp.	Col. John Barkiey	New Orleans	26 Apr. 49
Hq. Btry.	Cpt. William B. Cox	New Orleans	26 Apr. 49
Hq. 105th	Lt. Col. Tom Hall	Bogalusa	11 Apr. 47
Hq. Btry.	Cpt. Howard E. Foil	Bogalusa	11 Apr. 47
Btry. A	Cpt. Paul E. King	Bogalusa	11 Apr. 47
Btry. B	Cpt. Jesse D. Seal	Franklinton	11 Apr. 47
Btry. C	Cpt. Leon S. Poirier	Hammond	29 Jul. 48
Btry. D	Cpt. Paul E. King	Covington	16 Dec. 48
769th AAA			
Hq.	Cpt. Henry L. Riser	Baton Rouge	1 Jun. 48
Hq. Btry.	1st Lt. Donald W. Staples	Baton Rouge	1 Jun. 48
Med. Det.	Maj. Wood H. Scott	Baton Rouge	1 Jun. 48
Btry. A	Cpt. John B. Alexander	Baton Rouge	30 Jun. 48
Btry. B	Cpt. Raymond H. Metternich	Baton Rouge	30 Jun. 48
Btry. C	Cpt. Charles L. Carville	Plaquemine	27 Sep. 48
Btry. D	Cpt. O. J. Daigle, Jr.	Donaldsonville	18 Jun. 48
Hq. 527 AAA Bn.	Maj. Joseph H. Cunningham	New Orleans	23 May. 49
Hq. Btry.	Cpt. William B. Cox	New Orleans	23 May. 49
Med. Det.	Maj. Henry A. LaRocca	New Orleans	23 May. 49
Btry. A	1st Lt. Cecil A. Haskins	New Orleans	23 May. 49
Btry. B	1st Lt. Michael E. Poll	New Orleans	23 May. 49
Btry. C	2nd Lt. Vincent N. Beninate	New Orleans	23 May. 49
Btry. D	Cpt. Dalton H. Trepagnier, Jr.	New Orleans	23 May. 49
Hq. 773d Tank Bn.	'Maj. Charles G. Turner	Alexandria	18 Oct. 49
Hq. Co. & Svc.	Cpt. Neal B. Ryals	Alexandria	18 Oct. 49
Med. Det.	Maj. George Vash	Alexandria	27 Oct. 49
Co. A	1st Lt. Bert A. Adams	Leesville	17 Oct. 49

An Asian Adventure

UNIT	COMMANDER	LOCATION	DATE
Co. B	Cpt. Roy L. Dedmon	DeRidder	17 Oct. 49
Co. C	Cpt. Jessie Johnson	Ville Platte	27 Oct. 49
3628 Ord.	1st Lt. James G. Gusman	Alexandria	13 Dec. 49
3671 Ord. Co.	Cpt. Lloyd A. Randon	Alexandria	9 Dec. 46
122 Lt. Bomb.	Lt. Col. Hubbell F. Vincent	New Orleans	5 Dec. 46
122 Util. Flight	1st Lt. Donald H. Butler	New Orleans	5 Dec. 46
122 Weather	1st Lt. William T. Chapman, Jr.	New Orleans	5 Dec. 46
135 ACW	Maj. Orlando W. Stephenson, Jr.	New Orleans	19 May. 48
211 Air Sv.	Cpt. Milton O. Barth	New Orleans	5 Dec. 46

But what the War Department authorizes and what Congress in fact authorizes or allocates funds for are frequently at variance. But by February 2, 1950, the Army National Guard had authorized 4,436 units with a total strength of 348,196, approximately 100 percent of its projected goal as established by Congress. While the Air National Guard reached a strength of 43,494 within 488 units or 88 percent of the quota recommended by Congress. This was the total force of the National Guard when the invasion of South Korea by the North Korea People's Army occurred on June 25, 1950.

In quick succession, events of a volatile nature followed which put an army of the United States on a field of battle less than five years after World War II. On June 27 President Truman ordered U.S. air and sea units to aid South Korea while the Seventh Fleet patrolled the Straits of Formosa. The next day, however, North Korea captured Seoul, the capitol city of South Korea. The following day (June 30) President Truman ordered ground forces into Korea.

Truman had recommended that the wartime conscription machinery be retained despite the fact that it had officially ended. On March 31, 1947, such a plan was instituted as an emergency measure prompted by the aggressive actions of the Russians following World War II. A public law passed by Congress became official on June 24, 1948, and was to be ended by June, 1950. About 8.5 million young men between the ages of eighteen and twenty-five were registered with the option of either volunteering for one year service or be assigned to a reserve unit with annual training dates of not more than one month. By 1950 further legislation produced yet another Public Act enacted by the 81st Congress and then again by the 82nd Congress which extended the Act to July 1, 1953, the latter extending the required duration of service to twenty-four months.

The immediate effect on the National Guard was that it would be called by units into active service, while most of the army reserves would be called as individuals. The repeated enactments by Congress whereby the armed forces would be "on the ready" were not necessarily in anticipation of the events that occurred in Korea but as a means of meeting any emergency wherein the interests of world peace and those of the United States were involved. The conscription acts did, of course, provide the immediate structure upon which an armed force would be assembled to fight in Korea.

The tragedy in Korea was that the United States was in support of a southern portion of a divided ethnic group whose aims were autonomy and independence from the northern portion whose objectives were in direct contrast. The Koreans, collectively, had an identical history and identical culture but were divided in terms of ideology. The interference of outside powers came as a result of their geographical position in the contesting spheres of influences wielded by the world's great powers. As was the case when Germany overran Poland, Belgium, Holland, and France, the world balance of power was upset, and this brought about action from nations that considered themselves threatened. So it was in Asia in the cases of Korea and, later, Vietnam; they became the victims, and their land became the battleground in a contest for world influence. As early as January 12, 1950, Dean Acheson, in outlining American policy in relation to Asia, said that the defensive perimeter of the United States included South Korea.

The United States was also concerned about the situation in Vietnam where France was then trying to withstand Communist aggression. By the end of 1953 the United States was supporting the French efforts in Vietnam by paying two-thirds of the entire French military outlay or about one billion dollars. And President Eisenhower, who had succeeded Truman, stated that the fall of Indo-China would be of great concern to the United States; he later made a declaration embodying the Domino Theory that once one of those nations fell, all would fall. This presumption naturally intensified U.S. involvement. The proximity of Malayasia and the Philippines to the Korean Peninsula and Vietnam also made the defense of these countries imperative because it was within the United States's sphere of influence. To avoid the word *war*, the term *Korean Police Action* was used to describe the military operations in these theaters.

A total of 5,720,000 men and officers were in effect mobilized, of which 2,834,000 were for the army; 1,177,000 for the navy;

424,000 marines; and air force 1,285,000. From Louisiana the following National Guard units were ordered into Federal Service: 773rd Tank Battalion (heavy), October 5, 1950; 122nd Bombardment Squadron (L), April 1, 1951; 122nd Weather Station (Type A), April 1, 1951; 135th Aircraft Control & Warning Squadron, October 1, 1951.

During the thirty-seven months of warfare, deaths of the U.S. armed forces totaled 33,629, of which 596 were from Louisiana. The so-called "rotation" method, whereby men in a given unit served one year and were replaced, deterred the effectiveness of the war effort. This hindered unit continuity; it became more and more difficult to maintain efficient forces or sustain the *esprit de corps* over a long period of time. The rotation method also made it difficult for the individual to identify with his unit since his time with it was so limited. It was difficult to assess liability, to maintain an effective chain of command, and to properly condition the individual for the tasks at hand. An assembly line in an industrial plant would suffer from such a constant rotation of its personnel, much less a fighting unit.

The Korean War ended on July 27, 1953, and on August 5, Operation Switch began the exchange of prisoners. This war was caused by Russia's desire to further exert its influence; the United States managed to at least retain for South Korea a measure of autonomy though the threat from the north continues to the present day.

But in the summer of 1961 another crisis arose with Russian Premier Krushchev raising controversial issues regarding the city of Berlin. President John F. Kennedy, in the face of Russian aggressive tactics, resolutely declared: "We need the capability of placing in any area at the appropriate time a force which, combined with those of our Allies, is large enough to make clear our determination and ability to defend our rights at all costs. and to meet all levels of agressor pressure with whatever levels of force are required."

He then proceded to activate the National Guard and army reservists for one year or less; 150,000 men and officers were ready immediately. By October 1, 1961, 21,000 officers and men of the National Guard were on full-time duty, and 11 fighter squadrons were quickly dispatched to Europe to strengthen the American force at Berlin. It has been asserted by experts that the air support sent was the largest mass overseas flight in history.

Inducted into Federal Service for one year or less, from Louisiana, to meet the exigencies of the Berlin Crisis were the following:

UNIT	DATE OF ACTIVE DUTY	ACTIVE DUTY STATION
159 Evac. Hosp. (SM) Commanded by Colonel Lyman K. Richardson	October 1, 1961	Fort Sill, Okla.
204 Trans. Gp. (Trk.) Commanded by Colonel Francis C. Grevemberg	October 1, 1961	Fort Sill, Okla.
415 Ord. Co. (GAS) Commanded by Captain Samuel L. Johnson	October 1, 1961	Fort Campbell, Ky.
769 Signal Bn. (CC) Commanded by Lt.Col. O. J. Daigle, Jr.	October 15, 1961	Fort Polk, La.
3628th Ord. Co. (DAS) Commanded by Captain Charles J. Stelly	October 15, 1961	Fort Sill, Okla.

These Louisiana units were held on a standby basis pending further developments. But the strong display of U.S. arms and the firm resolve exhibited by President Kennedy tempered the rash Krushchev, and he retreated from a position of impudence to a conciliatory posture. Although the Russians' wall and barbed wire remained, further aggression was stymied.

Vietnam became the next arena for pressure tactics. The incendiary affairs in that unfortunate country began as a trouble spot for France whose influence in Indo-China began to wane in the German rout of World War II. Unlike Britain, which mothered and tutored its colonial subjects in parliamentary procedures that led to their independence, France's imperialism was repressive. Consequently, leaders for Vietnam independence soon fell under the influence of well-trained Communists who began an underground movement against the French. The Vietminh, the most disciplined among all dissenting groups under the leadership of Ho Chi Minh, soon became the dominant party. Ho Chi Minh had been schooled in Russian and was a volatile Communist besides being an ardent advocate of Vietnamese independence. By the time of the Japanese defeat, part of northern Vietnam had been liberated from their Nipponese rivals, and the Democratic Republic of Vietnam was proclaimed with Hanoi as its capitol and Ho Chi Minh as its president. Red China recognized the Hanoi government early in 1950 while the United States and Britain,

An Asian Adventure

in support of their World War II ally, recognized the Saigon regime of Bao Dai. From this point on, the United States became more and more enmeshed in the affairs of Vietnam.

France, with American aid, got mired in a war with the North Vietnamese which ended in a disgraceful defeat of Dienbienphu on May 7, 1954. By July 20, 1954, a "Geneva Agreement" truce was arranged between Hanoi and the French military command. The Seventeenth Parallel was agreed upon as a dividing line between the North and South Vietnamese. Bao Dai was succeeded by Prime Minister Ngo Dink Diem who was successful in gaining American aid. The United States went from sending simple aid to sending technicians, then a task force, then bombers, and finally fighting men who waged war for over ten years with huge expenditures of lives and money.

The National Guard was not mobilized for the Vietnam experience so gradual was the acceleration of the war efforts. But by the time the "policeaction" ended, with the United States pulling out its troops, South Vietnam had gone through several prime ministers, billions of American dollars, and had exhausted the patience of virtually every American citizen.

Soldiers were recruited by draft. Some National Guardsmen were called up but as individuals, but no Guard unit had the dubious honor or serving in this most terrible debacle in American history. They served as part of the Regular U.S. Army; 862 Louisianians lost their lives as a result of the Vietnam war. Unfortunately, the affair was never resolved—even to the extent of the Korean settlement. There were many reasons for the enormous loss of men and materiel, and historians will be assessing damages and causes for some time to come.

No matter what century, no matter what country, no matter the cause of the conflict, a mother always pays the painful price of her son's involvement, as is depicted in the figures of a mother bidding her son farewell. At top left the ready Guardsman is exemplified in the shadow of the Statue of Liberty, top center. The bottom of the drawing shows almost all of Louisiana with the locations of its fifty-one National Guard armories.

CHAPTER **14**

Reflections and the Future

Since World War II the National Guard has been strengthened until it represents an army in itself with ground troops, artillery, tanks, and a sophisticated air force. The tension and uncertainty of the Cold War era and even until the present *Detente*, the United States has been ever conscious of the potential threat from abroad. Greater emphasis has been placed upon the preparedness of the National Guard than at any time in history.

Pearl Harbor brought about a change, in the attitude of the high command; it also brought a unity in purpose, and concerted action. The pettiness and jealousy of the Regular Army toward the National Guard has been replaced by an awareness of the need for a homefront force capable of being mobilized quickly. The record of the National Guard in World War II brought home with a resounding emphasis of the value of that nucleus upon which an even larger segment of our fighting force was built. It was a miracle of manpower assembled and trained in time to go abroad and meet the enemy.

Our instincts are always greater than our pretentions; it is a natural phenomenon for man to protect himself. Whether it is a man in a cave with a stone ax, in the jungle with a spear, or on the plains with a bow and arrow, the instinct is to protect oneself. It is ironical that most of the great advances in technocracy have been put to a test on the battlefield initially in defense of a people or a principle and to vanquish an enemy. Surgical technique made its most rapid advances in history beginning with World War I because of the nature of the wounds of great numbers of men on the battlefields in Europe. In World War II, sulfa drugs and blood plasma were as important as ammunition.

Man's ideals and aspirations are interwoven inextricably with those of his country. And the extent to which he may pursue those goals of ideals and aspirations are limited in direct ratio to that resistance it may meet from outside forces. This resistance is defined by the word: *enemy*.

Since the dawn of history man has been struggling with political ideologies and the amassing or retention of worldly goods. If one is called into an army he will of course be up front, on stage, defending not only the political ideologies but often his country's borders. The lot of the soldier is a privilege as well as a duty.

> There lies a GI; he's been shot;
>   Where he is from, of what state,
> His name or regiment, I know not
>   But he has met the usual soldier's fate!

History is replete with evidence of vanishing races who chose peace at any price. In this age of propaganda, Marxists and their sympathizers shout, "Peace! Peace!" as if they invented the word. It is the potion that would lull and delude the complacent while the Communists pursue world conquest beyond the dreams of Alexander, Caesar, or Napoleon.

Democracy is cloaked in ideals without which no progress would be made in a turbulent and prosaic world.

Marxists are dedicated and disciplined. The discipline may be imposed by their rulers, but it is a force that must be recognized and met with at least equal or superior resistance. In a free society, discipline tends to be lax, but organizations such as the National Guard, manned by tens of thousands of citizens from every walk of life from thousands of cities and villages, are still maintaining the measure of discipline necessary for unified action in the face of an enemy. The individual who joins the National Guard requires altruistic motivation.

An army is an extension of its government, and in a true democracy it can only be a protector since its political makeup is representative of all the people. When the government is no longer democratic the army becomes an oppressor. An example is Cuba which proceeded from democracy to benevolent dictatorship and then to Communism; Portugal and India more recently have moved from democracies toward dictatorships. Other countries, particularly in South America, have gone from democracies to dictatorships in a short time. The army is a logical means of affecting a coup. In the United States the National Guard would be less likely to become the pawn of unscrupulous leaders than the Regular Army since the Guard is a more intimate and direct arm of the citizenry.

Today the United States of America stands almost alone in a world rife with aggression, contrasting ideologies in earnest opposition to our own. Our former allies, whose common interest, governmental and cultural, made it a natural alliance are fast fading from power and their influence in the council of nations has reached ebb-tide.

England, the most natural ally for freedom, is no longer a great power. And France, historically the first American ally, never recovered from humiliating defeat by the Germans.

The United States's influence in Indo-China has declined, and ties with Malaysia and the Philippines have been weakened as all countries adjust to accommodate continuing Communist aggression. The positions of Greece, Turkey, Portugal, and Italy in the North Atlantic Treaty Organization are uncertain because of the Communists. And India, once the democracy with the largest population, seems to have taken the road of totalitarianism.

The approach of the Bicentennial, which celebrates this country's independence, finds the United States faced with fighting for the same institutions and political ideals that were the goals of the Revolution.

Thomas Paine's famous statement is as applicable in 1976 as it was in the eighteenth century: "These are times that try men's souls. The summer soldier and the sunshine patriot will, in this crisis, shrink from the service of their country; but he that stand now, deserves the love and thanks of man and woman. Tyranny, like Hell, is not easily conquered."

Today the National Guard is stronger and better equipped than ever before. Throughout the fifty states it is, in size and caliber, worthy of any force in American history. It is more than just the home guard; it is the vanguard of peace and national defense. It is equipped and manned by average Americans who protect their nation. At the national level it consists of almost 500,000 persons with equipment valued at $7.2 million. Units are located in communities in every states, in Puerto Rico, the Virgin Islands, and the District of Columbia. They train a minimum of thirty-nine days a year annually and are summoned at various times to perform duties related to local emergencies. During 1974 alone more than thirty-six thousand Guardsmen were called up in forty-four states to protect life and save property in such catastrophes as storms, floods, fires, and street and prison riots.

There are twenty-seven hundred armories; in addition there are more than two thousand buildings used as warehouses, maintenance complexes, field training sites, and other facilities.

For the fiscal year, 1975, the National Guard was supported by $1.2 billion in federal appropriations. For 1976 that budget has been increased to $1.4 billion. In addition to its own equipment it is also in possession of $3.9 billion worth of Federal accouterments. To keep up with technical progress, large transfers are continually being sent to the Guard by the Federal government to replace worn and obsolete equipment.

Practically all of the army National Guard's 2,300 aircraft are helicopters of various types, but there are Light Observation: OH-6, OH-58; Troop and Gunship UH-1H/C/M "Huey"; Attack Gunship AH-1 "Cobra"; Support: CH-47 "Chinook," CH-54 "Skycrane," and OV-1 "Mohawk." A command and administrative: U-8, U-3, U-9, U-1 and U-6. Of its near half-million army and air officers and men, approximately 45,000 are technicians (employees) in company, detachment, and squadron type units totaling 3,275.

Its complement consists of (in round figures): 401,000 officers and men; 28,200 technicians; 25,500 blacks, and 4,150 women, in company and detachment units totaling 3,275.

The National Guard has a force structure of: eight combat divisions (5 Infantry, 2 Armored, 1 Mechanized); eighteen separate brigades (9 Infantry, 6 Mechanized, 3 Armored); 12 support-type brigade headquarters; 3 armored cavalry regiments; 158 separate combat battalions; 24 rear area operations support headquarters; 40 Special Forces companies and detachments; 681 additional companies and detachments.

At the opening of the Bicentennial year, the Louisiana National Guard is composed of 9,936 individuals who compose a land and air force, units of which are spread throughout the length and breadth

Reflections and the Future

of the state. As of July 1, 1975, the troop structure was composed of the following units:

LOUISIANA NATIONAL GUARD STATION LIST

July 1, 1975

UNIT	LOCATION	COMMANDER
Hq. La. Army & Air N.G.	Jackson Barracks	M.G. O. J. Daigle, Jr.
H.D. La. ARNG	Jackson Barracks	Cpt. Thomas J. Rodrigue, Jr.
241 Pub. Info. Det. (atchd. to HHD La. ARNG)	Jackson Barracks	Maj. Orleans A. Jambon
Hq. La. RCOM		
Commander	Jackson Barracks	B.G. Robert J. LeBlanc
356 Spt. Ctr.	Jackson Barracks	Col. Ralph D. Dwyer, Jr.
159th Cbt. Spt. Hosp.		
Commander	Jackson Barracks	Lt. Col. Rex F. Toole
256 Inf. Bde.		
Commander	Lafayette	B.G. Curney J. Dronet
H.C. 256 Inf. Bde (-)	Lafayette	Cpt. James W. Snyder
Det. 1 H.C. 256 Inf. Bde.	New Orleans	Cpt. Harold A. Kuhnell
Trp. E (-) 256 Cav.	Leesville	1st Lt. Robert E. Gillan
Det. 1 Trp. E 256 Cav.	DeRidder	1st Lt. Lynn A. Irvin
256 Engr. Co.	Opelousas	Cpt. Michael R. Fonger
812 Med. Det.	New Orleans	Cpt. Paul R. Lalumiere, Jr.
199 Spt. Bn.		
Commander	Alexandria	Lt. Col. Lucian J. Grass
H.D. 199 Spt. Bn.	Alexandria	1st Lt. Kenneth E. Ammons
Co. A	Lafayette	Cpt. James R. Lemaire
Co. B	St. Martinville	Cpt. Gregory M. Savoy
Co. C	Houma	Cpt. Curtis J. Prevost
Co. D	Winnfield	Cpt. Charles E. Crawford
1st Bn. 141 Arty.		
Commander	New Orleans	Lt. Col. Richard J. Gregory
Hq. Btry.	New Orleans	Cpt. Rene C. Jacques
Sv. Btry.	New Orleans	Cpt. Thomas J. Cuccia
Btry. A	New Orleans	Cpt. Clarke L. Lozes
Btry. B	New Orleans	Cpt. Russell A. Mayeur, Jr.
Btry. C	New Orleans	Cpt. Thomas J. Breslin, Jr.
1st Bn. 156 Inf.		
Commander	Shreveport	Lt. Col. Thomas O. Tyra
Hq. Co.	Shreveport	1st. Lt. Derryl W. Martindale
Spt. Co.	Shreveport	Cpt. James I. Cole
Co. A	Jonesboro	Cpt. Michael Synyard
Co. B	Shreveport	1st Lt. David L. Covington

1st Bn. 156 Inf. (cont'd)

Co. C (-)	Many	Cpt. Timothy T. Sloan
Det. 1 Co. C	Vivian	1st Lt. Silas W. Davis III

2nd Bn. 156 Inf.

Commander	Abbeville	Lt. Col. Joseph G. Martin, Jr.
Hq. Co.	Abbeville	Cpt. Charles L. Robichaux
Spt. Co.	Jeanerette	Cpt. Frank A. Catalano
Co. A	New Iberia	Cpt. Donald R. Belvin
Co. B	Franklin	Cpt. Thomas H. Lewis
Co. C	Breaux Bridge	Cpt. Clyde J. Guidry

3rd Bn. 156 Inf.

Commander	Lake Charles	Maj. Harry Montgomery
Hq. Co.	Lake Charles	Cpt. William J. Bennett
Spt. Co. (-)	Lake Charles	Cpt. Ronald G. Johnson
Det. 1 Spt. Co.	DeQuincy	1st Lt. Kenneth W. Harden
Co. A (-)	Natchitoches	Cpt. Dennis L. Smith
Det. 1 Co. A	Coushatta	1st Lt. Robert R. Wilson
Co. B. (-)	Crowley	1st Lt. Joseph W. Comeaux
Det. 1 Co. B	Eunice	2nd Lt. Glann J. Stelly
Co. C	Jennings	Cpt. Jimmy D. Potts, Jr.

204th Area Spt. Gp.

Commander	Jackson Barracks	Lt. Col. Murray F. Landry, Jr.
Hq. Co. 204 Area Spt. Gp.	Jackson Barracks	Cpt. Robert C. Derbyshire
156th Army Band	Jackson Barracks	C.W.2 Milton J. Boackle
39th M.P. Co. (-)	Jackson Barracks	Cpt. Joseph Graffia
Det. 1 39th M.P. Co.	Oakdale	2nd Lt. Harvey E. Scroggs, Jr.

165th Trans. Bn.

Commander	Monroe	Lt. Col. Harry T. Hyams III
H.D. 165th Trans. Bn.	Monroe	Cpt. Dolan R. Watson
1083rd Trans. Co.	Winnsboro	Cpt. Billy J. Burns
1086th Trans. Co.	Homer	1st Lt. George J. Fuller
1087th Trans. Co.	Minden	Cpt. William Thomas III

773rd Sup. & Svc. Bn.

Commander	Cp. Beauregard	Lt. Col. Robert L. Jordan
Hq. Co.	Cp. Beauregard	Cpt. Richard A. Burton
3671st Maint. Co.	Cp. Beauregard	Cpt. Jimmy F. Cockrell
3673rd Maint. Co. (-Det. 1)	Monroe	Cpt. Jay G. Blakeney
Det. 1 3673 Maint. Co.	Bastrop	1st Lt. Frank L. Carter

225th Engr. Gp.

Commander	Jackson Barracks	Col. Joseph L. Dabadie
Hq. Co.	Jackson Barracks	Cpt. James W. Shirah, Jr.

769th Engr. Bn.

Commander	Baton Rouge	Maj. Nolan R. Villar
Hq. Co.	Baton Rouge	1st Lt. Harold M. Rideau

Reflections and the Future 201

769th Engr. Bn. (cont'd)		
Co. A	Plaquemine	Cpt. Ronald R. E. Hebert
Co. B	New Roads	Cpt. Nick Cicero III
Co. C	Cp. Beauregard	1st Lt. Robert H. Wooten
Co. D	Donaldsonville	2nd Lt. Gerard W. Langlois
205th Engr. Bn.		
Commander	Bogalusa	Lt. Col. Ollie J. Blair
Hq. Co.	Bogalusa	2nd Lt. Clyde Woodward, Jr.
Co. A	Hammond	Cpt. Charles A. Adcox
Co. B (-)	Franklinton	Cpt. Clifford J. Schexnayder, Jr.
Det. 1 Co. B	Covington	2nd Lt. James H. Kostmayer, Jr.
Co. C (-)	Jackson Barracks	Cpt. William D. Schreck
Det. 1 Co. C	Slidell	1st Lt. Michael B. LaCour
Co. D	Thibodaux	Cpt. Timothy W. Toler
527th Engr. Bn.		
Commander	Bossier City	Maj. Ralph H. Brown
Hq. Co.	Bossier City	Cpt. Charles M. Partin
Co. A	Marksville	1st Lt. Lanny D. Cook
Co. B	Jonesville	Cpt. Ronald W. Burgess
Co. C	W. Monroe	1st Lt. Michael R. Morehead
Co. D	Ruston	Cpt. Freddie D. Mullins
2222nd Engr. Bn.		
Commander	Jackson Barracks	Lt. Col. Ralph E. Thompson
H.D. 2222nd Engr. Bn.	Jackson Barracks	Cpt. William E. Hutchison
2224 Engr. Co.	Jackson Barracks	Cpt. Paul E. Ayo, Jr.
2226 Engr. Co.	Jackson Barracks	Cpt. William J. Croft
2223rd Engr. Bn.		
Commander	Baton Rouge	Lt. Col. William H. Waters
H.D. 2223rd Engr. Bn.	Baton Rouge	Cpt. Donald J. Bringol
2225th Engr. Co.	Jena	1st Lt. Bennett C. Landreneau
2228th Engr. Co.	Gonzales	Cpt. Morton C. Hurston, Jr.
La. Air National Guard Units		
Hq. La. Air Nat. Guard	Jackson Barracks	Col. Carl L. Trippi
Hq. 159th Tac. Ftr. Gp.	New Orleans	Col. Edward J. Murphy
122nd Tac. Ftr. Sq.	New Orleans	Maj. James J. Hourin
159th Consol. Acft. Maint. Sq.	New Orleans	Maj. Donald M. Soignet
159th Combt. Spt. Sq.	New Orleans	Lt. Col. Frank P. Musso
159th Mobility Spt. Flt.	New Orleans	Maj. Elton G. Thompson
159th Wpns. Sys. Scty. Flt.	New Orleans	Cpt. Gerard A. Salles, Sr.
159th Tac. Clinic	New Orleans	Maj. Bruce B. Butler
159th Civil Engr. Flt.	New Orleans	Lt. Col. Ralph J. Melancon
159th Comm. Flt. Spt.	New Orleans	Cpt. Robert W. Givens
122nd Wea. Flt.	New Orleans	Lt. Col. John S. Cordero
214th Elec. Instl. Sq.	Jackson Barracks	Lt. Col. Charles E. Griffin

La. Air National
  Guard Units (cont'd)
236th Mbl. Comm. Flt.	Hammond	Maj. Robert G. Bolger
236th Flt. Fac. Flt.	Hammond	Maj. Alvin E. Porrier

It is an alert mobile force capable of being immediately assembled and put into action upon brief notice. At its disposal are: 4,322 vehicles and trailers; 10,595 small arms; 215 artillery pieces; 1,467 instrument and fire control equipment; 4,095 communication items; 1,148 special purpose items (bulldozers, graders and generators).

There are, organizational maintenance shops in strategic locations throughout the State. They are located in Shreveport, Monroe, Fort Polk, Plaquemine, Bogalusa, Lafayette, Abbeville, and Lake Charles, with three shops at Camp Beauregard and three at New Orleans.

The Louisiana National Guard has the following aircraft: Air National Guard: 15 F100-Ds; 5 F100-Fs; and 1 UC 131-Ds. Army National Guard: 13 OH 58s; 4 UH 1Bs; 7 UH 1H; and 1U3A.

The mission of the National Guard is set in precise terms:

> FEDERAL: "[It is to] provide reserve components of the Army and Air Force of the United States *capable of immediate expansion to war strength*, able to furnish units for service anywhere in the world, trained and equipped:
> (a) To defend critical areas of the United States against land, seaborne or airborne invasion; (b) To assist in covering the mobilization and concentration of the remainder of the reserve forces; (c) To participate by units in all types of operations, including the offensive, either in the United States or overseas."

STATE: "The mission of the National Guard of this state is to provide sufficient organizations so trained and equipped as to enable them to function efficiently at existing strength in the protection of life and property, and the preservation of peace, order and public safety, under competent orders of the State authorities."

STAFF ORGANIZATION, July 1, 1975

Adjutant General . . . . O. J. Daigle, Jr., M.G.
Assistant Adjutant General . . . . A. M. Stroud, Jr., B.G.
Chief of Staff . . . . Karl N. Smith, Col.
Director, Personnel and Administration . . . . . Sidney J. Scholl, Jr., Col.
Director, Plans and Training . . . . Reginald G. Booth, Col.
Director, Facilities Engineering . . . . William H. Hogan, Col.
Director, Supply and Services . . . . Henry J. Lala, Col.
Director, Maintenance . . . . George C. Duncan, Col.

Director, Military Support. . . . . Michael E. Poll, Col.
Chief of Staff (Air) . . . . Carl L. Trippi, Col.
Commander, Jackson Barracks. . . . . James L. Roberts, Col.
Commander, Camp Beauregard . . . . Joseph L. Dabadie, Jr., Col.
Public Affairs Officer. Ernest N. Souhlas, Maj.
Administrative Officer (Air) . . . . Maxime J. Montz, Jr., Maj.
State Judge Advocate. . . . . Eugene W. McGehee, Col.
Director, Medical Activities. . . . . Rex F. Toole, Jr., Lt. Col.
Director, Selective Service Section . . . . .Edward M. Hufft, Col.
State Chaplain . . . . John A. Tomasovich, Col. (CH)

THE ADJUTANTS GENERAL

1. JOSEPH DEVILLE de GOUTIN BELLECHASSE 1803-1804
2. FRANCOIS DUTILLET 1805
3. HENRY HOPKINS 1805-1811
4. ALEXANDER LANEUVILLE 1812-1827
5. ANATOLE PEYCHAUD. 1828-1831
6. FRANCOIS GAIENNIE 1832-1835
7. PERSIFOR SMITH 1836-1843
8. JOHN S. ARMANT. 1844-1846
9. CHARLES N. ROWLEY 1846-1852
10. HORATIO DAVIS 1852-1853
11. S. W. WESTMORE 1853-1854
12. SAMUEL LOVETT WALDO. 1855
13. MAURICE GRIVOT. . . . . 1855-1863 *
14. CHARLES LeDOUX ELGEE . . . . .1863 *
15. LEMUEL P. CONNOR . . . . .1863 *
16. THOMAS COURTLAND MANNING . . . . 1863 *
17. THEODORE G. HUNT 1864-1865**
18. JOHN L. SWIFT 1864-1865**
19. WILLIAM MITHOFF, JR.. . . . . .1865**
20. G. MASON GRAHAM. . . . . 1866-1867 †
21. GEORGE AUGUSTUS SHERIDAN . . . . . .1869 †

22. JAMES LONGSTREET........... 1870-1872 †
23. WILLIAM P. HARPER ....1872 †
24. HENRY STREET .... 1872-1875 †
25. JACK WHARTON............... 1875-1877 †
26. GEORGE BALDY....................1877 †
27. DAVID BRADFUTE PENN ....1877††
28. ISAAC W. PATTON 1877-1878
29. PIERRE GUSTAVE TOUTANT
    BEAUREGARD 1878-1888
30. WILLIAM G. BURT 1888-1890
31. THOMAS FLETCHER BELL 1890-1896
32. ALLEN JUMEL 1896-1904
33. DAVID THEOPHILIUS
    STAFFORD................ 1904-1912
34. OSWALD W. McNEESE 1912-1916
35. CECIL C. McCRORY 1916-1919
36. ALLEN T. HUNTER............. 1919-1920
37. LOUIS A. TOOMBS 1920-1928
38. RAYMOND H. FLEMING 1928-1948
39. RAYMOND F. HUFFT........... 1948-1952
40. RAYMOND H. FLEMING 1952-1956
41. RAYMOND F. HUFFT........... 1956-1960
42. RAYMOND H. FLEMING 1960-1964
43. ERBON WISE.................. 1964-1968
44. DAVID WADE 1968-1972
45. THOMAS BONNER (acting)....... 1969-1970
46. O. J. DAIGLE, JR. 1972-

* Confederate Louisiana
** Federal Louisiana
† Reconstruction Louisiana
†† First home-rule adjutant general.

Louisiana has flown under ten flags, more than any other state of the Union. Today Louisianians pursue life, liberty, and happiness under the Stars and Stripes, depending on the military leadership of Major General O. J. Daigle, Jr., Adjutant General of the state, shown bottom right.

CHAPTER 15

The Adjutants General

Researching the earlier adjutants general of Louisiana was sometimes hampered by a scarcity of records. Fortunately, more care has been taken in later years to preserve material related to the history of those who have held the highest military command in the state. From Joseph Deville de Goutin Bellechasse, the man considered to be the first adjutant general, to the present Major General O. J. Daigle, Jr., persons of varying complexities of character and background were encountered. Each represented the tempo of his times and was a prominent figure whose background and demeanor fitted him for his command. Bellechasse commanded during the fledging days when the Louisiana Territory first became a part of the United States and when the accouterments of war were muskets, cannons, horses, and sabers in contrast to General Daigle's highly mobile, sophisticated weaponry and communication systems. The following are brief sketches of the forty-six adjutants general:

JOSEPH DEVILLE DE GOUTIN BELLECHASSE
1803-1804

Napoleon had sent Pierre Clement Laussat to New Orleans to administer Louisiana when Spain retroceded the territory to France by the secret Treaty of San Ildefonso of October 1, 1800. Possession was delayed for political reasons and Laussat did not reach New

Orleans until March, 1803. In the meantime Napoleon decided to sell Louisiana to the United States, and Laussat arrived in time to make preparations for its transfer.

It was Laussat who appointed Bellechasse as chief of the Louisiana militia in 1803, commenting: "In the first place, I secured a chief for the Militia, and I was lucky indeed to lay my hands on an officer who had served for 24 years, who was not personally well disposed to the Marquis De Casa Calva [Spanish notable] on account of his having been dismissed from active service on favorable terms, and who enjoyed an excellent reputation and much popularity in the country. He is, besides, the owner of considerable property in the vicinity of the city and his name is Joseph De Goutin Bellechasse."

Given the rank of colonel, Bellechasse was placed in command of the militia on November 30, 1803. When the territory was transferred on December 20, he headed the three hundred men who participated in the ceremonies. And when the U.S. Congress, on October 1, 1804, created the Territory of Orleans, Bellechasse was appointed a member of the legislative counsel. However, he refused since he opposed the partition of Louisiana.

Bellechasse served with distinction on the governing council of Louisiana. He was also a delegate to the constitutional convention, which met on November 11, 1811, to frame the first constitution under which Louisiana was admitted to the Union.

He was a natural leader, but in a letter dated March 13, 1804, Colonel Bellechasse wrote to Governor W. C. C. Claiborne giving his reasons for resigning his post: "Ill health, insufficiency of means, and impossibility of explaining myself in the English language."

FRANCOIS DUTILLET
1805

Francois Dutillet, appointed adjutant general by Governor William C. C. Claiborne, was a veteran of the War of 1812 and served as a justice of the peace. He was born in New Orleans on July 5, 1764, and died there on March 18, 1844.

HENRY HOPKINS
1805-1811

Little is known about Henry Hopkins other than that he was a native of Baltimore, Maryland, a veterans of the United States Army, and that he settled in New Orleans. He received his appointment on November 1, 1805, from Governor Claiborne and resigned on November 11, 1811.

ALEXANDER LANEUVILLE
1812-1827

Alexander Laneuville was the first of the adjutants general to serve a long tenure, holding that office for sixteen years. The information on Laneuville is sparse, but records do indicate that he was a captain in the artillery in the United States Army and was a city court judge when he died on March 25, 1844. Laneuville served five governors—W. C. C. Claiborne, Jacques Phillips Villere, Thomas Bolling Robertson, Henry Schylet Thibodaux, and Henry S. Johnson, who ascended to the governorship from the presidency of the state Senate.

ANATOLE PEYCHAUD
1828-1831

Anatole Peychaud is another adjutant general about whom little is known. He served under four governors, Henry S. Johnson, Pierre Derbigny, Armand Beauvais, and Jacques Dupre. His appointment was confirmed on February 5, 1829.

FRANCOIS GAIENNIE
1832-1835

Francois Gaiennie served four years under Governor Andre Bienvenu Roman. Born in New Orleans in 1791, he was the son of Jeanne Marguerite (*dit* Mannette) Sarde of New Orleans and Rene Urbain Gaiennie of France. An Alderman of the city of New Orleans, he served during the War of 1812 as first lieutenant of the Fourth Regiment, Louisiana militia, known as Morgan's Fourth.

In 1823 he became commander of that Fourth Regiment. On May 29, 1826, he married Desiree Lalande de Ferrier, who was the daughter of Marie Hyacinthe Arnoult and Louis Lalande de Ferrier.

He was elected to the state legislature, taking office on January 1, 1827. In 1829 he was promoted to brigadier general of the First Louisiana Brigade. The following year he was elected an alderman for the city of New Orleans. He retired from public life and moved to a plantation on the Red River near Cloutierville.

He met death in a duel against General Pierre Bossier in Natchitoches Parish on September 18, 1839. The duelists used rifles at forty paces. Mrs. Gaiennie died in New Orleans on March 12, 1854.

PERSIFOR SMITH
1836-1843

Persifor Smith was born in Philadelphia, Pennsylvania, in 1799. After being graduated from Princeton University, where he was first in his class (1812 or 1814), be began to practice law. Arriving in New Orleans in 1820, he quickly settled down and married Mademoiselle Bareau, daughter of Francois Bareau.

In 1836 he commanded a company of Louisiana volunteers and went to Florida with them, joining General Zachary Taylor to fight the Seminoles. He served as a brevet brigadier general in the Mexican War, saw action at Monterrey, and then was transferred to General Winfield Scott. When a regiment of mounted riflemen was formed, President Polk appointed Smith its colonel. But he earned a brevet major general rank for gallant and meritorious conduct in the battles of Contreras and Churubusco, Mexico. *Brevet* denoted temporary rank.

Smith was a professional soldier serving in the military divisions of California, Texas, and Kansas. He died on May 17, 1858, en route to Fort Leavensworth. His wife died in 1853. He had served as adjutant general under Governors Edward Douglass White and Andre Bienvenu Roman.

JOHN S. ARMANT
1844-1846

John S. Armant was a wealthy sugar planter, and his memory endures in the name of a large sugar refinery and plantation near Vacherie. Born in September, 1801, he was the son of Rose Carmelite Cantrelle and J. B. Armant. He married Amelie Fuselier De La Claire and became wealthy and influential.

Appointed adjutant general by Governor Alexandre Mouton, he served for a while under Governor Issac Johnson. He was also a state senator for many years and remained a leader in the sugar industry.

His wife preceeded him in death, dying on August 21, 1852; he died on August 12, 1859, in his fifty-eighth year. Their tombs are in the Catholic Cemetery at St. James.

CHARLES N. ROWLEY
1846-1852

Charles N. Rowley was a native of North Granville, Washington County, New York, the son of Mehitable Needham and Samuel Rowley. He was christened Calvin but changed his name to Charles when he began practicing law in Troy, New York. Hearing of the sugar boom in Louisiana, he headed South with money to invest. He purchased extensive acreage near Vidalia, where he began his military career by joining the Sparrow Volunteers. He became paymaster of the Fourth (Montezuma) Regiment of the Louisiana militia. He became a colonel on June 5, 1844, and an aide to Governor Mouton.

On February 15, 1846, he was appointed adjutant and inspector general by Governor Issac Johnson. He was reappointed on March 13, 1850, by Governor Joseph Marshall Walker and was confirmed on March 24, 1846, by the Louisiana Senate.

Rowley was married, first to Jane Kemp, widow of Francis S. Girault, and upon her death to Eugenia M. Soria of Natchez, Mississippi. He died on July 10, 1869, in Rio de Janerio, Brazil.

HORATIO DAVIS
1852-1853

Horatio Davis was born in Pennsylvania in 1790, the son of Colonel Samuel Boyer Davis. He attended St. Mary's College at Baltimore, Maryland, and served in the United States Army. His wife was Naomi DuBourg. He was a warden of the St. Louis Cathedral.

Davis was appointed adjutant general by Governor Joseph Marshall Walker. At the age of sixty-three he died (October 17, 1857) and was buried in St. Louis Cemetery No. 1, New Orleans.

S. W. WESTMORE
1853-1854

S. W. Westmore was born M. West Moore in Charleston, South Carolina, in 1806. His father, Stephen Moore, a prominent banker of Charleston, secured a West Point appointment for his son. S. W. Westmore graduated from West Point with a commission of lieutenant and at the age of twenty-three was sent to New Orleans. He served with distinction in the Mexican War under General Zachary

Taylor. Just after the war he killed a fellow officer in a duel, an incident that preyed heavily upon his mind throughout his long life.

Because there was another man in the city of New Orleans named Samuel W. West Moore, he had his name legally changed to Samuel M. Westmore.

He married a New Orleans lady and had two sons, Robert and William. His only daughter became Mrs. King and lived in Charleston. His son William served as a hospital steward under Westmore's brother, Dr. Preston Moore, who was surgeon general of the Confederacy. William, who was completely deaf, was forced to give up his position and return to New Orleans. He studied at Charity Hospital and graduated as a physician but died a few years later. General Westmore's first wife died of yellow fever, and his second wife, Louise Hartz, whom he married in 1876, lost her mind when her child died soon after birth.

Westmore was appointed adjutant general by Governor Joseph Marshall Walker and was reappointed by Governor Paul Octave Hebert, his close friend.

The general gave his daughter and son-in-law a fine plantation in South Carolina. His son Robert located in New York City where he became an outstanding journalist. General Westmore lived to be ninety and died in an accident on February 4, 1896.

SAMUEL LOVETT WALDO
1855

Samuel Lovett Waldo, appointed by Governor Paul Octave Hebert, served a very short time as adjutant general—from May through October of 1855. He was for some years a member of the state militia and must have made a very good impression, for he was relatively young at the time of his appointment. He died October 19, 1855, at the age of thirty-nine.

MAURICE GRIVOT
1855-1863*

Maurice Grivot was appointed adjutant general by Governor Hebert and received reappointments by Governors Robert Charles Wickliffe and Thomas Overton Brooks. Well educated, Grivot practiced law in New Orleans; he died on March 7, 1875, at the age of sixty-one.

CHARLES LeDOUX ELGEE *
1863

Charles LeDoux Elgee was born in Rapides Parish and was a close friend of the Confederate governor, Thomas Overton Moore, who appointed him adjutant general. He was at one time a captain in the Second Cavalry Regiment of Louisiana and on the staff of Governor Moore. Elgee's mother was a LeDoux, of a Louisiana French family, and his father, John K. Elgee, was born in Ireland and migrated to Louisiana, eventually settling in Rapides Parish to practiced law.

In 1863 Louisiana was federally occupied, and thirteen parishes— Orleans, St. Bernard, Jefferson, Plaquemines, St. John, St. Charles, St. James, Ascension, Assumption, Lafourche, Terrebonne, St. Mary, and St. Martin—were under Federal jurisdiction. Adjutant General Elgee's power was restricted to that area controlled by the Confederacy, and his service was only for about one month. He died November 15, 1864.

LEMUEL P. CONNER *
1863

Lemuel P. Conner was another adjutant general who served the Louisiana Confederate state government and was appointed by Governor Moore. At this period of Louisiana's history there were two governors. Thomas Overton Moore for the Confederacy and General George F. Shipley who was military governor of the portion within Union lines.

Conner was a delegate to the state's constitutional convention of January 26, 1861, which resulted in the secession of Louisiana from the Union. He had represented the parishes of Madison, Tensas, and Concordia. He was also active in the state militia prior to the war and attained the rank of major in the Confederate army. Conner, like Elgee, served about one month.

THOMAS COURTLAND MANNING *
1863

Thomas Courtland Manning was born in Edenton, North Carolina, on September 14, 1831, the son of Sarah Houghton and Joseph Manning. He received his education at public schools of Edenton, and the University of North Carolina, where he received an honorary law degree in 1878 though he did not graduate.

He began his adult life by teaching school in Edenton and at the same time studied law and was eventually admitted to the North Carolina Bar. He married Mary Blair on January 18, 1848, and practiced law in Edenton until 1855 when he moved to Louisiana. He was a States' Right Democrat. Settling in Alexandria in Rapides Parish, he continued his law career. He was a member of the secession convention and was on Governor Moore's staff. When war began he was a lieutenant in the local military force that joined the Confederacy.

Governor Moore appointed Manning adjutant with the rank of brigadier general, in 1863. In 1864 Governor Henry Watkins Allen appointed him an associate justice of the Louisiana supreme court. In 1887 he became chief justice and in 1882 was again appointed to the supreme court. He served as vice-president of the state democratic convention that decided Louisiana's choice for president in 1876 (Samuel Jones Tilden).

He gained national recognition when President Grover Cleveland appointed him United States minister to Mexico in 1886. He had been appointed to fill a vacancy for the United States Senate by Governor William Pitt Kellogg in 1887 but was denied a seat by Congress. He died on October 11, 1887, in New York City while attending a meeting of the board of trustees of the Peabody Educational Fund, of which he was a member.

Manning was a man commanding demeanor and keen intellect. He served as adjutant general during the difficult time when Louisiana was under divided jurisdiction during the Civil War. His abilities were respected on both sides, and he is recorded as one of the intellectuals in Louisiana's history.

THEODORE G. HUNT **
1864-1865

Theodore G. Hunt was the eldest of five brothers, all of whom were noted for their legal abilities. His brother Randall Hunt was considered one of the greatest attorneys in North American.

Born in Charleston, South Carolina, on October 23, 1805, Theodore was the son of Louisa Gaillard and Thomas Hunt, the latter an immigrant from Nassau. One of Mrs. Hunt's two brothers was a United States senator (John Gaillard) from South Carolina for twenty-one years.

Well educated in the liberal arts, Theodore Hunt moved to New Orleans in 1833 and soon became a prominent and successful lawyer. His brother Doctor Thomas Hunt accompanied him to Louisiana, and he too gained notice in business and social circles.

Theodore Hunt became a district attorney, was elected to the state legislature, became a United States congressman, and was chosen as a judge of the First District court and also served as a judge of the criminal court. He joined the Fifth Louisiana Infantry as a colonel on May 10, 1861, at Deep Creek, Virginia. He led the Fifth Louisiana Regiment through the Peninsula campaign and the Seven Days battle. Resigning his commission, he transferred to the trans-Mississippi Department and was commissioned adjutant general of Louisiana with the rank of brigadier general.

While on duty in Shreveport as adjutant general, he married Mrs. Cornelia Ford. One son was born to this union—Randall Hunt. Theodore G. Hunt died in New Orleans on November 17, 1893, respected and admired.

JOHN L. SWIFT **
1864-1865

Captain John L. Swift was a member of the Union army, in command of the Forty-first Massachusetts Volunteers, Third Massachusetts Cavalry, and an acting aide-de-camp to Brigadier General C. Grover. Swift's appointment was one of military expediency during the Federal occupation of Louisiana. His residence in Louisiana lasted only as long as he was militarily necessary.

WILLIAM MITHOFF, JR. **
1865

William Mithoff, Jr., was born in Carrollton, Louisiana, now part of the city of New Orleans, on March 11, 1843. His father, a native of Osterado, Germany, was born September 11, 1811, and christened Hector William Mithoff; he later dropped the Hector. William, Sr., migrated from Germany to Pennsylvania, then to Ohio, Jefferson Parish, Louisiana (Harahan), and Fredericksburg, Virginia. He married Emma Margaret Thompson of Bordertown, New Jersey, who was the daughter of a Methodist minister. William and Emma then settled in Carrollton.

William, Jr., was educated in the New Orleans public schools and at the Louisiana Military Seminary at Pineville, forerunner of Louisiana State University, which was then under the presidency of William Tecumseh Sherman. Mithoff was a lieutenant with the New Orleans Volunteers and joined the Second Indiana Regiment as a Union soldier.

After the war he attended the University of Louisiana (now Tulane University) to study law, graduating in April, 1867. He married Gertrude Hyman, daughter of Dolores Gonzales and Chief Justice William Bryan Hyman, on September 10, 1869. William Mithoff, Jr., died on March 17, 1886, and was buried in Arlington National Cemetery, Washington, D.C. He was appointed adjutant general on July 3, 1865, by Governor James Madison Wells. Mithoff's sword is in the National Guard museum at Jackson Barracks, a gift from one of his daughters.

GEORGE MASON GRAHAM †
1866-1867

George Mason Graham was born in Fairfax County, Virginia, on August 21, 1807, the son of Elizabeth Mary Anne Barnes Hove (widow of George Mason) and George Graham.

He received a West Point appointment through the influence of his father but did not complete the required course, resigning in April, 1826. He then entered the University of Virginia but quit in 1828. During 1828 Graham was sent to Louisiana by his father to assess the family's holdings in Rapides Parish, because the cotton season had been unproductive.

His first marriage was to the daughter of Richard Smith in Washington D.C., on October 2, 1834; she died on December 9, 1835. His second marriage was to a daughter of Captain N. G. Wilkinson, on September 7, 1847, but she died on March 19, 1855. His third wife was to the childless widow of one of his relatives; this marriage was pledged on October 2, 1867. Six children were born of his three marriages; a daughter, Amby B. Graham, married David T. Stafford, who served as Louisiana adjutant general from 1904 to 1912.

George Mason Graham served in the Mexican War and saw action at Monterrey. He had been elected major of the Rapides Parish Regiment prior to the Mexican War, and after the conflict he became a brigadier general of the brigade from Avoyelles and Rapides parishes. He was appointed adjutant general on March 23, 1866, with the rank of brigadier general. Governor James Madison Wells commented, "Well, gentlemen, I intend to appoint Graham—I know he's honest."

Graham became vice-president of the first Board of supervisors of Louisiana State University. He suffered a great loss of money and property as a result of the Civil War. His positions as adjutant general paid him an annual stipend of $3,000, which was his only income and in sharp contrast to his former wealth.

A fall from his horse on October 9, 1868, caused him to be paralyzed and he resigned his post as adjutant general because he felt he could not perform his duties adequately. Despite his infirmities, he lived to the age of eighty-three, dying on January 31, 1891.

GEORGE AUGUSTUS SHERIDAN †
1869

A native of Millbury, Massachusetts, George Augustus Sheridan was born February 22, 1842. He grew up in Millbury, attended school there, and entered Yale College.

When the Civil War began he was passing through Chicago and got caught up with the excitement of military enlistments and joined the Eighty-eighth Illinois as a private. He soon became a captain and made a tour of battles until he was seriously wounded at Chickamauga.

Upon recovering from his wounds, he moved to Louisiana where he became active in local Republican party politics. A gifted speaker, he commanded attention in political circles. Governor Henry C. Warmoth appointed him adjutant general in 1869, but the state legislature refused to appropriate sufficient funds to maintain the state militia, causing him to comment, "I have to state that the effective Militia of this State for the year mentioned consists of one Adjutant General; he was well organized, thoroughly drilled and moderately well equipped." Despite his pleas, the legislature did not respond; nor did they provide sufficient funds. Sheridan served one year as adjutant general without an army and was caught in the crossfire of partisan politics of Governor Warmoth's administration.

In 1872 Sheridan was elected Republican congressman-at-large from Louisiana but did not take his seat immediately because the election was contested by P. B. S. Pinchback. The seat was finally settled in favor of Sheridan.

Sheridan gained national attention when he challenged Robert

Ingersoll's attack on Christianity, giving his views in a candid, precise manner in his "Answer To Ingersoll." He resettled in Washington, D.C., where he was appointed recorder of deeds for the District of Columbia in 1877.

JAMES LONGSTREET †
1870-1872

James Longstreet was one of the great generals of the Confederacy, though the loss at Gettysburg has been attributed to him by many of his contemporaries. His post-Civil War alliances generated continued animosity towards him, and he remained controversial.

Born in Edgefield District, South Carolina, in 1821, he spent part of his early life in Alabama. Upon his graduation from West Point in 1842, he serve in Indian campaigns and the Mexican War. He was a major in the United States Army, at the outbreak of the war but resigned his commission and cast his lot with the Confederacy as a brigadier general. He took part in the first battle of Bull Run and against McClellan in the Peninsular campaign. At the second battle of Bull Run he distinguished himself as a commander. At Fredericksburg he adeptly commanded the Confederates' left.

At Gettysburg he commanded the Confederate's right wing and directed some of the bitterest fighting. He also served in Tennessee, especially at Chattanooga and near Knoxville but rejoined Robert E. Lee in 1864. He was wounded while leading an attack.

After the Civil War, Longstreet settled in New Orleans. He became a Republican, thereby alienating himself with southerners in general. He was also a personal friend of General U. S. Grant. He entered the insurance business, became involved with Reconstruction, and its scandals implicated him by association if not by conviction.

Longstreet was appointed adjutant general on May 13, 1870, by Governor Henry C. Warmoth and served for two years in that capacity, resigning on April 19, 1872. He continued his association with the carpetbaggers and had the ingnominious duty of firing upon former Confederates and civilians during the dispute between the White Leaguers, who supported McEnery for governor, and the forces of Kellogg, who contested the election of 1874. In this battle at the foot of Canal Street, a rebel yell was shouted by the White Leaguers, and observers stated that Longstreet blanched when he heard the sound.

The Adjutants General

Influential in national politics, he was appointed minister to Turkey by President Grant and served as commissioner of Pacific railroads under William McKinley and Theodore Roosevelt.

Longstreet retired to Gainesville, Georgia, suffering from cancer of the eye and generally poor health. He died there on January 2, 1904, of pneumonia.

WILLIAM P. HARPER †
1872

When James Longstreet resigned as adjutant general, Governor Warmoth appointed William P. Harper on June 14, and he held position until November 21, 1872. He served only five months as adjutant general and resigned when he was elected civil sheriff of the parish of Orleans.

Harper was born in New Orleans on November 5, 1835, to a family with early identity in Louisiana. His mother was a native of New Orleans, as was his father, Captain H. S. Harper, who was chief of police during the tenures of Samuel J. Peters and Joshua Baldwin. The Harpers were originally from Pennsylvania, but his maternal French ancestors had found refuge in New Orleans during the slave uprisings in Santo Domingo at the turn of the nineteenth century.

Educated in the public schools of New Orleans, William Harper was graduated from college in Mississippi. In 1861 he was with the Seventh Louisiana Infantry, being a member of the Second Company of Crescent Rifles. He fought with Hay's Brigade at First Manassas and engaged in many more battles, being attached to Stonewall Jackson's corps in Virginia. He participated in the Valley campaign and action near Richmond and was with Lee when he surrendered at Appomattox.

Harper was wounded at the Battle of Sharpsburg (Antietam) and was captured by the enemy. After recovering from his wounds while in prison, he was exchanged. Upon his return to the field he was recommended by Brigadier General Francis T. Nicholls to be adjutant general of the Second Louisiana Brigade.

He was again wounded and captured at the Battle of Rappahannock and was sent back to Johnson's Island where he remained for one year and was then exchanged. He returned to his brigade where he served until the end of the war. Prior to his appointment to the post of adjutant general, he was secretary of the Louisiana

Equitable Company and had been a captain of the Seventh Louisiana Regiment.

William P. Harper died on December 3, 1875 at the age of forty, and his body was interred in Metairie Cemetery. His wife died on October 5, 1920; five children survived.

HENRY STREET †
1872-1875

Henry Street was born in Brooklyn, New York, and came to New Orleans as a member of the Seventh New York Regiment during the Civil War, remaining there at its end. For many years, he maintained a residence at Carondelet House located at 18 Dryades Street.

Active in Republic politics, Street gained some notice and for a time held a position in the Office of Internal Revenue. He commanded the First Regiment of the Knights of Pythias with the rank of colonel. He was also a mason.

He was appointed adjutant general on November 13, 1872, with the rank of brigadier general by Governor Warmoth and served a while under Kellogg. He died in November, 1897, in New Orleans and was buried in Brooklyn.

JACK WHARTON †
1875-1877

Jack Wharton is another adjutant general of whom little is known. He was a native of Baltimore, Maryland, but how he or why he came to New Orleans is not known.

He lived at 330 St. Charles Street for some years and was a member of the Mississippi Steam Fire Company No. 2. In all probability Wharton was another Union soldier who stayed in the South after the war and became a member of the local militia.

Governor William P. Kellogg appointed him adjutant general. He died at the age of fifty on April 7, 1882, and was buried in the family tomb at Hagerstown, Maryland. He was a United States marshal at the time of his death.

GEORGE BALDY †
1877

George Baldy is an obscure figure who served a brief time as adjutant general. The *Daily Democrat*, a New Orleans newspaper, published a brief news item revealing that he was indeed adjutant general. In the *Daily Democrat* on May 15, 1877, appeared Special Order No. 6, of January 18, 1877, and another brief item appeared on May 17, 1877, indicating that Baldy held the position. In the files of the National Guard there is also a document bearing his title and name.

DAVID BRADFUTE PENN ††
1877

David Bradfute Penn ran for lieutenant governor in the election of 1872 with John McEnery, the aspirant for governor. Although they claimed the election, it was nullified by the Returning Board of the carpetbag government, and the Republican William Pitt Kellogg and his ticket were declared the victors.

Penn was born in Lynchburg, Virginia (1836), but lived in New Orleans from the age of thirteen, his father having settled there some years before. College, Civil War, and Reconstruction interrupted what could have been a notable career, for Penn was a brilliant student with a prestigious family background.

There is some mystery concerning his role as adjutant general. Little evidence of his activities exists, but his alma mater, Virginia Military Institute, in a profile of him, states that he was appointed adjutant general by Governor Nicholls and "held this position until the government was fully established." Nicholls, in that election of 1876, which was bitterly disputed by the Republican forces under Stephen B. Packard, established a de facto government upon learning the results of the returns. In doing this he appointed a supreme court, assembled a legislative branch and swore in five hundred men to keep peace and order. Penn was most likely appointed commander of that five-hundred-man force and as such was recognized as the adjutant general, since he was indeed the highest military officer appointed by the governor. Penn, who served only until the Nicholls government was formally recognized by Congress and its investigative committee, should nevertheless be credited with being the first adjutant general of the post-Reconstruction era. His was the briefest term of all, but it was official.

David B. Penn attended Spring Hill College at Mobile, Alabama, and then entered Virginia Military Institute, graduating in the class of 1856 with high honors. His fellow cadets chose him to be the recipient of the statue of George Washington, an honor accorded to the valedictorian. He then studied law at the University of Virginia and in the law office of his brother-in-law in Richmond. He returned to New Orleans in 1858, and organized a company that became part of the Louisiana Seventh Regiment. He was soon to be promoted to major and was among the first men to arrive in Virginia to fight for the Confederacy.

Noted for his bravery and devotion to duty in the war, he was wounded twice, was taken prisoner on two occasions, and was an intimate friend of Stonewall Jackson who had taught at V.M.I. during Penn's attendance there. Penn died November 15, 1902.

ISAAC W. PATTON
1877-1878

Born in Fredericksburg, Virginia, Isaac W. Patton was the scion of one of that state's most distinguished families. His grandfather was Hugh Mercer, a general in the American Revolution; he was killed at the Battle of Princeton. John M. Patton, Isaac's father, a practicing lawyer in Richmond, served the Fredericksburg District as a representative in the U.S. Congress and was a member of the governor's council. Isaac received his early education at Fairfax Institution near Alexandria and upon graduation began studying law in his father's office.

He joined the army at the outbreak of the Mexican War and was appointed a second lieutenant in the Tenth U.S. Infantry by President Polk, a friend of the Patton family. Assigned to the command of General Zachary Taylor, Patton arrived at the battle scene too late for action. At the end of the war he was transferred to the Third Artillery Regiment where he served until 1855, at which time he resigned from the army. In 1855 he married Frances F. Merritt, daughter of a prominent physician.

In 1857 he moved to Madison Parish, Louisiana, bought a plantation, and planted cotton. His father-in-law had holdings below New Orleans which Patton planted in sugarcane. He was one of the few men in Louisiana history to have managed or owned plantations at opposite ends of the state—he planted sugarcane in the south and cotton in the north.

When Louisiana seceded he volunteered and was made captain of a company stationed at Proctorsville. He was later sent to take command of the batteries at Chalmette. When Farragut's fleet breached the defenses of the Mississippi River, Patton withdrew his forces to Camp Moore in Tangipahoa Parish to avoid surrendering. Later he became a colonel in the Twenty-Third Louisiana Infantry and served at the seige of Vicksburg, where he received a grievous hip injury and was taken prisoner. Shortly afterward he was exchanged. He saw action at Mobile, Alabama, took part of the fighting at Spanish Fort, was with the surrender and again taken prisoner, but was soon released.

At war's end he became a commission agent, speculating in cotton and sugar. In 1872 he was elected criminal sheriff and in 1874 was a captain of a company that engaged in the battle on September 14, when the White League fought Federal troops and the Metropolitan Police in an effort to seat John McEnery instead of William P. Kellogg in the disputed election.

Governor Francis T. Nicholls appointed Patton adjutant general. Patton died February 5, 1890.

PIERRE GUSTAVE TOUTANT BEAUREGARD
1878-1888

One of the most colorful figures in southern military history was P. G. T. Beauregard. Born in St. Bernard Parish, just south of New Orleans on May 28, 1818, he personified the Creole who was derivative of Louisiana's early French and Spanish settlers. Historians have referred to him as the Great Creole, and his somewhat pompous commanding manner, plus his rich family heritage and soldiery added to his legend.

The family's name was actually Toutant-Beauregard but while at the United States Military Academy at West Point, New York, he dropped the Toutant as part of his surname and used only Beauregard because it placed him near the top of the roll call of students.

Beauregard was graduated with honors from West Point in the class of 1838 and became a second Lieutenant in the Corps of Engineers. In the Mexican War he was wounded twice, and he was cited for gallantry. He served on the staff of General Winfield Scott and achieved fame in the taking of Mexico City.

A career soldier, he was named superintendent of the military academy at West Point in 1860, but when civil war seemed imminent, he resigned and offered his services to the South. His resignation became effective in February, 1861, and soon after he was made a brigadier general of the Confederacy and sent to command the forces at Charleston. Acting upon the instruction of his government, he fired on Fort Sumter and started the Civil War. In June of 1861, he took command of the easternmost of the two Confederate armies assembled in Virginia. He planned, gave the preliminary orders at the First Battle of Manassas, and was second in command, at the onset. Promoted to Major General he was transferred to the western front in 1862. At the Battle of Shiloh he was second in command, and when General Albert Sidney Johnston was mortally wounded he assumed the direction of the Confederate forces. He directed the retreat to Corinth, Mississippi, and fortified the town for a seige, but ill health forced him to give up the command to General Braxton Bragg.

After a rest he was entrusted with the defenses of the Georgia and Carolina coasts and repulsed successive attacks at Charleston. In the spring of 1864 he was again in Virginia and at Drewry Bluff inflicted a severe defeat on upon General Benjamin F. Butler, who later became known as "Beast Butler" in New Orleans. He directed the defense of Petersburg until General Robert E. Lee arrived. He served in the Carolinas in the closing months of the war and surrendered to William T. Sherman. Beauregard was an excellent engineer and an expert in fortifications.

When the Civil War ended he returned to New Orleans and became involved in the business and cultural affairs of the city. He organized the Southern Historical Society in 1869 which later moved to Richmond. One of the founders of L'Athenee, he served as its president for eleven years. And when his war colleague General John B. Hood died in 1879, Beauregard almost single-handedly organized a Hood Memorial Association to obtain funds to care for his ten orphaned children. He also managed to get Hood's memoirs published which added to the estate.

In 1888 he became commissioner of public works but ran afoul of the politicians who were instrumental in appointing him by firing the incompetents. Beauregard was naive about public officials; thoroughly honest, personally, he could not conceive of putting political patronage above his principles. His mere association with the Louisiana Lottery tarnished his fine image.

Named adjutant general by Governor Francis T. Nicholls in 1878, he also received reappointments from Governors Louis Alfred Wiltz and Samuel Douglas McEnery. He was uniquely qualified by experience and education to hold the highest military office in the state.

Bold, versatile, and innovative, General Beauregard proposed that the militia be supplied with uniforms with phosphorescent backs so that the men could be seen by their comrades in the rear while remaining invisible to the enemy in front.

Camp Beauregard in Alexandria is named after this extraordinary man, and an equestrian statue of him commands the main entrance to the City Park in New Orleans.

Another interesting aspect of his life was the presidency of the Louisiana Immigration and Homestead Company, which promoted and fostered the movement of white immigrants from the north of the United States and Europe to Louisiana.

Loved and admired, he remains one of the most celebrated military heroes in southern history. He died on February 20, 1893, and was buried with an impressive ceremony well attended by the high and low from New Orleans society. Two military bands led the procession playing appropriate funeral dirges. The bands were followed by the Washington Artillery, National Guard units, the Louisiana Field Artillery, and the Veterans of the Army of Northern Virginia and Tennessee.

WILLIAM G. BURT
1888-1890

William G. Burt was born in Edgefield District, South Carolina, on February 2, 1843. Only seventeen years old when the Civil War began, he volunteered and became a private in Company C of the First South Carolina Regiment. He saw action early and proved his capabilities under fire and was appointed a first lieutenant while still in his teens. His rise in the military ranks of the Confederate army was rapid, and he was promoted to lieutenant colonel of the Twenty-second South Carolina Regiment of Infantry which was part of Elliott's Brigade. Burt was one of the youngest colonels in the service. In 1864 he was promoted to the rank of full colonel "for distinguished valour and skill" at the "Crater" at Petersburg, Virginia. He was present and in command of his regiment at the surrender at Appomattox.

In 1866 Burt moved to Bossier Parish in Louisiana and became a planter. Highly respected, intelligent, and with an enviable war record, he soon became prominent in affairs of the Democratic party. He was treasurer and president of the Police Jury and the Agricultural Society of Bossier Parish.

Appointed adjutant general by Governor Nicholls on November 13, 1888, to succeed General Beauregard, who wanted to retire from the post, Burt served for two years with the rank of brigadier general. He lost his wife while still a relatively young man but remained a widower. He died at Bellvue, in Bossier Parish, at midnight on August 30, 1890.

THOMAS FLETCHER BELL
1890-1896

Thomas Fletcher Bell was another Virginia native to serve as adjutant general of Louisiana. Born in Lancaster County in 1838, he grew up there. In 1857 he attended the University of Missouri and after graduation went to Cumberland University in Tennessee to study law. Upon completing his law studies, he settled in Kansas City, Missouri. The nation was expanding greatly to the west during this period, and it was not uncommon for enterprising young men to seek their fortunes away from their native states.

During the Civil War he was with the Missouri State Guard at Booneville but later became a private in Hunter's Missouri Regiment. This was a delicate transition for Bell because Missouri was evenly split during the Civil War; sentiment was high for the Confederacy and the Union, dividing its citizens and in some cases causing bitter and bloody disputes.

By January, 1863, Bell had advanced to the rank of captain and was on the staff of Colonel Charles S. Mitchell. The end of the war found him at Shreveport, and he was present at that city's surrender. He remained in Shreveport to practice law, and by 1872 was prominent in that field.

When William G. Burt died suddenly, Governor Nicholls appointed Bell to the post of adjutant general on November 14, 1890, with the rank of brigadier general. He had been active in the campaign of Samuel Douglas McEnery for governor and became widely known throughout the state. He had presided over an antilottery convention in Baton Rouge in 1890, which established his political views, and he became a popular choice for adjutant. When Murphy J. Foster became governor, he reappointed Bell, extending his tenure to six consecutive years.

ALLEN JUMEL
1896-1904

Allen Jumel's father, Albert, was an officer in Napoleon's imperial Guard and was a chevalier of the Legion of Honor. He came to America in 1825 and received an appointment as sword master at the United States Military Academy at West Point, New York, the following year. Jumel was born February 19, 1835, at West Point while his father was an instructor there. And in 1836 the family, attracted by the French culture, moved to Louisiana.

Albert Jumel died of yellow fever in New Orleans in 1839 and Allen settled in Iberville Parish in 1844. He attended Centenary College, finishing in 1850. He entered the Confederate service in 1862 as captain of the Second Louisiana Cavalry and spent the rest of the war at such places as Labadieville, Camp Bisland, Pleasant Hill, Monett's Ferry plus many scouting expeditions. Wounded three times, he became a prisoner when in command of a flag of truce that was violated. Jumel, feeling personally responsible for the incident since he was in command, offered himself as hostage for the freedom of the others in the party. Exchanged after two months, he was in New Iberia at the time of the surrender.

In 1866 Allen Jumel won an election for sheriff in Iberville Parish. He was in the steamboating business from 1869 until 1876 when he was elected auditor of the state of Louisiana. He held the position for two terms winning reelection in 1880. He also was elected to a state Senate seat from 1884 until 1888 and became a state representative in 1892, serving until 1896. Allen Jumel served Governor Murphy J. Foster during his second term and the entire term of Governor William Wright Heard. He died July 26, 1915.

DAVID THEOPHILIUS STAFFORD
1904-1912

David T. Stafford was born on September 12, 1849, on Edgefield plantation near Cheneyville in Rapides Parish, Louisiana. He was the son of Sarah Catherine Wright and General Leroy Stafford, a prominent Confederate officer from Louisiana.

After receiving his early education at the public schools of Cheneyville, he entered the Louisiana Seminary of Learning near Pineville.

Upon reaching maturity he left Cheneyville for Alexandria and went into steamboat freight and warehouse business. He next began farming at which he remained for ten years. Entering politics he became active in ridding the state of carpetbag rule and joined the Knights of the White Camellia, a forerunner of the Ku Klux Klan. He fought with the Citizens League in the battle on Canal Street against the carpetbag government on September 14, 1874.

In Rapides Parish he was a justice of the peace and later a sheriff for sixteen years. In 1904 Governor Newton Crain Blanchard appointed him adjutant general; four years later he was reappointed by Governor Jared Young Sanders. He had married Amy Blanchard Graham, daughter of former Adjutant General George Mason Graham. Twelve children were born to them. General Stafford died in Alexandria, Louisiana on January 18, 1926.

OSWALD W. McNEESE
1912-1916

Governor Luther Egbert Hall appointed Oswald W. McNeese adjutant general on June 3, 1912. Born on October 18, 1880, in Lake Charles, he was the son of Susan Bilbo and John McNeese. John McNeese had settled Calcasieu Parish in 1870, migrating from Maryland. He practiced law, became superintendent of the parish educational system, and was prominent in civic affairs of the area. McNeese State University is named for him.

Oswald McNeese attended Louisiana State University and later engaged in business affairs of his home community becoming assistant cashier of the Lake Charles National Bank.

He gradually ascended the military ladder until he became adjutant general. Appointed a first lieutenant in the First Louisiana Infantry in 1903, he soon became a captain and then a major in the Louisiana National Guard. Efficient and intelligent, McNeese impressed Louisianians with the excellence of his performances.

In World War I, he was commissioned a major in the 173rd Infantry Brigade of the Eighty-seventh Division, becoming an assistant chief of staff. He was also an assistant instructor for company and platoon commanders of the division school. He went to France with the Advance School Detachment of the Eighty-seventh Division, where he completed a course for field officers at Langres, France.

Upon his discharge from the U.S. Army following World War I,

McNeese was commissioned a lieutenant colonel of Infantry Officer Reserve Corps and under War Department General Order No. 74, was designated as eligible for general staff duty. He was made an assistant chief of staff of the Eighty-seventh Division, Organized Reserves.

McNeese left an impressive record in many areas of the military. He was chief of staff of the Thirty-first Division, G-1 Personnel, War Department General Staff, 1932-1936. He worked in the planning branch of G-1 on manpower procurement for war. He sat on the Joint Army and Navy Selective Service Committee that formulated the proposed law and regulations for manpower procurement through Selective Service. He wrote and secured War Department approval of the Model State Plan for Selective Service. He was detailed to procure similar plans for the forty-eight states and the District of Columbia, and The plan was adoped when Selective Service became effective in 1940.

McNeese also served as chief of the Regulation and Planning Division of the National Guard Bureau; was chairman of the War Department General Staff of the National Guard Committeee; and was also on Joint National Guard and Organized Reserve Committee. He was an executive of the Second Military Area, Seventh Corps Area Service Command, Omaha, Nebraska, until his retirement on August 9, 1942.

CECIL C. McCRORY
1916-1919

Cecil C. McCrory was born on November 23, 1880, at Hope Villa in the northeastern part of Ascension Parish, Louisiana. The son of Mr. and Mrs. Jackson, "Mink" McCrory spent his early life on a farm near what is now Hobart in Ascension Parish. Competing in a written educational examination sponsored by the Ascension Parish Police Jury, McCrory made the highest grade and won a scholarship.

He graduated from the original Baton Rouge High School when it was on St. Louis Street. Receiving a B.S. Degree from Louisiana State University in mechanical engineering, he continued graduate work, qualifying for a Master's degree in electrical and chemical engineering. As a member of the cadet corps at LSU, he was captain of Company C, a member of the 1901 class baseball team, and of Kappa Sigma Fraternity.

McCrory combined a great intellect with rugged outdoor activity.

Horseback riding, quail hunting, and fishing were frequent diversions. As adjutant general he rode horseback in the presidential inaugural parade marking the reelection of Woodrow Wilson in 1916.

From 1902 to 1906 he was commandant of cadets at LSU and from 1903 to 1906 was assistant professor of mathematics under the noted mathematician, Colonel James William Nicholson.

At the age of thirty-six he was appointed adjutant general with the rank of brigadier general by Governor Ruffin G. Pleasant on June 6, 1916, and served until September 22, 1919.

He first gained attention in the National Guard as a lieutenant of the First Louisiana Regiment and became captain of Company B, Lafayette, on October 21, 1908. By June 15, 1910, he was a regimental adjutant and on June 1, 1914, was promoted to major of the Second Battalion.

He was responsible for the reorganization of the National Guard when it took the field in the Mexican border incident. Preparation for World War I was also under his tutelage as head of the National Draft System in Louisiana.

After his resignation as adjutant general he devoted his time to farming at Hope Villa, but he found time to be campaign manager for Colonel Frank P. Stubbs who ran for governor in 1920.

On May 16, 1927, he accepted the position of agriculture agent for Caldwell Parish with the LSU Agricultural Extension Service. In 1929 he transferred to Caddo Parish and was agent there for fifteen years.

His wife was Estelle Buffington Bullion of Hope Villa, who was the daughter of Civil War officer Octavius Alonzo "Doc" Bullion; they had six children. General McCrory died on December 9, 1944, and was buried at his homestead in Hope Villa.

ALLEN T. HUNTER
1919-1920

It seems incredible that so little is known about so recent an adjutant general as Allen T. Hunter. There is evidence that he was born in 1878 and was the son of Judge Edward Hunter who was a lawyer in Rapides Parish. Hunter was also a member of the Louisiana legislature when World War I was declared.

Appointed September 22, 1919, by Governor Ruffin G. Pleasant, he held office when the nation was reveling in the victory of World

War I and giving little attention to the home front and its defense. Hunter served while the great majority of the National Guard were still technically a part of the U.S. Army. After the return of the veterans Hunter began reorganization. He resigned on July 1, 1920.

LOUIS A. TOOMBS
1920-1928

Louis A. Toombs served ably as adjutant general under three governors—John M. Parker, Henry L. Fuqua, and Oramel H. Simpson. Toombs was the first of the modern adjutants general who were exceptionally well qualified for the position and who advanced the National Guard in terms of personnel, equipment, and training to an extent that made the past Guards seem comparatively primitive. This includes the men who followed him—Fleming, Hufft, Wise, Wade, and Daigle. This is not to imply that any of those gallants of the past were not suited for the office, but the Toombs administration marked the beginning of a period of continued excellence in the management of the affairs of the Louisiana National Guard.

Toombs began his military career as private in the Texas National Guard Infantry during 1894-1895. Next he is found a second lieutenant in the Mississippi Volunteers, Company B, Third Infantry, from June to December in 1898 and later a first lieutenant in the same outfit from 1898 to 1899, during the Spanish-American War. When peace was established he became a captain in the Mississippi National Guard Infantry from 1899 until 1900. How and why Toombs left Texas for Mississippi is not known but whatever he did for a living he was determined to be a soldier.

He was first lieutenant, Signal Corps, Louisiana National Guard, from June 4, 1902, to December 6, 1904, and again a captain, this time with Company A, Second Infantry, from March 12, 1905, until December 6, 1906, and from August 5, 1907, to December 9, 1907, was a first lieutenant in Company A, Second Infantry.

Toombs became a colonel, inspector of rifle practice, a rank he held from September 5, 1908, to June 3, 1912. Then he was back to major in the Ordinance Department, but still state inspector of rifle practice, from March 6, 1914, to June 25, 1917.

He was also a major in the U.S. Reserve Corps from June 26, 1917, to October 6, 1918, and was called to active service on June 12, 1917, when he became assistant adjutant general of the Central

Department of Chicago. He was appointed Assistant adjutant general of the Eighty-eighth Division, on September 10, 1917, while at Camp Dodge, Iowa, and became a full adjutant of the Eighty-eighth on March 12, 1918, while still at Camp Dodge. Promoted to lieutenant colonel in the Adjutant General's Department of the U.S. Army on October, 1918, Toombs embarked for France with the Eighty-eighth Division. He was appointed provost marshal of the American forces in Italy on February 12, 1919, and became provost marshal of Belgium, on May 20, 1919, two rare distinctions.

He was repeatedly recommended for promotion to higher positions. An official report was signed by General R. L. Bullard, dated February 1, 1919, endorsing recommendation for Toomb's appointment to the Adjutant General's Department of the regular Army. Under the same date Major General William Weigel, commanding the Eighty-eighth Division also added his recommendation, indicating the exemplary efficient, prompt, and unerring judgment in Toombs's handling of complicated administration.

Perhaps his most distinguished service abroad is that revealed in the recommendation that the Distinguished Service Medal be awarded him based on his service as provost marshal of Italy during the critical period when, at the time of the peace conference decision on the Fiume question, he deftly prevented friction between the members of the American Expeditionary Force and the subjects of the king of Italy. By authorization of Congress, he was presented the medal on October 5, 1921.

An official communication from the Ministry of Foreign Affairs of Italy, dated June 20, 1919, apprised General Toombs that he was appointed an officer of the Order of the Crown of Italy as a token of appreciation for his services.

On September 12, 1919, he was made assistant adjutant general of the Eastern Department of the army, while stationed at Governor's Island, New York. He was discharged from the army at Jackson Barracks on October 31, 1919.

Toombs became adjutant general of the Louisiana National Guard with the rank of brigadier general on July 1, 1920, having been appointed by Governor John M. Parker. He was, however, federally recognized as a lieutenant colonel in the Adjutant General's Department on November 27, 1920, and promoted to the grade of colonel on January 22, 1922, in the same department.

In 1922 and 1923 General Toombs was detailed by the secretary of war to be a member of General Staff in Washington. He served on two important committees while with the General Staff and was federally recognized as a brigadier general in command of the Sixty-first Infantry Brigade of the National Guard.

Toombs's career was further distinguished by his fulltime service and devotion to the Louisiana National Guard. Under him the Guard made rapid advances; most important, he was primarily responsible for its post-World War I reorganization. He laid the cornerstone for what was to follow.

RAYMOND HARTWELL FLEMING
1928-1948   1952-1956   1960-1964

One of the most remarkable of all the adjutants general was Raymond H. Fleming who served twenty-eight years under nine different governors. Twenty of those twenty-eight years were consecutive, and he served two intermittent four-years terms. One of the most popular figures in Louisiana's long history, he enjoyed the respect from the governor, the public at large, and the men in the ranks of his command.

Born in Waxahachie, Texas, on July 5, 1889, to Viola Middleton and Jesse H. Fleming, he grew up in his native state. He received a Bachelor of Arts degree in 1915 at Trinity University at San Antonio. Later in his life Trinity bestowed an honorary Doctor of Science degree upon Fleming.

On March 11, 1917, he married Elna V. Harrison; this union bore two children, Raymond H. Fleming, Jr., and Doris E. Raymond, Jr., served as cadet colonel of the Reserve Officers Training Corps at Louisiana State University during his senior year and became a captain commanding Battery B of the Eighteenth Field Artillery Battalion in Germany during World War II. He was killed in action. Doris became Mrs. Vernon Kennedy. General Fleming was a Presbyterian.

After settling in Louisiana he enlisted as a private in the First Field Artillery of the Louisiana National Guard on May 23, 1916, and served in the Mexican border affair with the First Battalion Field Artillery (Washington Artillery). On February 28, 1917, he was mustered out of the service with the rank of sergeant. Upon reinduction into the Louisiana National Guard, he was commissioned a second lieutenant on April 9, 1917, in the field artillery and assigned to the Battalion Washington Artillery.

During World War I, Fleming served with the 141st Field Artillery which trained at Camp Beauregard where he became captain and commanding officer of Battery D. His detachment was sent to France, arriving at Brest on September 2, 1918. One week later they were sent to Messac, and from there marched twenty-one miles to Coetquidan where the unit underwent another period of training. News of the Armistice of November 11 reached them while they were still at Coetquidan. They returned to the United States in April of 1919 and were mustered out of Federal service on May 19, 1919.

Following this demobilization, Fleming, as captain, reorganized and commanded Battery A, of the 141st Field Artillery of the Louisiana National Guard. This unit was the first post-World War I unit to be reorganized and activated.

Fleming's genius for organization, his military acumen, and constancy of purpose soon became evident, and his rise in the Louisiana National Guard was rapid. From 1920 to 1928 he rose from captain to brigadier general and on July 18, 1928, at thirty-nine was appointed adjutant general by Governor Huey Pierce Long.

Great improvements in the National Guard physical plants became the hallmark of General Fleming who, using the work relief programs of the federal government, instituted his own program of refurbishing existing buildings and erecting new ones. Attention was given to National Guard personnel with drives for recruits and specific training programs. Fleming was innovative with a continuity of plans and efforts, and as a result, few National Guard units were in the excellent state of Louisiana's when World War II began.

Fleming was ordered into Federal service as state director of the Louisiana Selective Service System in October, 1940. He had assumed command of the Fifty-fifth Cavalry Brigade, Twenty-third Cavalry Division, as early as January 20, 1940. But he continued to serve as adjutant general of Louisiana while directing the World War II Selective Service operation.

At the end of World War II, General Fleming began the arduous task of reorganizing the National Guard. On September 30, 1946, he assumed command of the Thirty-ninth Infantry Division of the National Guard of Louisiana and Arkansas and on May 9, 1947, was promoted to major general.

From September 1, to October 11, 1948, he again served the Selective Service System but on a national scale as assistant director of the agency at national headquarters. His broad, intimate experience in this field served him well as a chief advisor regarding Selective Service.

National recognition of his abilities continued as he became the first chief of the army division of the National Guard Bureau, a newly created agency for National Guard affairs. First he was named acting chief of the National Guard Bureau in September, 1950, and made chief on August 14, 1951. He held this position until his federal recognition was mandatorily terminated by reason of age in accordance with federal law on February 28, 1953. He served two additional terms as adjutant general, 1952-1956 and 1960-1964. General Fleming served as chief of the National Guard Bureau during an interim period when he was not adjutant general of Louisiana which is indicative of the broad respect he enjoyed.

He served as adjutant general during the administrations of Huey P. Long, Alvin O. King, Oscar K. Allen, James A. Noe, Richard W. Leche, the first term of Earl K. Long, Sam Houston Jones, Jimmie H. Davis, and Robert F. Kennon.

Honors accorded him were many; in addition to the Distinguished Services Medal, he received the Commendation Ribbon with Medal Pendant, the Mexican Border Service Medal, World War I Victory Medal, American Campaign Medal, World War II Victory Medal, National Defense Service Medal, Armed Forces Reserve Medal, American Defense Medal, the Distinguished Service Medal of the State of Louisiana with Fleur de Lis, the War Cross of Louisiana, the Longevity Medal of Louisiana, the Emergency Service Medal of Louisiana, the Washington Artillery Medal, the National Guard Association of the United States Distinguished Service Medal, and the Distinguished Service Medal of Alabama.

General Raymond H. Fleming devoted most of his life to the interests of the National Guard. His works have left an indelible stamp. He originated the plans for the gigantic maneuvers held in 1939 and 1940 preparatory to World War II when twenty million acres of land were leased to the U.S. Armed Forces without cost. This land continued to be used as a training ground through the duration of World War II.

The state plan implementing the Selective Service Act of World War II was perfected by General Fleming. His work in organizing standby disaster relief facilities was coordinated with federal, state, and local agencies. His efforts in this field were prodigious and served as a model for future emergencies. He made a studious approach to all problems and plans.

He attended the School of Fire at Fort Sill, Oklahoma, in 1918; the Field Officer Course, Field Artillery School at Fort Sill in 1924; the Command and General Staff School of Fort Leavenworth, Kansas, in 1925; and the Army War College, Washington, D. C., in 1928. He was one of the few National Guard officers who wore the service ribbon of the Mexican border, World War I, World War II, and Korea.

Although his primary interest was to the National Guard, General Fleming devoted much time to civic affairs. Besides being a member of the National Guard Association of the United States and member of the Adjutants General Association of the United States and one of its past presidents, he was also a member of the board of directors of the National Guardman Publishing Company; the American Legion; Military Order of World Wars; Veterans of Foreign Wars; Theta XI Fraternity; the Masonic Order; the Sojourners; the New Orleans Chamber of Commerce; the advisory board of the Salvation Army; and the Young Men's Business Club of New Orleans, of which he was a president. He was also a president of the Army and Navy Club of New Orleans.

A beloved figure, who devoted his life to his country and fellow men, General Fleming's record is one of the most distinguished in Louisiana's history. His tenure as adjutant general is the longest in National Guard history. He is also the only adjutant to serve three different periods, 1928-1948, 1952-1956, and 1960-1964; the period from 1928 to 1948 was the longest single tenure among all adjutant generals. He died on November 23, 1974, at the age of 85.

RAYMOND FREDERICK HUFFT
1948-1952   1956-1960

An apt description of Raymond F. Hufft would be, "He was a soldier's soldier." It would indicate the military respect he enjoyed, but he was also a citizen-soldier, having come up—like his predecessor, the gallant Fleming, from the ranks. One of the most respected and likeable persons ever to hold the rank of adjutant general, he was also the youngest.

Hufft was the most decorated soldier in Louisiana history and one of the most decorated in the United States. And his life was as exciting as a Hollywood scenario. The sobriquet that Napoleon affixed to Marshal Ney, "the bravest of the brave," would fit Hufft as well. He had an affinity for being in the right place at the right time, risking his life for a fellow soldier, and generally exhibiting exemplary conduct. He was born to be a soldier; having an unbeatable combination of qualities: raw courage and extraordinary intellect.

He entered World War II a first lieutenant and came out of it a lieutenant colonel, with more medals than his broad chest could display and the admiration of all who heard of his exploits. He served in both the Pacific and European theaters.

Born in New Orleans on August 4, 1914, he was the son of Casilda Holyland and Frederick J. Hufft. He received his early education in the Orleans Parish public schools, graduating from Warren Easton High School in the Class of 1933. He attended Louisiana State University and later Spencer Business College in New Orleans. As a youth, Hufft availed himself of the opportunities available during the depression years. He joined the Civilian Military Training Camp in 1934. This program afforded young men an opportunity to work for a small stipend and receive a limit amount of military training. This was his first experience with regimentation, and it obviously excited his interest, for in June, 1934, upon completing the C.M.T.C. enlistment, he joined the Louisiana National Guard by enlisting in the 108th Cavalry. By 1937 he had risen to the rank of first sergeant, and he became a second lieutenant in the Officers Reserve Corps in 1940. He trained at the Advance Rifle Instructor School, Camp Perry, Ohio, during periods from 1938 to 1940. Promoted to first lieutenant on November 17, 1940, he next entered the U.S. Coast Artillery School at Fort Monroe, Virginia, and returned to command Battery B, 105th Coast Artillery Antiaircraft.

Called into federal service on January 6, 1941, as a first lieutenant, attached to the 105th Separate Battalion Coast Artillery, he trained at Camp Hulen, Texas, and left for the Asiatic-Pacific Theater on January 19, 1942. Attached to the Holly Task Force in the Phoenix Islands of the South Pacific he was battalion commander but did not receive the rank of captain until April 10, 1942. He was frequently advanced to commands before attaining the commensurate rank.

Captain Hufft returned to the United States after a year's duty in the Pacific, arriving on March 12, 1943, and was immediately assigned to the post of Battalion Commander (airborne) at Fort Eustis, Virginia; his promotion to major came on June 23, 1943.

On November 13, 1943, he left for the European war as battalion commander of the First Special Services Force. He became a lieutenant colonel on February 17, 1944, and was placed in command of the Forty-fifth Regimental Combat Team. Hufft attained a measure of fame while in the European operation of the U.S. Army. He was with the first troops to enter Rome and with the first to invade France. While leading a counterattack against the Germans in southern France he rescued a wounded officer during street fighting, and for his heroism he was awarded the Silver Star. He was also the first officer of the Seventh Army to cross the Rhine River into Germany. This crossing was made in company with three men on the night of March 25, 1945, in preparation to the crossing of the main body of troops. Hufft and his three men reconnoitered the landing area in the darkness and at great personal risk. For this action he received the Distinguished Service Cross.

He was in command of a battalion of the Forty-fifth Infantry Division in the Ardennes pocket and Rhineland campaigns. As commanding officer of an Airborne Task Force, he succeeded in casuing the surrender of a German lieutenant and seventy-five of his men. He led a patrol seven miles behind the enemy's lines. Next he was successful in a raid upon an enemy fortress and then moved an ammunition truck from under perilous enemy fire. For these three heroics he received three Bronze Star medals.

On April 17, 1945, he was seriously wounded and was lying among the dead when a medic happened to notice some movement made by the unconscious Hufft. He was attended to in time to save him and then sent to the United States to recover, arriving at the Oliver General Hospital in Augusta, Georgia, on July 21, 1945; the war ended while he was recuperating. He was separated from active duty on October 27, 1946. He had participated in the battles of New Guinea, Rome-Arno, Casino, Southern France, and central Europe.

Lieutenant Colonel Hufft returned to Louisiana recognized as a hero. Governor Earl K. Long appointed him adjutant general on June 3, 1948, with the rank of brigadier general; Hufft was only thirty-three years old. On November 1, 1948, he received the appointment of brigadier general in the Adjutant General's Corps of the National Guard of the United States. General Hufft was appointed state director of the Louisiana Selective Service System on July 13, 1948, and as director of Louisiana Civil Defense he became the Louisiana state coordinator for disaster relief.

The rank of major general was bestowed on Hufft on October 14, 1949. Having served four years for Earl K. Long, Hufft again received the appointment of adjutant general on May 16, 1956, and director of Selective Service on May 18, 1956, and Louisiana state coordinator for disaster relief as well. He received a second appointment to director of Civil Defense on July 1, 1956. His second term as adjutant general ended in 1960.

General Hufft received the following medals while serving his country: Distinguished Service Cross; Silver Star with two oak leaf clusters; Bronze Star with three oak leaf clusters; Purple Heart with two oak leaf clusters; French Croix de Guerre with palm; Parachutist Badge; Combat Infantry Badge; Asiatic Pacific Theater Ribbon; European Theater of Operations Ribbon with six battle stars and bronze arrowhead; African Theater of Operations Ribbon with one battle star; American Defense Service Medal, Allied Ribbon; German Army of Occupation Medal; Unit Presidential Citation, Louisiana Distinguished Service Medal; Armed Forces Reserve Medal; Louisiana Longevity Medal; Louisiana Emergency Service Medal; Louisiana War Cross; Dominion of Canada Honorary Life Membership in the Army, Navy, and Air Force of Canada.

He was an honorary life member, National Guard Association of Louisiana; honorary life member, Louisiana National Guard Officers' Club of New Orleans; member of the National Guard Association of the United States, member National Defense Committee, American Legion Department of Louisiana; Veterans of Foreign Wars; Military Order of World Wars. He was also a member of the Young Men's Business Club, president of the New Orleans Athletic Club; member of Delta Phi Theta Fraternity; member of State Veterans Reemployment Rights Committee; chairman of the National Security Committee; member of the Chamber of Commerce of New Orleans; member New Orleans Army Advisory Committee; vice-president and general manager of Radio Station WNOE, New Orleans.

General Hufft married Dorothy Robinson on June 11, 1939. Four children were born to this union—James Michael, Mrs. Rayme Hufft Miller, Robin Ann, and Cindy Ann. He died on August 14, 1972, loved and mourned by all who knew him and respected by those who admired his fearless courage.

Major General Raymond Frederick Hufft has joined that list of notables in Louisiana's history whose lives have contributed to the protection and progress of the homeland. Fear was alien to him; his heart was brave, and his deeds were noble; he was a model and an inspiration. Louisianians and the nation owe him much.

> Beat the drums slowly
> Let proud banners wave
> Play a tune of glory
> O'er our hero's grave!

ERBON WISE
1964-1968

Erbon Wise's appointment as adjutant general by Governor John J. McKeithen broke a Louisiana tradition for he was not a National Guard officer. He was, however, a thoroughly capable and knowledgeable military man.

Born in Claiborne Parish in 1920 to Edmond W. and Eula Bridewell Wise, he was reared in a rural atmosphere. Upon graduation from Boyce High School, he entered Northwestern State College at Natchitoches, where he was graduated. He began his military career on December 29, 1941, by enlisting in the United States Army Air Force. He gained a commission on June 30, 1942, as a finance disbursing officer in England, France, and Germany, with the Twelfth, Eighth and Nineth air forces. One of the first finance officers to arrive in England, he participated in the invasion of Normandy in World War II and was active in the financial affairs of U.S. expeditionary forces. He also saw duty as a finance officer with the French Provisional Air Force.

On February 15, 1946, Major Wise received an honorable discharge and became a member of the Reserves where he rose to the rank of lieutenant colonel by 1960.

Colonel Wise attended ten annual tours of active duty at the National Security seminars. He also attended Navy-Marine amphibious exercises at Camp LeJeune, North Carolina, in 1963 and made an inspection visit to the North American Air Defense Command at Colorado Springs in 1964. In 1964 he was graduated from the U.S. Army Command and General Staff College at Fort Leavenworth, Kansas.

Before he was appointed adjutant general, Wise had twenty-two continuous years of military service as an active soldier or reservist. Among the honors he received were: the Bronze Star, the European Theater of Operations Ribbon with four campaign stars, the Distinguished Unit Emblem and the Meritorious Unit Emblem, German Army of Occupation Medal, World War II Victory Medal, and Armed Forces Reserve Medal. Governor John J. McKeithen bestowed the rank of brigadier general upon Wise when he designated him adjutant general and promoted him to major general on June 8, 1967.

Active in business and civic affairs, General Wise was president of Wise Publications Inc., publishers of the *Daily Recorder* of Lake Charles; the *Daily Legal News* of Leesville; the Cameron *Reporter;* *Orange County Court Report* of Orange, Texas; and the *Calcasieu Auto Register* of Lake Charles; the *Southwest Builder*; the *Southwest Star* of Sulphur; and the Vinton *News*.

Wise was also chairman of the board of directors of the *West Bank Guide* of Harvey and a partner, in Wise-Maker Publications, publishers of the *Official Daily Court Record* of New Orleans and the *Jefferson Daily Legal News* of Gretna. In addition he was a director of the Louisiana Press Association, former presdient of Community Newspaper Representatives of Louisiana, Inc., chairman of the Military Affairs Committee of the West Calcasieu Association of Commerce, a member of the Association of the United States Army, and a member of the Navy League.

General Wise's wife is the former Willie Marie Norris of Natchitoches; they have four children. Erudite and distinguished, Wise brought vast experience to the state's highest military post where he advanced its traditions and interests. On three occasions during his tenure, he was awarded the Louisiana Emergency Service Medal for Disaster Relief and Civil Disturbance.

DAVID WADE
1968-1972

David Wade, appointed adjutant general by Governor John J. McKeithen, effective August 1, 1968, brought to the National Guard his wide military knowledge. Born June 15, 1911, in Homer, Claiborne Parish, he attended the public schools there. After high school he entered Homer Junior College from which he graduated; he then entered Louisiana Polytechnic Institute at Ruston, where he majored in engineering.

He began his military career in the Louisiana National Guard by serving from 1928 until 1930. In February, 1935, Wade joined the

Army Air Corps as a cadet, and received his wings at Randolph Field, Texas. In late 1935 he became an Air Corps pilot with additional squadron duties, where he served until the latter part of 1941.

From November, 1941, until October, 1943, he was an assistant director and, later, director of training at Big Spring, Texas. From Big Spring he was sent to Blythe, California, to assume command of the Thirty-fourth Combat Crew Training School. He also became the commanding officer of the Ninth Bombardment Group at Blythe. In March, 1945, he began a twenty-six-month tour of duty in command of the Ninth in the Marianas and the Philippines ending in April, 1947, when he was assigned the command of the Nineteenth Bombardment Group on Guam.

Returning to the United States in November, 1947, David Wade entered the Armed Forces Staff College at Norfolk, Virginia, from which he was graduated. He became vice-commander of the United States Air Force Security Service in July, 1948, and remained with this unit until 1950 when he was made deputy commander of the Ninety-third Bombardment Wing at Castle Air Force Base in California.

With the outbreak of the war in Korea, Wade was made commander of the Ninety-eighth Bombardment Wing which bombed strategic targets in North Korea. His service in Korea lasted from April, 1951, until October of the same year when he was transferred to command the 303rd Bombardment Wing, stationed at Davis-Monthan Air Force Base, Arizona.

His training and skills in aerial warfare repeatedly demanded his transfer to different unit commands where his expertise was needed. During the period of 1952-1954, Wade commanded the Ninety-second Bombardment Wing and then was put in command of the Fifty-seventh Air Division at Fairchild Air Force Base in Washington state. From 1954 until 1955 he was in command of the Twenty-first Air Division, at Forbes Air Force Base in Kansas, and in April, 1955, was assigned to headquarters of the Strategic Air Command (SAC) as inspector general and in July, 1956, became its chief of staff.

On January 1, 1958, Wade was made commander of the First Missile Division at Vandenburg Air Force Base, California, which was the first operational missile unit in United States Air Force history. His responsibility was dual, for he was in charge of maintaining an operational capability with intercontinental ballistic missile systems while providing operational readiness training for missile crews

The Adjutants General

manning the Strategic Air Command missile sites and support for the orbiting satellite programs.

From Vandenburg, General Wade was sent to Torrejon Air Base near Madrid, Spain, and in July, 1961, assumed command of the Strategic Air Command, Sixteenth Air Force, which included the units in Spain and Morocco.

On August 1, 1963, he was promoted to lieutenant general in command of the Strategic Air Command's Second Air Force, headquarters at Barksdale Air Force Base, Louisiana. He took command of the Eighth Air Force on August 1, 1966, and remained at this post until his retirement on March 1, 1967.

General Wade was the first adjutant general with a military service devoted exclusively to the Air Force prior to his appointment to command the Louisiana National Guard. Able, well versed in military affairs, he brought much distinction to his office. His military record was one of steady and rapid advancement. In 1937 he was a second lieutenant in the Reserve but a permanent one with the Regulars in 1938. He became a first lieutenant on October 4, 1940; a captain on April 6, 1942; just two weeks later on April 30 a major; a lieutenant colonel on August 8, 1942; and a full colonel by October 26, 1943; a brigadier general on June 23, 1953; a major general by August 5, 1957; and a lieutenant general on August 1, 1963.

Due to General Wade's extraordinary organizational ability, he was appointed superintendent of state police and director of the State Department of Public Safety for a period of one year—February 1, 1969 through January 31, 1970—during which period Brigadier General Thomas Bonner served in his stead as adjutant. General Wade, like Beauregard and Longstreet, was a lieutenant general before assuming the post of adjutant general. However, upon assumption of the duties of adjutant his rank was adjusted to the grade of major general, the highest rank federally recognized for adjutants general. Longstreet and Beauregard were, of course, lieutenant generals in the Confederate States of America, and Wade held that rank with the United States Army Air Force.

Among the many honors bestowed upon the distinguished General Wade were the Distinguished Service Medal, Legion of Honor with one oak leaf cluster, the Distinguished Flying Cross, the Soldier's Medal, the Air Medal with one oak leaf cluster, the Air Force Commendation Medal, the American Campaign Medal, the Asiatic-Pacific Campaign Medal, the World War II Victory Medal, the

National Defense Service Medal, the Korean Service Medal, the Air Force Longevity Service Award Ribbon with one silver and one bronze oak leaf cluster, the Philippine Liberation Ribbon, the Republic of Korea Presidential Unit Citation, the Philippine Independence Ribbon, and the United Nations Service Medal. He was also awarded the Louisiana Distinguished Service Medal and the Louisiana Longevity Service Medal.

Prior to his appointment as adjutant general, General Wade served for fourteen months as director of institutions for the state of Louisiana, receiving this appointment on May 1, 1967.

While in the Army Air Force he logged over ten thousand hours flying time as a pilot in almost every type of military aircraft, including the most modern jets. His term as adjutant general was marked by great advances in the Air National Guard. One of the most qualified men ever to hold Louisiana's highest military post, he added to the progress and luster of the Louisiana National Guard. General Wade is married to former Leta Marie Tollett; they have one daughter, Mrs. Kay Wade King.

THOMAS BONNER
(Acting adjutant general)
1969-1970

General Thomas Bonner was assistant adjutant general to General David Wade. When Governor John J. McKeithen appointed General Wade superintendent of the state police and director of the Louisiana State Department of Public Safety, General Bonner became acting adjutant general and remained so from February 1, 1969 through January 31, 1970. When General Wade resumed his position, General Bonner again became assistant.

Dedicated and able, General Bonner has served the Louisiana National Guard for thirty-three years since his enlistment as a private in 1936. He entered World War II as a second lieutenant of the National Guard and an aide-de-camp to Brigadier General Louis F. Guerre, commander of the Sixty-first Infantry Brigade, Thirty-first Infantry Division.

His record as an operations officer for the 345th Infantry of the Eighty-first Division in the Ardennes, the Rhineland, and central Europe was brilliant. His bravery in the face of the enemy and his initiative and complete dedication to state service earned him the

Legion of Merit, the Silver Star, the Bronze Star, Belgium's Croix de Guerre with palm, the Combat Infantry Badge, the EAME Medal with three battle stars, the American Defense Medal, the American Campaign Medal, the World War II Victory Medal, the Armed Forces Reserve Medal, Louisiana's Distinguished Service Medal with fleur de lis, the Emergency Service Medal with ten fleur de lis, and the Thirty-year Longevity Medal. He is a member of the American Legion, the Veterans of Foreign Wars, the Military Order of the World Wars, the Association of the United States Army, the National Security Committee of the New Orleans Chamber of Commerce, the National Guard Association of the United States, the National Guard Association of Louisiana, the American Association of Retired Personnel, and the Federal Executive Board of New Orleans.

In 1946 he was appointed operations and training officer of the Louisiana National Guard and was successful in recruiting cadres and obtaining armory facilities throughout the state in the postwar reactivation of the Guard. For twenty-three continuous years he has maintained close liaison with the National Guard Bureau, Departments of the Army and Air Force, and with important military officials through the United States.

His military education includes the Infantry School Officer Communications Course, 1941; Infantry School Officer Advance Course, 1943; Command and General Staff.

General Bonner was born in Louisiana on November 8, 1911; he married to the former Mercedes Vulliet and and is the father of four sons. He is presently the director of the Selective Service System of Louisiana.

O. J. DAIGLE, JR.
1972-

Major General O. J. Daigle's elevation to adjutant general is especially timely during the period of the bicentennial commemoration since his forbears have figured in Louisiana's colonial history. He is the first adjutant general since Beauregard to represent the French culture of south Louisiana.

His wife, too, the former Jeanne Aline Waguespack, affectionately called Jeanette, whom he married on December 26, 1942, has ancestors who are identified with Louisiana's beginnings. She was born at Evergreen plantation near Edgard, Louisiana. Her German

Waguespack (Waggenspack) antecedants were among those immigrants whom John Law brought to the Louisiana Territory from the Palatinate sector of the old Teutonic Empire early in the eighteenth century.

General Daigle was born in Donaldsonville on July 10, 1922, the son of Eva Courreges and O'Neil James Daigle, Sr. He was christened in the Roman Catholic faith and grew up in Donaldsonville, where he attended the public schools. World War II interrupted his college education, but after the war he reentered Louisiana State University and received a B.S. degree in Agriculture in 1950.

Industrious, versatile, and with great initiative, Daigle was able to advance in the business community while fulfilling military duties. In 1943 he completed ROTC at LSU and became an officer candidate at the infantry school at Fort Benning, Georgia. On May 28, 1943, he was commissioned a second lieutenant and assigned to Fort McClellan, Alabama, where he served with the Twenty-first Battalion of the IRTC as an instructor and assistant S-3. A tour of duty took him to the Sixty-fifth Infantry Division at Camp Shelby, Mississippi, the Antilles Department as Department I-E Officer, and the New Orleans Port of Embarkation where men and material of the U.S. Armed Forces are shipped in large numbers and quantity.

He became a first lieutenant on March 9, 1945, and a captain the following year on June 8. By June 17, 1948, he had become an officer of the Reserve Corps with the 417th, OR Comp Group, stationed at Thibodaux.

His National Guard service began on June 18, 1948, when he was named commander of Battery D of the 769th AAA AW Battalion serving in this assignment until June 6, 1950. From June 7, 1950, until March 31, 1951, Captain Daigle was executive officer of the HHB 769th AAA AW Battalion. On March 14, 1951, he became the battalion commander of the 769th AAA AW and on June 12, was promoted to the rank of major, and on June 13, 1955, he became a lieutenant colonel.

During the Berlin crisis when Krushchev was threatening Europe, the 769th Signal Construction Battalion, with Daigle as commander, was called into Federal service on October 15, 1962, and sent to Fort Polk attached to the Forty-ninth Armored Division. During this call-up he served as battalion commander and as assistant post G-3. The battalion stood ready in case events in Berlin deteriorated, but a year later on October 14, 1962, the situation eased and the 769th returned to National Guard service.

Daigle became a full colonel on October 16, 1962, with the HHD La ARNG and remained at this post until November 30, 1963. On May 1, 1963, he was assigned to the HHC 225th Engineer Group (construction) and was its first group commander. He was deputy commander of Headquarters Emergency Operations on December 1, 1967, and on November 1, 1968, became its commander. He became a brigadier general on December 10, 1968, and on April 1, 1971, was named director of Emergency Operations La ARNG. Upon Brigadier General Bonner's retirement from the Guard, Daigle was named assistant adjutant general by General David Wade. Daigle was appointed adjutant general on May 9, 1972, and promoted the same day to major general, the rank he now holds.

General Daigle's military training was varied and constant. He attended the U.S. Infantry School in 1943; Riot Control School in 1964; Umpire School in 1965; Armored Maintenance School in 1967; Engineer's Refresher Course in 1968; Command and General Staff College in 1968; Civil Defense Management Course in 1969; and the National War College Defense Strategy Seminar in 1969. He took Civil Disturbance Orientation in 1970; the Disaster Recovery Course in 1970; the Army War College Senior Reserve Commander's Orientation Course in 1971; the Combat Surveillance Orientation Course in 1971; the Senior Officer Engineer Orientation Course in 1971; and Civil Affairs Specialist Training Institute in 1973.

While attaining high military rank he also progressed in the business world. He founded Daigle Pontiac-Buick Company in 1955 and became its president and president of O. J. Daigle Volkswagen, Inc., in Gonzales. Prominent in financial circles, he is president of the First National Bank of Gonzales; vice-president of Southern Securities; a partner in Daigle and Mire Real Estate Company; and the Circle Jay-Dee, a real estate holding company in Gonzales.

He is a member of the Military Order of World Wars; the American Legion; the Louisiana Cattlemen's Association; the Louisiana Wildlife Federation; the Louisiana Automobile Dealers Association; the Washington Artillery Association; the National Guard Association of the United States; the National Guard Association of Louisiana; a member of the Reserve Forces Policy Board; a member of the Advisory Council Istrouma Area of the Boy Scouts of America; a member and past president of the National Guard Association of

Louisiana; a member and past chairman of the Ascension Parish United Givers Association; a past president of the Baton Rouge Deanery Council of Catholic Men; a past chairman of the Industrial Development Board of Ascension Parish; a past member of the Volunteers of America Advisory Board; and a member of the Louisiana State University Foundation; a present member of the Louisiana Highway Safety Commission; and a past president and member of Delta Sigma Phi Fraternity of Louisiana State University; and member of the Samurai Interfraternity Council.

He received the Legion of Merit; the World War II Victory Medal; the American Campaign Medal; the Army Commendation Medal; the National Defense Service Medal; the Louisiana Longevity Medal with two fleur-de-lis; the Louisiana War Cross; the Louisiana Emergency Service Medal with five fleur-de-lis; the Louisiana Cross of Merit; and the Louisiana Distinguished Service Medal. His name is listed in the U.S. Infantry Hall of Fame, Fort Benning, Georgia.

Through his efforts, the most extensive renovation in the history of Jackson Barracks and Camp Beauregard is now taking place. At Jackson Barracks, streets and buildings have been given names relevant to Louisiana National Guard history. A chapel has been established, and the headquarters building is known as Fleming Hall in memory of General Raymond H. Fleming.

At Camp Beauregard, lakes, dams, roads, homes, office buildings, an airstrip, a deep water well, barracks, noncommissioned officers' clubs, enlisted men clubs, and post exchanges have been built or improved. It will eventually be possible to train five thousand men during the summer months.

General Daigle is also a member of the Reserve Forces Policy Board, the principle policy advisory board to the secretary of defense and Congress on Reserve affairs.

The parents of four children, Stephen John, Debra Ann, Arthur David, and Jane Elizabeth and the grandparents of Stephen J. Daigle, Jr., General and Mrs. Daigle actively contribute to the progress and welfare of Louisiana. They reside at number five, Jackson Barracks. Connoisseurs of the arts, they have an enviable collection of Louisiana paintings. The general is recognized as an art critic and appraiser.

A self-made man, Major General Daigle has enjoyed eminent success in two distinct professions, the military and private business. His businesslike building and training programs have expanded the Guard to its present record number. His keen mind, coupled with a sensitive appreciation for the traditions of the National Guard, make General Daigle uniquely qualified to guide the modern militia with its advanced techniques and sophisticated weaponry and logistics. He is also the adjutant general who initiated research and recording of the history of the Louisiana National Guard. Much of the material herein is a result of his interest in that historical preservation.

* Samuel Cooper's name has appeared as an adjutant during the American Civil War, but he was the adjutant general of the entire Confederacy and not of Louisiana. Much of his correspondence has found its way in some National Guard files, and upon first glance one might assume that he was indeed an adjutant general of Louisiana, but further inspection clearly eliminates this possibility. The office in the Confederacy was created for him as an honorary position. At the time of the Civil War he was aged and infirm.

CHAPTER 16

Jackson Barracks

New Orleans' very name conjures scenes of antiquity. The romantic past is easily imagined as one goes from the French Quarter, to the riverfront, to the antebellum homes in the Garden District, to the old U.S. Mint and other historic sights.

Equally steeped in history is the complex of buildings and parade grounds known as Jackson Barracks. Situated astride the boundary between Orleans and St. Bernard parishes, it rests on the east bank of the Mississippi River and is a sweeping greensward of about one hundred acres. The newer buildings along three city streets that cross its grounds tend to obscure the magnificent colonial buildings that grace the grassplots.

Visitors and local residents often fail to seek out Jackson Barracks because the word *barracks* evokes a grim utilitarian image that few would care to see. But the barracks are among the most beautiful buildings in Louisiana. Built before the Civil War, the two-storied structures have wide galleries and supporting columns. Fourteen fine buildings either face the river or overlook a quadrangle planted with moss-draped oak trees. No other small area in Louisiana can boast of so many antebellum buildings. As sturdy as the bricks they are made of, the fourteen edifices serve as homes for the adjutant general and his staff officers. Through the generations decaying buildings have been replaced, but these fourteen have withstood the ravages of time and weather as reminders of a glorious past. They are visible links with the oldest traditions of the Louisiana National Guard.

The best viewing point of the Louisiana National Guard administrative base is from the levee along the Mississippi River.

Today, the most notable contrasts between the relatively new buildings and the old are in the slavemade bricks as compared to concrete blocks and the virgin timbers compared to synthetic siding.

The Louisiana militia got its first headquarters when the United States acquired the Louisiana Territory in 1803 and with it the old barracks in the Vieux Carre. Local citizens petitioned Congress to sell the barracks, claiming the need of more warehouse space in the area. The buildings were sold but immediately released for billeting the U.S. garrison. This strange transaction must have been a local mystery for some time because the lease involved a considerable amount of money. The interest on the $170,000 was equal to the rent, according to one account.

In 1826, during the nineteenth congressional session, a plan and estimate for a barracks was tendered by General Thomas Jessup, quartermaster general, but brought no results. Another plan was submitted in 1828 but Congress ignored it. A proposal by General Edmund C. Gaines in 1829 failed to obtain the desired one-thousand-man garrison, but on July 19, 1832, an appropriation for $87,000 was approved and signed by President Andrew Jackson.

Location was not specified; the only stipulation in the congressional appropriation was that the barracks be in the vicinity of New Orleans. Advocates of the installation were primarily concerned with obtaining the necessary funds.

In a letter dated May 13, 1833, Governor A. B. Roman opined that he favored a location within a half-hour march from any point in the city and suggested a site on Bayou Road. Mayor D. Prieur of New Orleans recommended a site on the river or Bayou St. John but was properly against any site across the river. The proposal of Colonel David E. Twiggs prevailed; he preferred a site below the river since any force approaching New Orleans from the gulf would use the river, Lake Pontchartrain, or an overland route from Lake Borgne. A site below New Orleans would be a strategic defensive spot to all three egresses, and alert Germans and Acadians along the coasts could quickly send warning couriers by horse.

On December 14, 1833, two lots were bought from Mr. and Mrs. Pierre Cotteret for the sum of $31,500. By January 15, 1835, a hospital and warehouse were completed, and progress had been made on another hospital, a guardhouse, an encircling wall, and two watchtowers.

The name of Colonel David E. Twiggs appears repeatedly on work records of the project, indicating that he was the first commandant of Jackson Barracks, though at that time the complex had not yet been given the name of the victorious general at the battle of New Orleans.

As the work progressed various alterations in plans were considered necessary. A magazine and a bakehouse were added, requiring one hundred more workmen. The magazine was estimated to cost $3,530 and had gotten underway by October 10, 1837. An interesting article appeared in a New Orleans paper in 1838 describing plans:

> A main feature of the same [barracks] being high protective walls, defended by armed round towers at the angles of the enclosure. The whole being intended to serve as a citadel, for the reception and safety of the families of the citizens in case of an insurrection or other casualty, and therefore made strong; as also to serve as barracks for troops in garrison in the city. . . . The barracks occupy a parallelogram of about 300 feet on the river and by 900 in depth. All the ground in the rear, however, belongs to the general Government to the depth of forty arpents, [an arpent is an old French measure for 1.26 acres] and can be used for the benefit of the troops. The garrison was intended to consist of four companies of infantry but ample accommodation exists for much more than that number. The quarters of the commandant occupy the middle of the front, those of the Staff and Officers on either flank. The companies are quartered in a hollow square which is thrown back far enough to give space for a large and handsome parade ground. In the rear of these quarters are the hospitals, store house, and corps des garde; and still in rear and beyond the walls is the post magazine, as well as other building necessary for the comfort and convenience of the troops. In front of the whole is a commodious wharf for the landing of supplies, etc.
>
> This work was begun on 24th February 1834 and completed 31st December 1835 at a cost, including the enclosure of the public grounds at $182,000.00.

The first troops were in the Barracks by February of 1837, and during this interim socials, parades, and inspections went on for the amusements of the soldiers and their families.

Colonel George Croghan, inspector general of the United States Army, reported in an official dispatch of May 6, 1844:

> There is perhaps no post in the country at which the soldiers live better. They have a pretty good garden of their own, besides which

they have hourly opportunities for exchanging with the market people and fruits that they may desire. The companies, even living as they do, contrive to save out of their regular ration allowance $30 each per month on an average. Here, for the first time, I have found that salt beef is preferred to pork and that the latter is seldom issued and then in small quantities. The mess rooms and kitchens are as clean and neat as anyone could desire.

When war with Mexico was declared on May 12, 1846, an excerpt from the *Daily Picayune* stated, "The volunteers seemed to be all in good spirits and as comfortable as the nature of their case would admit, but all were impatient to be off and on their way to attack the foe. One or two additional companies were marched into the barracks yesterday which swelled the number there to be 1200, we are told."

On January 19, 1847, Special Order No. 22 designated the "New Orleans Barracks" as a hospital for the sick and wounded of the Mexican War. This brought about a purchase of land from a Mrs. Prudence Desilets, the widow of one Louis Badins. The act of sale for lots thirteen and fourteen was recorded in the Register of Conveyances of the city of New Orleans.

A military hospital was completed by March, 1849, overseen by General George M. Brooks, Major Tompkins, and Captain Chase. The compound consisted of four two-story buildings each facing a square of one hundred yards, capable of accommodating one thousand patients. In the center of the square was an octagonal building that served as the surgery center and the medical dispensary. It cost $150,000 and was built under the direction of W. P. Kelsey.

The dedication ceremonies of the hospital drew distinguished guests from points far from New Orleans. Present were Henry Clay, statesman and orator from Kentucky; Isaac Johnson, governor of Louisiana; General Edmund Pendleton Gaines, oldest officer in the U.S. Army; Major General Patterson, of Philadelphia; General John A. Quitman, of Natchez; and many others. Someone said the hospital "is not equalled by any similar edifice in the Union."

Nevertheless, soon after the dedication the garrison was withdrawn (July 14, 1849), and by December 20 only twenty soldiers occupied the barracks. The hospital buildings deteriorated; green lumber shrank to such a degree that the buildings soon became dilapidated. By General Order No. 2, Headquarters of the Army, on September 26, 1853, it was abandoned and the small garrison transferred to Texas.

But on April 7, 1854, the U.S. War Department acceeded to a request that the hospital buildings at New Orleans Barracks be used for sick and disabled seamen and that it be transferred to the U.S. Treasury Department. The U.S. Marine Hospital, then located in Algiers, was in need of repairs. Use of the barracks was more practical especially since it was more easily accessible to patients on the east bank of the river. Perhaps the fact that Jefferson Davis, a Mississippian, was the Secretary of War and P. G. T. Beauregard of Louisiana was the U.S. Army officer who made the feasibility study, affected the decision. The instituted arrangement, however, was only temporary, since the War Department reserved the right to its services on demand.

On January 11, 1861, the Louisiana militia, on the heels of a threat of secession, seized the barracks and remained there until April 29, 1862, when Union forces captured New Orleans. Admiral David Farragut turned the post over to General Benjamin Butler, and it remained a Union garrison until well into Reconstruction days.

On July 7, 1866, Special Order No. 143 officially named the post Jackson Barracks in honor of General Andrew Jackson, hero of the Battle of New Orleans. Its first occupants after that order were the First U.S. Infantry and Battery K, First U.S. Artillery, who were transferred there. Soon after, an assessment was made of the property; the land was estimated to be worth $100,000 and the buildings and equipment were appraised at $350,000 for a total value of $450,000.

In 1888 the last of the four original buildings of the hospital had been torn down; it was 168 feet long and 31 wide with two stories. With it went most of the enthusiasm for retaining the barracks as a military post, and in 1889 Senator Gibson introduced a bill to give the entire complex to Tulane University. Fortunately, the Senate Committee on Military Affairs decided otherwise.

Jackson Barracks was again used as a military post during the Spanish-American War when a regular garrison was maintained there, in addition to several units of the Louisiana militia. The Louisiana Field Artillery detachment remained until the end of the war. At about this time there were plans for its enlargement, but funds were not forthcoming from Congress.

From 1900 until 1914 it remained an army post, most often for artillery units. In October of 1912, part of the property was lost to the river when the levee had to be set back. Two of the towers, the commanding officer's quarters, and part of the encircling wall were also lost as were a number of large oak and magnolia trees.

During World War I fourteen buildings were added to the compound including mess halls, hospital wards, and additional barracks at a total expenditure of $60,000. Following the war, interest in perpetuating Jackson Barracks again began to wave. The U.S. government decided to discontinue its use as a military post.

But due to the efforts of Adjutant General Louis A. Toombs and Governor John M. Parker, Jackson Barracks was saved by a request to use the facilities for the newly reorganized National Guard. The secretary of war, on October 22, 1921, issued a revocable license to that effect, and the state obtained possession on February 1, 1922, by immediately moving in its National Guard. Officers of the Guard established residences in the usable buildings for which they paid a small monthly stipend. The Washington Artillery and Headquarters Troop, 108th Cavalry, were the first units to formally locate there under the newly arranged lease.

Some of the buildings, since they were now the onus of the state were rented to the federal government for the personnel associated with their cavalry and field artillery units. By the end of 1923 the adjutant general, in a report to the governor, was able to say, "Jackson Barracks Reservation is being operated without cost to the State." But despite this arrangement between state and federal governments, which proved advantageous to both, the War Department still wanted to declare Jackson Barracks surplus and recommended its sale. In 1926 Congress authorized the War Department to sell all surplus army posts that it deemed unnecessary for military purposes and Jackson Barracks was on the list.

General Louis A. Toombs again went to the rescue, proposing that the state purchase the barracks from the U.S. government. The flood of 1927 depleted the financial resources of the state, but negotiations had begun before the flood and undoubtedly spared Jackson Barracks. Huey P. Long, at the urging of General Toombs, made the following proposal to the Secretary of War: "In accordance with an act of Congress approved June 28, 1930, etc.; I desire, as Governor of the State of Louisiana, to withdraw the option and in lieu of such proposed purchase, the State of Louisiana desires to lease said property under the provisions of the above mentioned act. I have the honor of transmitting to you a form of lease for your consideration."

The lease was signed and filed on November 7, 1930, which

granted the state of Louisiana use of the barracks as a National Guard post for a nominal fee for twenty-five years, beginning December 5, 1930.

During the 1930s the game of polo was instituted at Jackson Barracks, and matches became a regular feature, not only between the units stationed at the barracks but also against the military of other cities.

With the election of Franklin D. Roosevelt in 1932, national work programs provided employment and the means to improve and refurbish public facilities at Jackson Barracks. A three-story administration headquarters was built that conformed with the architecture of the originals. Roads were also built, giving easy access to all areas of grounds; drainage, sidewalks, and parking areas for motorized vehicles were installed. Forty acres of land, partly underwater, were reclaimed by draining, filling the low spots, and grading. The total outlay provided by the federal government was in excess of one million dollars.

Jackson Barracks was the site for Selective Service conference for a number of years prior to the enactment of the Selective Service Act. When events in Europe became critical, representatives from fifteen states, in conjunction with officials of the War Department, met and studied plans for manpower procurement in case of a national emergency. The Selective Service plan designed and prepared by Adjutant General Raymond H. Fleming and the state staff was the first accepted by the U.S. General Staff in Washington and was used as a model by which other states drafted their plans.

Shortly after the completion of these facilities, on September 8, 1939, a limited national emergency was declared by President Roosevelt. All National Guard units in Louisiana were immediately ordered into federal service in early 1941. When an unlimited national emergency followed on May 27, 1941, Jackson Barracks was partly occupied by units of the U.S. Army which operated a port of embarkation. In time, all buildings, with the exception of the residence buildings, National Guard headquarters building, one warehouse, and a few garages were returned to the U.S. War Department.

The bakery that had been forgotten in the original construction and later authorized was to be once again established in Jackson Barracks for the 1940 maneuvers. The former polo grounds—that area on the river side of St. Claude Avenue—were converted into a huge open-air bakery from which the aroma of baking bread could be savored for blocks around. A new technique was developed to bake the bread very slowly with a one quarter inch crust that could preserve the interior for as long as six weeks, a valuable bread-making experience to be used in World War II.

On March 12, 1947, Jackson Barracks was again declared war surplus and returned to the state of Louisiana under the terms of the lease. Congressman F. Edward Hebert introduced House Resolution 3479, which proposed that the portion of Jackson Barracks to be declared surplus would be transferred by title to the military department of the state of Louisiana for National Guard use. But Hebert's proposal failed, and the barracks is still under a revokable lease whereby the War Department can appropriate the facilities in any emergency and at will.

The adjutant general's report for 1948-1949 valued the grounds and buildings at Jackson Barracks at $2,080,000 and estimated the grounds at 103.06 acres. In 1955 its value had increased to $4,000,000. In 1965 the disastrous Hurricane Betsy emphasized the need of more armories which would not only serve as facilities for the National Guard but also as a refugee centers. Subsequently, two 2-story buildings, one facing St. Claude Avenue and the other facing North Claiborne, were constructed. Each contains 47,000 square feet of floor space for supply rooms, drill halls, rifle ranges, arsenals, classrooms, administrative offices, kitchens, and locker rooms. They were built at a cost of $1,378,000, of which $387,000 was contributed by the state of Louisiana.

Today (July 10, 1975), the complex comprises 115 buildings; it is still the headquarters for the National Guard of Louisiana, the residence of the adjutant general, Major General O. J. Daigle, Jr., and his administrative offices. There are eight buildings which serve exclusively as offices, and there are armory facilities for the following units:

> Headquarters and Headquarters Detachment
> Louisiana Army National Guard
>
> 241st Public Information Detachment
> (Field Service)
>
> 356th Support Center (Rear Area Operation)
>
> 159th Combat Support Hospital
>
> Headquarters and Headquarters Company,
> 204th Area Support Group

156th Army Band

39th Military Police Company (Guard) (—Detachment 1)

Headquarters and Headquarters Company, 225th Engineer Group (Construction)

Company C (—Detachment 1) 205th Engineer Battalion (Construction)

Headquarters and Headquarters Detachment, 2222nd Engineer Battalion (Maintenance)

2224th Engineer Company (Construction Support) (Type B)

2226th Engineer Company (Float Bridge)

Headquarters, Louisiana Air National Guard

214th Electronics Installation Squadron (Air National Guard)

A massive rehabilitation program, under the administration of major General Daigle, has been initiated to modernize the interior of all residential quarters, the exterior and interior of the office and work buildings to make them not only more habitable but more beautiful.

Among the major projects either completed or scheduled for completion is the conversion of the former Headquarters and Headquarters Detachment Armory into an interdenominational chapel. Funded entirely by private contributions, it will provide the members of the Guard and their families a place for religious services, weddings, baptisms, funerals, and quiet meditation. The streets in Area A between the river and Dauphine Street have been named after such military personages as Grant, Lee, McClellan, Beauregard, and Jessup.

Buildings have been dedicated to the memories of such outstanding Louisiana Guardsmen as Generals Fleming, Hufft, Guerre, and Edmonds; an enlisted bachelor quarters honors the memory of Corporal Wilmer E. Hathaway who was killed in action during World War II.

A modern, well-stocked post exchange has been established by the Army and Air Force Post Exchange Service for the benefit of the Guardsmen, their families, members of other reserve and active component personnel. In addition, retired personnel of all services are entitled to take advantage of this facility. In the case of reservists they may purchase on the basis of one day for each day of military duty performed, such as Unit Training Assemblies, Full Time Training Duty, and Annual Training.

Through Louisiana Legislative Act 688 of 1974, the Louisiana Military History and Weapons Museum has been created and provided a domicile in Jackson Barracks. It provides and/or transfers budgetary control to the Military Department, state of Louisiana, and authorizes the adjutant general to take all necessary steps toward its development. The old powder magazine has been chosen as its site and is presently under renovation. For the first time weapons used by Louisiana militiamen in all the wars in which they have fought will be displayed in one museum. Further plans call for gun and heavy equipment emplacements around the exterior of the building and an information office at the entrance to the area.

Of the original building started in 1833, the fourteen white-columned sentinels, two round towers, and a powder magazine remain.

Currently, an interesting function operating out of Jackson Barracks and Camp Beauregard is the Work Release Rehabilitation Program. Inmates from Louisiana institutions are housed, fed, and assigned to work for wages in the business community or to perform on-the-job training in various skills at both installations (plumbing, carpentry, painting, electricity, administration, maintenance, etc.). The Work Release Program was initiated by the 1968 state legislature under authorization of Act No. 187 as a prerelease tool.

It provides opportunity to individuals who, in the judgment of the director of institutions, need specific training and further transitional preparation for community life. The program has helped hundreds of persons to return to society as self-supporting citizens. It is significant that such a tedious yet worthy program has come under the supervision of the National Guard—where administrative competence and trustworthiness are unquestioned.

Jackson Barracks has become a tradition, a venerable institution that has served Louisiana and the nation through generations. Its permanence has endured even to exceed that of the state capitols. Its identity with Louisiana's turbulent past has created an aura of stability; its old buildings, walls, and grounds have become monuments to history. The ravages of time, wars, and political fights have left scars, but Jackson Barracks survives.

Through its sally gate, history has paraded Ulysses S. Grant, Robert E. Lee, Zachary Taylor, Henry Clay, Edmond P. Gaines, George S. Gaines, P. G. T. Beauregard, George B. McClellan, Arthur MacArthur, and John J. "Black Jack" Pershing, who reviewed the troops there in 1921. For nearly a century and a half thousands of American soldiers have paused here for training, hospitalization, or embarkation to foreign battle fields. Though technically the barracks remains federal property, Louisiana still has use of it through leases that are automatically renewable upon each date of expiration. It should always be preserved and maintained as one of the great treasures of Louisiana.

Prize possessions: Redemption (right) and Resurrection

CHAPTER 17

Redemption and Resurrection

Among the Louisiana National Guard's most prized possessions are two bronze howitzers, relics of a momentous victory and symbols of the restoration of home rule following the ousting of the Reconstruction carpetbag government in Louisiana.

The howitzers were captured from the Metropolitan Police on September 14, 1874, after the battle at the foot of Canal Street when New Orleanians opposed Federal troops in their attempt to establish local government. William P. Kellogg, the de facto carpetbag governor, offered a sizable cash reward for information concerning the cannons' whereabouts, but to no avail.

Minute Book No. 1 of the Washington Artillery, 1875-1879, page 323, contains this statement by Colonel W. M. Owen, who was a witness: "After the installation of the Nicholls' Government, two 12-pounder bronze howitzers that had been taken from the Metropolitan Police on 14th of September, 1874, and put away in a safe place, were resurrected, mounted and placed in the arsenal, thus adding to the armament."

In 1954 the cannons were taken to Alexandria to be repaired by an eighty-year-old wheelwright, the only man who could be found to fix their wheels. The cannons were featured in a public display at Gallier Hall with other relics during the Orleans Parish commemoration of the centennial of the American Civil War in 1961. Today, the cannon, which bear the names Redemption and Resurrection, are on permanent display in the headquarters building of the Louisiana National Guard at Jackson Barracks, timely reminders of a period when the state was redeemed and home rule resurrected from the ashes of the Civil War and Reconstruction. The only visible markings on the cannons are the words, *Made by C. A. Co. Boston* and their names.

Bibliography

BOOKS

Annals of America (1755-1783), Vol. II, *Resistance and Revolution*. Encylopedia Britannica, Inc., 1968.

Army Almanac. Harrisburg, Pa.: Stackpole Co., 1955.

Army Lineage Book, Vol. II, *Infantry*. Washington, D.C.: Government Printing Office, 1953.

Bartlett, Napier. *Military Records of Louisiana*. Baton Rouge: Louisiana State University Press, 1964.

Bernard, Antoine. *Histoire de la Louisiane: Des ses origines a nos jours*. Quebec: Universite Laval, 1953.

Booth, Andrew. *Records of Louisiana Confederate Soldiers and Louisiana Confederate Commands*. New Orleans: n.p., 1920.

Buchanan, A. Russell. *The United States and World War II*. New York and London: Harper and Row, 1964.

Buchanan, Lamont. *A Pictorial History of the Confederacy*. New York: Crown, 1951.

Carpetbag Misrule in Louisiana. Edited by James J. Fortier. New Orleans: Louisiana State Museum Publication, 1938.

Carter, Clarence Edwin. *Territorial Papers of the United States: The Territory of Orleans, 1803-1812*, Vol. IX. Washington, D.C.: Government Printing Office, 1940.

Casey, Powell A. *Louisiana in the War of 1812*. Baton Rouge: Claitors, 1963.

— — —. *The Story of the Washington Artillery in World War II*. Baton Rouge: Claitors, 1971.

Casso, Evans J. *Lorenzo: The History of the Casso Family in Louisiana.* New Orleans: Jackson Square Press, 1972.

Caughey, John Walton. *Bernardo de Galvez in Louisiana, 1776-1783.* Gretna, La.: Pelican Publishing Co., 1972.

Chandler, David G. *The Campaigns of Napoleon.* New York: Macmillan Co., 1966.

Churchill, Winston S. *Their Finest Hour.* Boston: Houghton Mifflin, 1949.

Clark, John G. *New Orleans: 1718-1812: An Economic History.* Baton Rouge Louisiana State University Press, 1970.

Davis, Edwin Adams. *Louisiana: A Narrative History.* Baton Rouge: Claitors, 1965.

Delery, Simon de la Souchere. *Napoleon's Soldiers in America.* Gretna, La.: Pelican Publishing Co., 1972.

Dieler, J. Hanne. *The Settlement of the German Coast and the Creoles of German Descent.* Philadelphia: American Germanica Press, 1909.

Donald, David. *Divided We Fought, 1861-1865.* New York: The Macmillan Co., 1961.

Douglas, Henry Kyd. *I Rode with Stonewall.* Chapel Hill: University of North Carolina Press, 1940.

Dufour, Charles L. *Gentle Tiger: The Gallant Life of Roberdeau Wheat.* Baton Rouge: Louisiana State University Press, 1957.

— — —. *The Mexican War: A Compact History, 1846-1848.* New York: Hawthorn Books, 1968.

— — —. *The Night the War Was Lost.* Garden City, N.Y.: Doubleday and Co., 1960.

— — —. *Ten Flags in the Wind.* New York: Harper and Row, 1967.

Dufour, Charles L., and Leonard Huber, eds. *The Battle of New Orleans.* New Orleans: Sesquecentennial Historical Booklets, the Battle of New Orleans 150th Anniversary Committee of Louisiana, 1965.

(1) Huber, Leonard V. *New Orleans as It Was, 1814-1815.*
(2) Eller, E. M., W. J. Morgan, and R. R. Bascoco. *Sea Power and the Battle of New Orleans.*
(3) Scott, Val McNair. *Major General Sir Edward M. Pakenham.*
(4) Casey, Powell A. *Louisiana at the Battle of New Orleans.*
(5) Watson, Elbert L. *Tennessee at the Battle of New Orleans.*
(6) Wilson, Samuel, Jr. *Plantation Houses on the Battlefield of New Orleans.*
(7) Dixon, Richard R. *The Battle on the West Bank.*
(8) Christian, Marcus. *Negro Soldiers in the Battle of New Orleans.*
(9) Meuse, William E. *The Weapons of the Battle of New Orleans.*

Dupuy, Ernest. *The Compact History of the United States Army.* New York: Hawthorn Books, 1961.

Elliott, James C. *The Modern Army and Air National Guard.* Princeton, N.J.: D. Van Nostrand Co., 1965.

Fair, Hardin J. *An Outline of Shreveport and Caddo Parish History.* Reprint from *Louisiana Historical Quarterly*, XVIII (October, 1935).

Fleming, Raymond H. *Problems of World War II.* Twenty copies privately published. New Orleans: 1955.

Fortier, Alcee. *A History of Louisiana.* 4 vols. Paris: Goupil & Co., 1903.

Fortier, James J. A., ed. *The Spanish-American War of 1898.* New Orleans: Louisiana State Museum Publication, 1939.

Fregault, Guy. *Le gran marquis, Pierre de Rigaud de Vaudreuil et la Louisiane.* Montreal: Fides, 1952.

Gayarre, Charles. *History of Louisiana.* New Orleans: F. F. Hansell, 1903.

Haroe, Jean-Baptiste Benard de la. *Historical Journal of the Settlement of the French in Louisiana.* Translated by Virginia Koenig and Jean Cain. Edited and annotated by Glenn R. Conrad. Lafayette: University of Southwestern, Louisiana, 1971.

Hatada, Takashi. *A History of Korea.* Translated and edited by Warren W. Smith, Jr., and Benjamin H. Hazard. Santa Barbara, Calif.: ABC-Clio, 1969.

Hill, Jim Dan. *The Minute Men in Peace and War: A History of the National Guard.* Harrisburg, Pa.: Stackpole, Co., 1963.

Historical Annual: National Guard of the State of Louisiana. Baton Rouge: Army and Navy Publishing Co., 1938.

Historical Militia Data (Mexican Border). Compiled by Works Project Administration, 1930s.

Historical Register and Dictionary of the United States. Vols. I and II. Washington, D.C.: Government Printing Office, 1903.

Hofstader, Richard, William Miller, and Daniel Aaron. *The United States: The History of a Republic.* Englewood Cliffs, N.J.: Prentice Hall, Inc., 1959.

Holmes, Jack D. L. *A Guide to Spanish Louisiana, 1762-1806.* New Orleans: private publication, 1970.

——— . *Honor and Fidelity: The Louisiana Infantry Regiment and the Louisiana Militia Companies.* Birmingham, 1965.

Jordan, Paul. *The Civil War.* National Geographic Senior Editorial Staff, produced by the National Geographic Special Publication Division. National Geographic Society,

Kendall, John Smith. *History of New Orleans.* Chicago and New York: Lewis Publishing Co., 1922.

Landry, Stuart Omer. *The Battle of Liberty Place.* New Orleans: Pelican Publishing Co., 1955.

Latour, A. LaCarriere. *Historical Memoir of the War in West Florida and Louisiana in 1814-1815.* Gainesville: University of Florida Press, 1964.

Lechie, Robert. *The History of the Korean War.* New York: G. P. Putnam's Sons, 1962.

Long, E. B., with Barbara Long. *The Civil War Day by Day: An Almanac.* Garden City, N.Y.: Doubleday, 1971.

Louisiana Almanac and Government Guide, 1966-67. New Orleans: Pelican Publishing Co.

Martin, Francois-Xavier. *The History of Louisiana*. Reprint; Gretna, La.: Pelican Publishing Co., 1963.

Matloff, Maurice, ed. *American Military History*. Washington, D.C.: Army Historical Series; Office of Chief of Military History, United States Army, 1969.

Menn, Joseph Karl. *The Large Slaveholders of Louisiana—1860*. New Orleans: Pelican Publishing Co., 1964.

Morris, Eric. *Blockade: Berlin and the Cold War*. New York: Stein and Day Publishers, 1973.

Nation's National Guard, The. Buffalo, N.Y.: Privately published by the National Guard Association of the United States; Baker, Jones Hausauer, Inc., 1954.

Nau, John Frederick. *The German People of New Orleans, 1850-1900*. Leiden, the Netherlands: E. J. Brill, 1958.

Owen, William Miller. *In Camp and Battle with the Washington Artillery of New Orleans*. Boston: Tichnor and Co., 1885.

Powell, James W. *Customs of the Service*. Kansas City, Mo.: Franklin Hudson Publishing Co., 1905.

Rand, Clayton. *Stars in Their Eyes*. Gulfport, Miss.: Dixie Press, 1953.

Reeves, Miriam C. *The Governors of Louisiana*. Gretna, La.: Pelican Publishing Co., 1972.

Robichaux, Albert. *Louisiana Census and Militia Lists, 1770-1789*, Vol. II. Harvey, La.: Dumag Printing Co., 1973.

Smith, Justin H. *The War with Mexico*, Vols. I and II. New York: Macmillian Co., 1919.

Snyder, Louis L. *The War: A Concise History*. New York: Julian Messner, 1960.

Stern, Phillip Van Doren. *The Confederate Navy*. New York: Doubleday and Co., 1962.

— — —. *Robert E. Lee: The Man and the Soldier*. New York: Bonanza Books, 1963.

War of the Rebellion: A Compilation of the Official Records of the Union and Confederate Armies. Washington, D.C.: Government Printing Office, 1880–1901.

Washington's Lost Plan Revived. Twenty-three-page booklet; reprinted by courtesy of the University of Chicago.

Wharton, Edward C. *A History of the Proceedings in the City of New Orleans*. New Orleans: A W. Hyatt, 1881.

Wiley, Bell Irvin. *Embattled Confederates*. New York: Harper and Row, 1964.

Williams T. Harry. *History of the United States*. New York: Alfred A. Knopf, 1966.

Wood, Sterling. *Riot Control*. Harrisburg, Pa.: Military Service Publishing Co., 1950.

Bibliography

ARTICLES

Casso, Evans J. "Details Revealed in Nicholls' Letters to His Wife." Donaldsonville (La.) *Chief*, August 15, 1974.

———. "Diary of a Cannoneer Made Public for the First Time." Donaldsonville (La.) *Chief*, August 15, 1974.

———. "Nicholls Lived and Died for Dixie." Donaldsonville (La.) *Chief*, January 31, 1974.

———. St. Maxent Founded Spanish Colony of Valenzuela." Donaldsonville (La.) *Chief*, March 21, 1974.

Rooney, William E. "The First Incident of Secession: Seizure of the New Orleans Marine Hospital." *Louisiana Historical Quarterly*, XXXIV (April, 1961).

Williams, T. Harry. "Louisiana Commemorates the Civil War: Centennial 1861-1961." Published by the Louisiana Civil War Centennial Commission, 1961.

Williams, T. Harry, and A. Otis Hebert. "The Civil War in Louisiana: A Chronology." Published by the Louisiana Civil War Centennial Commission, 1961.

"Washington Artillery, The." *Times-Picayune*, April 26, 1887.

PAPER and LECTURES

Casso, Evans J. "Civil War Music: An Anthology and the Origin of Civil War Music." Civil War Round Table, New Orleans, January 21, 1970.

———. "A Brief Review of the History of Louisiana, 1852-1912." New Orleans, Tuesday Discussion Group, 1973.

Deutsch, Eberhard P. "The Real Origin of the Secession Movement." Civil War Round Table, New Orleans, April 19, 1967.

Histories, Louisiana National Guard Units, 1956-57 (unpublished):
Headquarters and Headquarters Detachment
39th Infantry Division
105th Antiaircraft Artillery Battalion (AW) (SP)
141st Field Artillery Battalion
156th Infantry Regiment
199th Infantry Regiment
Headquarters and Headquarters Battery, 204th Antiaircraft Artillery Group
527th Antiaircraft Artillery Gun Battalion (90mm)
773rd Tank Battalion
935th Field Artillery Battalion

Index

Abercrombie, Wylie, 169
Acadia Parish, 52
Adams, Bert A., 188
Adams, John Quincy, 48, 50
Adams, William L., Jr., 187
Adcox, Charles A., 201
Alexander, John B., 188
Alexandria, 84, 111, 124, 150, 159, 160, 178, 186, 188, 189, 199, 225, 228, 263
Allen, Henry Watkins, 78, 84, 85, 214
Ammons, Kenneth E., 199
Andries, Harold W., 187
Andrus, Erwin C., 144
Apffel, C. C., 145
Aquillard, Nolan, 187
Armant, John S., 203, 210
Ascension Parish, 52, 65, 80, 168, 169, 213, 229, 248
Assumption Parish, 52, 65, 80, 168, 213
Avendano, Numo P., 145, 177, 188
Avoyelles Parish, 38, 135, 216
Ayo, Paul E., Jr., 201

Baker, Thomas A., 146, 187

Baldy, George, 204, 220, 221
Ball, A. Caron, 124, 126,
Banks, N. P., 79, 80, 83, 84
Bankston, T. M., 151
Barkley, John, 146, 152, 166, 188
Barth, Milton O., 189
Bassich, Cyril, Jr., 124, 188
Baton Rouge, 21, 23, 25, 35, 36, 37, 44, 51, 75, 79, 82, 85, 115, 136, 159, 168, 169, 180, 187, 188, 200, 226
Beauregard, P. G. T., 72, 78, 86, 93, 160, 204, 223–26, 243, 255, 259–60
Becker, Edward, 144
Beckett, George F., 187
Becnel, J. Sidney, iii, xii
Belgard, Cecil C., 144
Bell, Thomas Fletcher, 204, 226
Bellechasse, Joseph, 42, 45, 203, 207, 208
Belvin, Donald R., 200
Benezech, Edward P., 126, 188
Beninate, Vincent N., 188
Bennett, William J., 200
Bienvenu, Thomas F., 145
Bienville, Jean Baptiste Sieur de, 16,

272 Index

19, 20, 21–22
Bishop, Clarence A., 145
Black, Bryan, 124, 125
Black, Charles E., 126
Blackburn, Frank C., 144
Blair, Ollie J., 201
Blakeney, Jay G., 200
Blanque, Jean, 56
Bliss, Minter A., 145
Boackle, Milton J., 200
Bodet, Adrien, 126
Boh, John, 144, 186
Bolger, Robert G., 202
Bonner, Thomas, 204, 243–45, 247
Booth, Reginald G., 188, 202
Bossier Parish, 225–26
Boulet, Hughit J., 187
Breazele, Henry H., 145
Breslin, Thomas J., Jr., 199
Brien, Elisha S., 127
Bringol, Donald J., 201
Briscoe, Walter F., 69–70
Broussard, Samuel S., 187
Brown, Michael L., xiii
Brown, Ralph H., 201
Buchel, G. B., 127
Burgess, Ronald W., 201
Burns, Billy J., 200
Burt, William G., 204, 225–26
Burton, Richard A., 200
Buskie, J. Gilmore, 127
Butler, Benjamin F., 83, 90, 224–26, 255
Butler, Bruce B., 201
Butler, Donald H., 189

Cabot, George, 49, 50
Caddo Parish, 230
Calcasieu Parish, 228
Caldwell Parish, 230
Calhoun, Teal C., 187
Campbell, Joe W., 187
Carondolet, Francois Louis Hector, 24, 37, 38, 43
Carter, A. J., 167
Carter, Frank L., 200

Carville, Charles L., 188
Cassidy, Francis H., 127
Castille, Simon, 144, 187
Catalano, Frank A., 200
Cate, Thomas W., 151
Chaney Edgar L., 187
Chapman, William T., Jr., 189
Cicero, Nick, 201
Citrano, Paul J., 144, 187
Claiborne Parish, 240, 241
Claiborne, William C. C., 40–57 *passim* 208, 209
Clark, Dewitt H., 145
Clark, George, 124
Clarke, George, 125
Cockrell, Jimmy F., 200
Cole, Herbert C., 127
Cole, James I., 199
Comeaux, Joseph W., 200
Concordia Parish, 213
Connor Lemuel P., 203, 213
Cook, Lanny D., 201
Cordero, John S., 201
Covington, David L., 199
Cox William B., 188
Crawford, Charles E., 199
Croft, William J., 201
Crow, Frank M., 145, 187
Cuccia, Thomas J., 199
Culbertson, Floyd D., Jr., 187
Cunningham, Joseph A., 167, 188
Currier, Lawrence J., 126
Curtis, Henry B., 145, 157

Dabadie, Joseph L., Jr., 200, 203
Daigle, Jeanne Aline Waguespack, xii 245–46, 248
Daigle, O. J., Jr., iii, viii, ix, xi, xii, 34, 35, 169, 188, 192, 199, 202, 204, 206, 207
Davis, Horatio, 68, 69, 203, 211
Davis, Jefferson, 76, 78, 86, 156, 255
Davis, Silas W., III, 200
Dedmon, Roy L., 189
Defelice, Woodrow J., 187
Delahoussaye, Harry L., 187

Index

Denegre, Thomas B., 126
Denton, Dan N., 187
Derbyshire, Robert C., 200
Desonier, Roland P., 144
De St. Aubin, Albert, 128
Delamain, Frederick W., 145
Diaz, Demetrio D., 145
Dick Act, 4, 10, 11, 112
Dickey, George E., 145
Donaldsonville Cannoneers, 32, 55, 81, 169
Douglas, James D., 128
Dronet, Curney J., 199
Dufour, Charles L., xiv, 63, 92
Duke, L. G., Jr., 145
Dunbar, Harold W., 187
Duncan, George C., 202
Dunn, Robert G., 169
Dupont, Chester F., 186
Dutillet, Francois, 203, 208
Duval, Louis E., 127
Dwyer, Ralph D., 199

East Baton Rouge Parish, 52, 80, 168
East Feliciana Parish, 37, 52, 55, 168
Eddy, Bret W., 127
Edmonds, James E., 124–25, 165, 259
Edmondson, B. F., 127
Elgee, Charles Le Doux, 203, 213
Elliott, Joseph G., 146
Emancipation Proclamation, 77, 80, 84, 86, 89

Favrot, Gervais, 126
Flagg, Geddes B., Jr., 188
Fleming, Raymond H., xii, 14, 111, 126, 132, 134, 136, 157, 183, 204, 231, 233, 234, 235, 236, 248, 257, 259
Foil, Howard E., 188
Fonger, Michael R., 199
Ford, H. S., 127
Fort Bienvenu, 57
Fort Bute, 23, 35, 36
Fort DeRussy, 84

Fort Hopkins, 54
Fort Jackson, 70, 75, 79, 85, 160
Fort Mims, 51
Fort Petite Coquilles (Fort Pike), 51
Fort St. Charles, 51
Fort St. John, 51
Fort St. Leon, 51
Fort St. Phillip, 51, 52, 59, 70, 75, 79, 85, 160
Fortier, Michael, 53
Fox, Frederick H., 145, 152, 166
Fox, Lawrence J., 146
Francis, Alfred G., 144
Freeland, Frederick B., 124
Frost, Meigs O., 124
Fuller, George J., 200
Funderburk, Wilbur H., 145

Gaiennie, Francois, 203, 209
Galvez, Bernardo de, 22–23, 23–36 43
Garrison, James C., 188
Gassoway, Garish, 124–26
Gehr, Mires C., 144
Gillan, Robert E., 199
Gillis, Duncan, 145, 158, 188
Givens, Robert W., 201
Goldstein, Louis, 124, 126
Gouaze, Edmond C., 188
Graffia, Joseph, 200
Graham, G. Mason, 203, 216–17, 228
Grant Parish, 93
Grant, U. S., 8, 84–97 *passim*, 218, 259, 264
Grass, Lucian J., 199
Green, Harvey, 126
Gregory, Richard J., 199
Grevemberg, Francis C., 166, 192
Griffin, Charles E., 201
Grivot, Maurice, 80, 203, 212
Guerre, Louis F., 127, 144, 151, 259
Guidry, Clyde J., 200
Guill, William S., 186
Guillory, Earl C., 188
Gusman, James G., 189

Hall, Tom, 188
Hamilton, Peter, 124, 125, 126
Harden, Kenneth W., 200
Harper, William P., 204, 219, 220
Harris, Abe B., 127
Harvey, William B., 145
Haskins, Cecil A., 188
Hathaway, Wilmer E., 259
Haynes, Ira., 125
Haywood, Alba S., 187
Herbert, Ronald, R. E., 201
Henderson, W. H., 128
Hipple, James B., 164
Hitler, Adolph, 137, 139–41, 170
Hobson, W. N., 124
Hodges, Henry C., 125
Hogan, William H., 186, 202
Holdeman, Harold I., 188
Holliday, Joseph A., 144
Hopkins, Henry, 203, 208
Hoskins, William L., 126
Hourin, James J., 201
Huber, Eugene R., 188
Huber, Herman J., 144
Hufft, Edward M., 203
Hufft, Raymond F., 138, 204, 231, 236–40, 259
Hunt, Theodore G., 69, 203, 214–15
Hunter, Allen T., 204, 230–31
Hurston, Morton C., Jr., 201
Hutchison, William E., 201
Hyams, Harry T., III, 200

Iberville Parish, 52, 168, 227
Iberville, Pierre Le Moyne Sieur d', 16–19
Ingram, Van F., 187
Irvin, E. L., 127
Irvin, Lynn A., 199

Jackson, Andrew, 2, 7, 8, 51–59 *passim*, 68, 252, 255
Jackson Barracks, xii, 75, 91, 98, 115, 134–35, 166–67, 199–201, 216, 248, 251–64 *passim*
Jackson, T. J., "Stonewall," 81, 86 159, 219

Jacques, Rene C., 199
Jambon, Orleans A., 199
Jefferson Parish, 80, 213, 215
Jefferson, Thomas, 25, 39, 41, 43, 47, 48, 75
Jennings Cavalry, 108, 111, 114, 165
Johnson, Jesse, 189
Johnson, John B., 127
Johnson, Ronald G., 200
Johnson, Samuel L., 192
Johnson, Walter H., 188
Jones, Glynne M., 146, 178
Jordan, Levi, 144
Jordan, Robert L., 200
Jumel, Allen, 204, 227

Kellogg, William P., 92–97, 214, 218, 220, 223, 263
Kelly, Edwin L., Jr., 187
Kendall, Walter B., 127
Kennedy, John F., 13, 182, 191–92
Khoury, Kamiel, 187
King, Paul E., 188
Kostmayer, James H., Jr., 201
Kuhnell, Harold A., 199
Kuttner, J. B., 144
Kuttner, J. H., 127, 144, 161–63, 186

La Cour, Michael B., 201
Lafourche Parish, 32, 52, 80, 213
Lala Henry J., 202
Lalumiere, Paul R., Jr., 199
Landreneau, Bennett C., 201
Landry, Murray F., Jr., 200
Laneuville, Alexander, 203, 209
Langlois, Gerard W., 201
La Rocca, Henry A., 188
Lazarus, Harry A., 187
Le Blanc, Robert J., 187, 199
Ledig, Walter D., 145
Lee, Robert E., 8, 79, 84–86, 94, 156, 218–19, 224, 259
Lemaire, James R., 199
Lemarie, Stanley, 124–26
Lemell, Alexander, 54
Lewis, Thomas H., 200
Life, Arthur R., 146

Index

Lincoln, Abraham, 74, 77, 79, 84, 86, 90
Lindsley, P. W., 151
Livingston Parish, 168
Longstreet, James, 86, 94, 96, 204, 218, 219, 243
Louisiana Purchase, 26, 38, 42, 47–50, 75
Lowley, J. H., 127
Lozes, Clarke L., 199

McCord, Harry E., 126
McCrory, Cecil C., 204, 229–30
McDonald, Dorsey W., 145
McEnery, John, 92–95, 103, 218, 221, 223, 224, 226
McGehee, Eugene W., 203
McGehee, Schaumberg, 124
McGowan, Henry W., 114
McHugh, Thomas, 124, 126
McNeese, Oswald W., 114, 204, 228–29

Madison Parish, 213, 222
Maloney, Guy R., 124, 125
Manning, Thomas Courtland, 203, 213–14
Marino, Frank A., 186
Martin, Joseph G., Jr., 200
Martin, Tom B., 127
Martindale, Derryl W., 199
Mason, James, 124
Melancon, Ralph J., 201
Metternich, Raymond H., 188
Milhet, John, 22
Miller, Roy S., 144
Mithoff, William, Jr., 203, 215–16
Mittlesteadt, C. W. Robert, 186
Mogabgab, Eugene, 126
Montgomery, Harry, 200
Montz, Maxime J., Jr., 203
Mook, George W., 187
Moore, Thomas O., 74, 78, 84, 213–14
Morehead, Michael R., 201
Moret, Lucien J., 126
Morgan, Snyder, 126

Mullins, Freddie D., 201
Murphy, Edward J., 201
Murrell, Hampden P., 187
Musso, Frank P., 201

Napoleon, 25, 26, 41, 43, 64, 65, 72, 76, 196, 207, 208, 227
Natchitoches Parish, 31–33, 38, 43, 44, 52, 54, 84, 210
Nathan, Harold, 124–26
National Defense Acts, 4, 11, 12, 133, 143
Neville, C. W. J., 128
New Orleans, 8, 16, 19–25 *passim*, 33–94 *passim*, 102, 123, 135–36, 150, 159, 165, 167, 170, 176, 178, 183, 186, 188–89, 201, 202, 207–27 *passim*, 237, 240, 245, 251–53, 255, 263
Nicholls, Francis T., 90, 96–104 *passim*, 156, 219–26, 263

O'Donnell, Peter, 126
Olivier, Christian L., Jr., 144, 187
Opelousas Territory, 32–38 *passim*, 52, 54, 55, 80
Orleans Parish, 54, 80, 136, 213, 219, 237, 251, 263
Ouachita Parish, 52
Owen, Allison, 82, 111, 124, 126
Owen, W. Miller, 263

Parker, James, 124
Parrino, Paul S., 145
Partin, Charles M., 201
Patton, Isaac W., 204, 222–23
Pauley, Leonard E., 187
Pauley, Raymond H., 187
Pedneau, Thomas A., 146, 152
Pellegrin, Sidney A., 187
Penn, Davis B., 92, 94–95, 204, 221–22
Peychaud, Anatole, 203, 209
Phillips, Fred R., 111
Pipes, Rip D., 187
Pitre, Earl L. J., 188

Pittman, Beuford A., 145
Plaquemines Parish, 52, 75, 80, 136, 213
Pointe Coupee Parish, 32–38 *passim*, 52–54, 81
Poll, Michael E., 188, 203
Poirier, Alvin E., 202
Poirier, Leon S., 188
Posey, Lloyd, 124
Potts, Jimmy D., Jr., 200
Prevost, Curtis J., 199
Prince, Percy S., 127
Pugh, Phillip H., Jr., 127

Railey, Charles R., 128
Randon, Lloyd A., 189
Rapides Parish, 38, 52, 213–14, 216, 227–28
Ratigan, W. J., 124
Rauch, Bernard J., 145
Redding, Joseph A., 127, 145, 164, 187
Rentz, Erin E., 145
Richardson, Lyman K., 192
Ricker, Robert B., 144
Riddle, Daniel M., 186
Rideau, Harold M., 200
Riser, Henry Leroy, 169, 187, 188
Roberts, James L., 203
Robichaux, Charles L., 200
Robinson, Joseph F., 126
Robotham, G. W., 128
Rodrigue, Thomas J., 199
Rogers, G. K., 146
Romero, Zachary J., 144
Roosevelt, Franklin, 139–42, 184–85, 257
Rosato, Frank J., 144
Roux, Edwin P., xiii
Rowley, Charles N., 68, 203, 211
Roy, Howard O., 144
Roy, Mary-Alice, xiii
Rucker, Robert M., iii, xiii, 115
Rutter, W. S. 127
Ryals, Neal B., 188

St. Bernard Parish, 80, 136, 213, 223, 251
St. Charles Parish, 32–33, 52–53, 80, 168, 213
St. Helena Parish, 44, 52, 150–51, 168
St. James Parish, 32–33, 52, 80, 168, 213
St. John Parish, 32–33, 52, 80, 168, 213
St. Martin Parish, 52, 54, 80, 213,
St. Mary Parish, 52, 80, 213
St. Tammany Parish, 44, 80, 150–51
Sales, Gerard A., Sr., 201
Savoy, Gregory M., 199
Schexnayder, Clifford J., Jr., 201
Scholl, Sidney J., Jr., 202
Schopfer, Henry G., Jr., 186
Schreck, William D., 201
Scott, Wood H., 145, 187–88
Scroggs, Harvey D., Jr., 200
Seal, Jesse D., 188
Shaugnessy, Francis X., 146
Sheridan, George Augustus, 203, 217
Sherman, William T., 8, 9, 82, 85, 86, 216, 224
Sherrard, Raymond, 126
Shirah, James W., Jr., 200
Short, Paul C., 186
Simpson, Sidney, 128
Sirgo, Stanley, xiii
Sloan, Timothy T., 200
Smith, Dennis L., 200
Smith, Jean Mason, 126
Smith Karl N., xiii, 202
Smith, Persifor F., 68, 69, 203, 210
Smith, Stuart E., 146
Snider, Samuel E., 187
Snyder, James W., 199
Soignet, Donald M., 201
Souhlas, Ernest N., xiii, 203
Speck, Carlos D., Jr., 188
Spiess, Frank G., 145, 171, 174–75
Spivey, Samuel P., 187
Sprol, Jonas C., 145
Stafford, David T., 204, 227–28
Staples, Donald W., 188
Starnes, Karl L., 146, 152

Index

Stauffer, Walter, 124, 125
Stelly, Charles J., 192
Stelly, Glenn J., 200
Stephens, Ralph H., 144
Stephenson, Orlando W., Jr., 189
Street, Henry, 204, 220
Stroud, A. M., Jr., 202
Stubbs, Frank P., Jr., 111, 126–27, 230
Swift, John L., 203, 215
Sword, Earl F., 188
Sylvest, M. J., 151
Synyard, Michael, 199

Tangipahoa Parish, 44, 81, 150, 223
Taylor, Louis J., 114
Taylor, Zachary, 62, 66–70, 79, 210–12, 222
Tensas Parish, 213
Terrebonne Parish, 80, 213
Thomas, William, III, 200
Thompson, Elton G., 201
Thompson, Ralph E., 201
Toler, Timothy W., 201
Tolson, Gus, 125
Tomasovich, John A., 203
Toole, Rex, F., 199
Toombs, Louis A., 132–33, 204, 231–33, 256
Toujan, O. J. 151
Tracy, Uriah, 48–49, 81
Treaty of Fontainebleau, 20, 21
Treaty of Ghent, 59
Treaty of Guadalupe Hidalgo, 67
Treaty of San Ildefonso, 25, 41, 47
Treaty of San Lorenzo, 24, 25
Treaty of Utrecht, 21
Trepagnier, Dalton H., Jr., 188
Trippi, Carl L., 201, 203
Trousdale, George W., 187
Turner, Charles G., 175, 188
Tyra, Thomas O., 199

Utley, T. E., 127

Vash, George, 188

Vaudry, James W., 145
Vigliero, John, 124, 126
Villar, Nolan R., 200
Villere, Jacques, 45–46, 52, 56–57, 209
Vincent, Hubbell F., 180, 189
Vuillemot, Charles, 187

Wade, Davis, 204, 231, 241–44, 247
Waldo, Samuel L., 203, 212
Walton, James B., 69–70, 80, 82–83
Warmoth, Henry C., 88, 91, 101, 102, 217–18, 220
Warren, E. W., 127
Washington Artillery, 55, 69–70, 74–75, 80–83, 98, 100, 102, 103, 111–12, 115, 123–26, 134–35, 155–58, 167, 176, 184, 225, 34, 256, 263
Washington, George, 4, 5, 8, 82, 124, 113
Washington Parish, 44, 150–51
Waters, William H., 201
Watson, Dolan R., 200
Wells, James M., 91, 216–17
West Baton Rouge Parish, 52, 168
West Feliciana Parish, 37, 52, 55, 168
Westmore, S. W. 203, 211–12
Wharton, Jack, 204, 220
White, James A., 144
Whitehouse, Stanley O., 144, 186
Wigginton, Lynn Mary, xiii
Wilkerson, Jack C., 187
Wilson, Earl J., 188
Wilson, Robert R., 200
Wilson, Woodrow, 110–12, 129–30
Wise, Erbon, 204, 231, 240–41
Womack, Charles M., 187
Wood, Elmer E., 126
Woodward, Clyde, Jr., 201
Woolfley, Francis A., 183
Wooten, Robert H., 201
Wulff, Fred A., Jr., 146, 152

Yarborough, Neill A., 187
Young, Richard A., 127

www.ingramcontent.com/pod-product-compliance
Lightning Source LLC
Chambersburg PA
CBHW030337240426
43661CB00052B/1664